How To Neutralize Curses

Dag Heward-Mills

Parchment House

HOW TO NEUTRALIZE CURSES

First published 2017 by Parchment House
3rd Printing 2019

Find out more about Dag Heward Mills at:

ⁿHealing Jesus Campaign
Email: evangelist@daghewardmills.org
Website: www.daghewardmills.org
Facebook: Dag Heward-Mills
Twitter: @EvangelistDag

ISBN : 978-1-68398-197-8

Contents

SECTION 1

THE REALITY OF CURSES

CHAPTER 1

Why This Book About Curses?

Therefore hath **THE CURSE DEVOURED THE EARTH, and they that dwell therein are desolate: therefore the inhabitants of the earth are burned, and few men left.**

Isaiah 24: 6

Notice from the scripture above that it is curses that devour the earth and not demons or evil spirits.

1.   Modern Christians must have a proper respect for curses.

Then shall I not be ashamed, WHEN I HAVE RESPECT unto all thy commandments.

Psalm 119: 6

Modern Christians are more aware of evil spirits and devils than they are of curses. Modern Christians respect the reality of demons but do not fear and respect the reality of curses.

It is my prayer that as you read this book, you will develop a proper and healthy respect for the reality of curses. I believe in the reality of demons, evil spirits and devils. I bind them daily and I cast them out of my life. I have written many books about demons. *However, I also believe that curses are the real reason why these evil spirits have the chance to work and cause frustration, evil and death. It is evil spirits that implement curses!* Curses provide the legal framework for evil spirits to carry out their wickedness. Curses are real whether you believe in their existence or not!

You must begin to have respect for the presence of curses which determine and fashion human life as we know it today! Most of what we are experiencing today are determined by curses and blessings that were spoken years ago. Indeed, one of the chief characteristics about heaven is that there will be no more curse.

... but ye have not looked unto the maker thereof, NEITHER HAD RESPECT unto him that fashioned it long ago.

Isaiah 22: 11

2

2. **It is the duty of a minister of God to point out curses when they are present.**

It is not wrong for a pastor to detect the presence of a curse. Do not fight the word of God! Do not deny the existence of a curse when the word of God says so. It is not wrong for a pastor to say or to declare that a person or a group of people are laboring under a curse! It is indeed the responsibility of a good minister of God to identify curses when God shows them to him. Listen to what the prophet Malachi said to the people of Israel. He said to them, "You are cursed with a curse!" He was not wrong in pointing out the curse. He was right in identifying that a curse was real and present. It is only when you point out a curse that it can be overcome. If you deny that the curse exists, how will you ever fight against it or neutralize it?

YE ARE CURSED with a curse: for ye have robbed me, even this whole nation.

Malachi 3: 9

3. **Do not be offended when a curse is identified and pointed out.**

In the days of Malachi, the people of God were not to be offended when he informed them about the presence of a curse. Do not be offended with what I am writing in this book about curses that affect different groups of people. I am not writing these things to put down any group of people but to identify the curse so that you can neutralize it. A large part of this book is dedicated to neutralizing and overcoming the curse. Do not let me become your enemy because I share with you the truth in God's word about curses and blessings.

Just as the prophet Malachi spoke the truth and told the people that they were under a curse, I am also sharing with you about the presence of the curse.

Am I therefore become your enemy, because I tell you the truth?

Galatians 4: 16

4. Every curse can be neutralized.

I believe that every curse can be neutralized! I am writing this book so that everyone who is open to the word of God will recognize the curse and overcome it through the wisdom of God. How can you neutralize something if you say it does not exist? Your denial of its existence is your greatest weakness!

Do not use the teachings of this book to degrade, insult or humiliate any group of people. That is wrong. Use the teachings of this book to lift up people out of all identified curses.

This is a book of hope! It is a book of victory! It is a book that declares your superiority over curses through the wisdom and power of God. I believe that every group of people in the world - the rich, the poor, men, women, Jews, non-Jews, blacks and whites are respected by God and have the opportunity to escape and overcome every withering curse that is at work in their lives. God respects you and expects you to rise up and be great.

Do not use this book to cheat, enslave or rob anyone. You are cursed if you do so! Please use this book to overcome, to neutralize, to obliterate and to quench all types of curses that may be working in your life. Read the scripture below and take heart in God's will for your equality with all men and your victory over all curses.

Then Peter opened his mouth, and said, Of a truth I perceive that GOD IS NO RESPECTER OF PERSONS: But IN EVERY NATION HE THAT FEARETH HIM, AND WORKETH RIGHTEOUSNESS, IS ACCEPTED with him.

Acts 10: 34 - 35

CHAPTER 2

What is the Curse?

And THERE SHALL BE NO MORE CURSE: but the throne of God and of the Lamb shall be in it; and his servants shall serve him:

Revelation 22:3

Life on earth is dotted with continual frustration, persistent unhappiness, desolation, unexplained misfortune, death, emptiness, frequent harassment, confusion, futility, war, constant conflict and poverty. Such a description has only one definition – a curse!

Most people are not even aware of the fact that there are curses in the earth. This book is intended to help you recognize the curses in the earth and have a proper respect for them. Anyone who does not have a proper respect for curses may live to regret it.

One of the most pervading things on earth today is 'the curse' and its terrible effect. There are several ancient curses that are at work as well as thousands of new and more modern curses. Just think about what life is like on this earth and you will immediately accept that there is a curse on the earth. It is not so easy to define the curse so we must turn to the Bible and see what a curse really is. Let us look at ten biblical definitions of a curse.

Ten Biblical Definitions of a Curse

1. A curse is an appeal to some supernatural power to inflict evil on someone, which may cause misery or lead to death. An appeal was made to Balaam by Balak the king of Moab to curse Israel.

    If you say that there is a curse on someone, you mean that there seems to be a supernatural power causing unpleasant things to happen to them. You can refer to a curse as something that causes a great deal of trouble and harm. You are hereby delivered from whatever causes you a great deal of trouble and harm!

    And he took up his parable, and said, Balak the king of Moab hath brought me from Aram, out of the mountains of the east, saying, Come, curse me Jacob, and come, defy Israel.

How shall I curse, whom God hath not cursed? or how shall I defy, whom the Lord hath not defied?

Numbers 23:7-8

2.   A curse is any expressed wish that some form of adversity or misfortune will befall or attach itself to someone.   In particular, a 'curse' may refer to a wish that harm or hurt will be inflicted on another person, by any supernatural power, such as God, through a spell, a prayer, magic, witchcraft or a spirit.   To reverse or eliminate a curse is called removal or breaking and is often believed to require equally elaborate rituals or prayers.

God has placed a curse on all those who worship idols. Don't have anything to do with idolatry and you will escape one of the most severe curses on earth.   Do not serve money!   Do not worship money!   Do not do anything because of money and you will be delivered from a powerful curse!

CURSED be the man that maketh any graven or molten image, an abomination unto the Lord, the work of the hands of the craftsman, and putteth it in a secret place. And all the people shall answer and say, Amen.

Deuteronomy 27:15

3.   To be cursed is to be sentenced to demotion and inferiority. The serpent was cursed by God and thereby sentenced to demotion and subjected to inferiority. By God's grace, you will never be sentenced to demotion and inferiority like the serpent! The serpent was sentenced to the lowest position on earth. The serpent was also sentenced to eat from the ground forever. This is the lowest any creature can ever fall to. When you are cursed, you are sent into the lowest position. You are doomed to inferiority and downgraded permanently.   God is coming into your life at this time to lift you up by His power.

And the Lord God said unto the serpent, Because thou hast done this, thou art CURSED above all cattle, and above every beast of the field; UPON THY BELLY SHALT THOU GO, AND DUST SHALT THOU EAT all the days of thy life:

Genesis 3:14

4. To be cursed is to have continual sorrow. It is the repetitive, continuous, frequent, unrelenting and sustained sorrow that defines something as a curse. Adam was sentenced to sorrow for the rest of his life. This is the reason for the continual sorrowing of mankind. The unrelenting sadness, depression and darkness that affect the whole world are evidence of the curse that exists. Receive the joy that comes from the Holy Spirit and be lifted above this curse!

And unto Adam he said, Because thou hast hearkened unto the voice of thy wife, and hast eaten of the tree, of which I commanded thee, saying, Thou shalt not eat of it: CURSED is the ground for thy sake; IN SORROW SHALT THOU EAT OF IT ALL THE DAYS OF THY LIFE;

Genesis 3:17

5. To be cursed is to continually have everything work against you all the time. To be cursed is to experience evil, misfortune and death when you should have received goodness, good fortune and life.

THORNS ALSO AND THISTLES SHALL IT BRING FORTH to thee; and thou shalt eat the herb of the field;

Genesis 3:18

6. To be cursed is to sweat, to struggle, to be agitated, to suffer. The fighting, the struggling, the toil and the labour in our world are the evidence of the curse. Receive the grace to rise above the struggles, the toil and the futility in the earth.

And unto Adam he said, Because thou hast hearkened unto the voice of thy wife, and hast eaten of the tree, of which I commanded thee, saying, Thou shalt not eat of it: CURSED is the ground for thy sake; in sorrow shalt thou eat of it all the days of thy life;

Thorns also and thistles shall it bring forth to thee; and thou shalt eat the herb of the field;

IN THE SWEAT OF THY FACE shalt thou eat bread, till thou return unto the ground; for out of it wast thou taken: for dust thou art, and unto dust shalt thou return.

Genesis 3:17-19

7. To be cursed is to be continually frustrated, unhappy and to receive the opposite of what you deserve for all your hard work. Cain was cursed and that was the outworking of his curse. Emptiness, vanity, frustration, grasping and longing for good things is the greatest evidence of a cursed existence. In spite of going to school, working and toiling; emptiness and futility dog the human race.

And the Lord said unto Cain, Where is Abel thy brother? And he said, I know not: Am I my brother's keeper? And he said, What hast thou done? the voice of thy brother's blood crieth unto me from the ground.

And now art thou CURSED from the earth, which hath opened her mouth to receive thy brother's blood from thy hand; When thou tillest the ground, IT SHALL NOT HENCEFORTH YIELD UNTO THEE HER STRENGTH; a fugitive and a vagabond shalt thou be in the earth.

Genesis 4:9-12

8. To be cursed is to be never established, a fugitive, continually on the run, continually a beggar, a tramp, a vagabond and a worthless person. To be a vagabond is to live under a curse. God is lifting you from every vagabond-like existence!

And the Lord said unto Cain, Where is Abel thy brother? And he said, I know not: Am I my brother's keeper? And he said, What hast thou done? the voice of thy brother's blood crieth unto me from the ground.

And now art thou CURSED from the earth, which hath opened her mouth to receive thy brother's blood from thy hand; When thou tillest the ground, it shall not henceforth yield unto thee her strength; A FUGITIVE AND A VAGABOND SHALT THOU BE IN THE EARTH.

Genesis 4:9-12

9. To be cursed is to be made a servant of servants. A servant of servants is permanently blighted (prevented from growth and prosperity), continually confused and confounded. To be a servant of servants is to be continually unable to rise, hounded by unhappiness and desolation. You are delivered from all forms of inescapable servanthood!

And he said, CURSED be Canaan; A SERVANT OF SERVANTS shall he be unto his brethren.

Genesis 9:25

10. To be cursed is to be surrounded, bedevilled, continually harassed, continually tormented, unable to escape and continually arrive at a doomed and damned end. Whether going in or whether coming out, you come to the same conclusion and confusion. God is giving you the wisdom key that will deliver you from the enemies that surround you!

CURSED shalt thou be when thou comest in, and CURSED shalt thou be when thou goest out.

Deuteronomy 28:19

These important definitions of a curse reveal that a cursed person is truly surrounded. To be cursed is to be surrounded. Nothing works and nothing will work when you are surrounded.

All definitions of a curse bring you to this conclusion. You are surrounded!

They compassed me about like bees ...

Psalm 118:12

Let us try to understand what it means to be surrounded. If you are surrounded by death, you will find it in every direction you go. Therefore, if you are cursed to die, whichever direction you turn, you will still die. You could die just making a cup of tea. You could go on a long journey and still die. A curse does not depend on a person's ability to escape. A curse comes to pass because there is no way to escape from it. Christians must therefore have a proper respect for curses and blessings.

To be cursed is to be besieged. To be besieged is to be surrounded with all supply routes and relief points completely blocked out. You will notice that many things in this life do not make sense. Many things do not have good explanations for the way they are. Many things are the complete opposite of what you would expect.

The curse creates an inexplicable and unmistakable picture. That picture results in the same story being told about those under the curse whenever, however and wherever they may be! Consider the story of Africa! Whether African nations were colonised or whether they experienced apartheid, whether they were never colonised or whether they had revolutions, democracy, and independence, it has all given rise to the same picture in Africa.

What is the explanation for the poverty-ridden state of Africa? Whichever country you go to in Africa the same picture is portrayed. Are we besieged and surrounded? You cannot get away from it, no matter where you go or what you do.

When there is a curse on a family for example, none of the girls are able to get married. Whether they are tall, short, fair or dark, pretty or ugly, the result is the same. No marriage!

Human beings have the curse of death hovering over their heads. Whether you are rich, poor, famous, unimportant, European, American, African, black or white, death is the enemy you will have to meet. There is no escape from this enemy no matter who you are.

It is important to understand a curse in this way if you want to overcome it. The Bible is the only book that tells us how to come out when we are surrounded. When a small city is surrounded by a mighty king with his armies, death and destruction seem inevitable. There is no escape and there is no way out of the city. Whatever you do, the result will be the same – death!

Are You Cursed? Are You Surrounded?

Do you have any situation in your life which makes you feel surrounded with no way out? Is everything you do leading to the same point of failure and frustration? Perhaps a real curse is in operation. Too many Christians spend a lot of time trying to find out if there is a curse from their grandmother or from their ancestors. That is not what is necessary. Why bother to find out if your grandmother, your great grandfather has brought about a curse into the family? The Bible tells us there is a curse in the earth. As for the curse it is real and it is present! No matter how much faith you have, your faith does not go above what is written in the Bible. Instead of wasting your time trying to find out if there is a curse in your family, you must assume that there is one. What you need to do is to find out how to come out of a situation in which you are surrounded. Like everyone else on earth, you are most likely surrounded. Once you understand what it means to be surrounded, you can work your way out of it.

> **All nations compassed me about: but in the name of the Lord will I destroy them.**
>
> **They compassed me about; yea, they compassed me about: but in the name of the Lord I will destroy them.**

They compassed me about like bees; they are quenched as the fire of thorns: for in the name of the Lord I will destroy them.

Psalm 118:10-12

I can assure you that your family is as wicked as any other family on earth. I am sure that your family has an equal number of bad people, sinners, witches and wizards as any other family. Just as you are thinking that someone's family has witches and wizards, someone is also thinking that your family has witches and wizards. Stop wasting your time searching for the sources and the origins of curses and witchcraft. I do not have to counsel you personally to know that there is a curse operating somewhere.

The Bible has told us clearly that there is a curse operating under the sun. Whether you are in Ghana, Nigeria, Romania, America, England, Germany or Malaysia, you will sweat before you eat. You will discover that the same frustrations of death and futility are found everywhere. One of the greatest signs that we have transitioned out of this world will be the absence of the curse and all that it represents. In heaven, this famous scripture "...THERE SHALL BE NO MORE CURSE..." (Revelation 22:3) will be fully manifest. Do not think too far when you are thinking of a curse. The curse is everywhere. It is working and causing a great frustration and emptiness in everything we do on earth. Solomon, the wisest person, knew that there was a great curse at work. Actually, it takes wisdom to identify that a curse is in operation somewhere.

Solomon Described the Curse on this Earth

What do you think Solomon meant when he said, "ALL IS VANITY"? Everything he did ended up the same way: vanity, uselessness, emptiness, damnation, frustration and confusion! Life on earth has a curse of frustration, vanity and the futility of grasping for things. Adam's punishment for his rebellion has

13

been very severe indeed. Solomon tried to escape the curse by doing many different things. No matter what Solomon did, he ended up in the same place – vanity! He discovered for himself that life was full of vanity. Let's have a look at the different things that Solomon tried.

Solomon said, "Come on, let's try pleasure. Let's look for the 'good things' in life." But he found that this, too, was meaningless. So he said, "Laughter is silly. What good does it do to seek pleasure?" After much thought, he decided to cheer himself with wine. And while still seeking wisdom, he clutched at foolishness. In this way, he tried to experience the only happiness most people find during their brief life in this world.

Solomon also tried to find meaning by building huge houses for himself and by planting beautiful vineyards. He made gardens and parks, filling them with all kinds of fruit trees. He built reservoirs to collect the water to irrigate his many flourishing groves. He bought slaves, both men and women, and others were born into his household. He also owned large herds and flocks, more than any of the kings who had lived in Jerusalem before him.

Solomon collected great sums of silver and gold, the treasure of many kings and provinces. He hired wonderful singers, both men and women, and had many beautiful wives and concubines. He had everything a man could desire!

So he became greater than all who had lived in Jerusalem before him, and his wisdom never failed him. Anything he wanted, he would take. He denied himself no pleasure!

Solomon even found great pleasure in hard work. But as he looked at everything he had worked so hard to accomplish, it was all so meaningless – like chasing the wind. There was nothing really worthwhile anywhere. He described it aptly and said it's all emptiness and vanity.

For what hath man of all his labour, and of the vexation of his heart, wherein he hath laboured under the sun? For all his days are sorrows, and his travail grief; yea, his heart taketh not rest in the night. This is also vanity.

Ecclesiastes 2:22-23

It is actually a good thing when you discover that a curse is in operation. Why is that? When you know about a curse, you can pray for wisdom to circumvent it and thwart its effect. Throughout this book you will learn about many curses and how real they are. You will also discover how God's wisdom can make you survive and overcome curses in this life.

CHAPTER 3

The Global Curses

And **THERE SHALL BE NO MORE CURSE:** but the throne of God and of the Lamb shall be in it; and his servants shall serve him:

Revelation 22:3

There are three categories of curses that are clearly found in the Scripture.

1. The Global Curses

2. The Bible Curses

3. The Custom-made Curses

The Global Curses are curses that came upon the earth from the very beginning and have consistently and continuously affected the whole wide world.

The Bible Curses are common things we all know that the Bible has named as cursed. Any activity or action that crosses certain lines brings about these Bible curses. All through the Bible, you find examples of these Bible curses being played out.

Custom-made Curses are curses pronounced by individuals on others because of an offence committed against the individual. A curse causeless shall not come but such curses have power when they do have a cause!

As the bird by wandering, as the swallow by flying, SO THE CURSE CAUSELESS SHALL NOT COME.

Proverbs 26:2

In this chapter and the two that follow after, we will have a look at Global Curses, Bible Curses and a few Custom-made Curses.

The Global Curses

1. The curse on men.

And unto Adam he said, Because thou hast hearkened unto the voice of thy wife, and hast eaten of the tree, of which I commanded thee, saying, Thou shalt not eat of it: cursed is the ground for thy sake; in sorrow shalt thou eat of it all the days of thy life;

Thorns also and thistles shall it bring forth to thee; and thou shalt eat the herb of the field;

In the sweat of thy face shalt thou eat bread, till thou return unto the ground; for out of it wast thou taken: for dust thou art, and unto dust shalt thou return.

Genesis 3:17-19

2.   The curse on women.

Unto the woman he said, I will greatly multiply thy sorrow and thy conception; in sorrow thou shalt bring forth children; and thy desire shall be to thy husband, and he shall rule over thee.

Genesis 3:16

3.   The curse by Noah.

And he said, Cursed be Canaan; a servant of servants shall he be unto his brethren.

Genesis 9:25

4.   The curse on Israel.

But it shall come to pass, if thou wilt not hearken unto the voice of the Lord thy God, to observe to do all his commandments and his statutes which I command thee this day; that all these curses shall come upon thee, and overtake thee:

Deuteronomy 28:15

5.   The curse on those who hate Israel.

The Jews are a blessed people. It is a dangerous thing to hate them and to fight them. During the Second World War, Adolf Hitler and his murderous team killed six million Jews, but at the end of the day, about seven and a half million Germans were also killed. The nation of Germany was destroyed at the end of 1945 but the nation of Israel was born after 1945. People who walk into a life of hating Jews are walking straight into a curse. There is no need for you to enter into the curse that awaits all those who hate and curse God's people.

Decide to love them and enter into the blessing of the Lord. It is this blessing that many ministries seek to enter into by supporting Israel and doing things to help Israel.

The church of God must realise the blessing that is available to those who love Israel.

Let people serve thee, and nations bow down to thee: be lord over thy brethren, and let thy mother's sons bow down to thee: cursed be every one that curseth thee, and blessed be he that blesseth thee.

Genesis 27:29

And I will bless them that bless thee, and curse him that curseth thee: and in thee shall all families of the earth be blessed.

Genesis 12:3

CHAPTER 4

The Top Bible Curses

And MOSES CHARGED THE PEOPLE the same day, saying, THESE SHALL STAND UPON MOUNT GERIZIM TO BLESS the people, when ye are come over Jordan; Simeon, and Levi, and Judah, and Issachar, and Joseph, and Benjamin: AND THESE SHALL STAND UPON MOUNT EBAL TO CURSE; Reuben, Gad, and Asher, and Zebulun, Dan, and Naphtali.

Deuteronomy 27:11-13

Moses was the author of most of the top Bible blessings and curses. He declared these curses for the people of God as he established Israel as a nation.

The top Bible curses are listed as things that you must avoid. You must live your life in such a way as to avoid ever stepping into any of these things. If you do not have a proper respect for these written curses, they will envelope your life and colour everything you do. A visit to the Yad Vashem Memorial in Israel will help you to have a proper respect for the curses declared by Moses.

Without a proper respect for these curses, you will constantly do things which will bring these curses into your life. I notice many people who do not have a proper respect for the curses in the world. It is interesting because I believe that life is largely determined by the blessings and curses that have already been spoken into the atmosphere.

1.   THE CURSE ON IDOL WORSHIPPERS.

People who love money and worship money as an idol are cursed, (even if they are pastors). No idol is worth worshipping. You always find a curse on people who follow money and serve it instead of serving God. Pastors who serve money instead of serving God bring a curse on themselves and their ministries.

People who give up their ministries to seek after prosperity only attract the curse on idol worshippers. They set it up in the secret places of their heart and follow it secretly instead of following God. This only brings frustration, emptiness and misfortune. And that is a curse!

All through the Bible, it is this one thing that invokes God's anger. You will notice that God never commented on the number of wives Abraham, Isaac, David, Jacob and Solomon had. But He was furious about their gods. God is always angry when you have an alternative to Him. God is always angry when there is something or someone else that can make you move, sacrifice and change your life. When God is not able to make you move and do things for Him but money and jobs are able to do that, He is angered because He recognizes you have another god.

> CURSED IS THE MAN WHO MAKES AN IDOL or a molten image, an abomination to the LORD, the work of the hands of the craftsman, and sets it up in secret...
>
> Deuteronomy 27:15 (NASB)

> Ye shall make you NO IDOLS nor graven image, neither rear you up a standing image, neither shall ye set up any image of stone in your land, to bow down unto it: for I am the LORD your God.
>
> Leviticus 26:1

> THOU SHALT NOT MAKE UNTO THEE ANY GRAVEN IMAGE, or any likeness of any thing that is in heaven above, or that is in the earth beneath, or that is in the water under the earth: Thou shalt not bow down thyself to them, nor serve them: for I the LORD thy God am a jealous God, visiting the iniquity of the fathers upon the children unto the third and fourth generation of them that hate me;
>
> Exodus 20:4-5

> There shall not be found among you any one that maketh his son or his daughter to pass through the fire, or that useth divination, or an observer of times, or an enchanter, or a witch, Or a charmer, or a consulter with familiar spirits, or a wizard, or a necromancer.

> For all that do these things are an abomination unto the LORD: and because of these abominations the LORD thy God doth drive them out from before thee.
>
> Deuteronomy 18:10-12

> But the fearful, and unbelieving, and the abominable, and murderers, and whoremongers, and sorcerers, and

IDOLATERS, and all liars, shall have their part in the lake which burneth with fire and brimstone: which is the second death.

Revelation 21:8

2. THE CURSE FOR THOSE WHO DISHONOUR FATHERS AND MOTHERS.

CURSED IS HE WHO DISHONORS HIS FATHER OR MOTHER. And all the people shall say, 'Amen.'

Deuteronomy 27:16 (NASB)

Whoso curseth his father or his mother, HIS LAMP shall be put out in OBSCURE DARKNESS.

Proverbs 20:20

For Moses said, Honour thy father and thy mother; and, whoso curseth father or mother, let him die the death:

Mark 7:10

Dishonouring parents will draw curses faster than most things. Your lamp will go out and you will enter obscurity and darkness when you dishonour fathers. The power of God is unleashed upon those who have no time to fear and respect fathers. A father is a God-ordained position. It is a heavily defended, fortified, spiritual place. Disrespect and disregard for that place have great consequences. Watch out for those who turn off the lamp in their lives by dishonouring their fathers and their mothers.

3. THE CURSE ON THOSE WHO CHEAT AND DECEIVE.

BUT CURSED BE THE DECEIVER, which hath in his flock a male, and voweth, and sacrificeth unto the LORD a corrupt thing: for I am a great King, saith the LORD of hosts, and my name is dreadful among the heathen.

Malachi 1:14

Then Joshua called for them and spoke to them, saying, "WHY HAVE YOU DECEIVED US, saying, 'We are very far from you,' when you are living within our land? NOW THEREFORE, YOU ARE CURSED, and you shall never cease being slaves, both hewers of wood and drawers of water for the house of my God."

Joshua 9:22-23 (NASB)

There is a curse for those who deceive. Don't join them. If you passed your exams by cheating, you have provoked a curse. You may have had eight "A"s but it is a cursed set of "A"s. Your future is cursed because you obtained those "A"s through deception.

Do not cheat during elections. There is a curse for those who cheat to gain power. You may be in power but you will be cursed because you cheated to win the elections. You must fear God's word. You must fear stealing, you must fear cheating. You must fear the coming of the curse.

It is not easy to pray your way out of an accursed situation. It is not easy to deliver people who have cursed themselves by cheating and stealing. Pastors often waste their time praying for accursed people. There are often no results for such prayers.

When men of God pray for accursed people, it looks as though the pastor is powerless to deliver the people. It is not easy for anyone to dislodge a legitimate and well-deserved curse.

As the bird by wandering, as the swallow by flying, SO THE CURSE CAUSELESS SHALL NOT COME.

Proverbs 26:2

4.   THE CURSE ON THIEVES.

Some nations are blessed with honest and sacrificial leaders who labour to build their countries and help the ordinary people. On the other hand, many nations have been run by thieves who have stolen the wealth of their nations. They have systematically stolen the monies of their countries. Some of these thieves are more sophisticated than others. Some steal openly and others steal in a remarkably subtle and clever way. Whatever the style of stealing, it always attracts a curse. There is a curse on thieves and that curse is proclaimed by God. This curse on thieves cannot be averted by a prophet who prophesies good things to governmental thieves. This is why politicians who have stolen the wealth of nations rarely enjoy their booty. They and their families are plagued with curses and are unable to climb out of their damnation. You will never be a thief by the grace of God! And this curse will never come upon you!

> Then said he unto me, THIS IS THE CURSE that goeth forth over the face of the whole earth: FOR EVERY ONE THAT STEALETH shall be cut off as on this side according to it; and every one that sweareth shall be cut off as on that side according to it.
>
> I will bring it forth, saith the Lord of hosts, and it shall enter into the house of the thief, and into the house of him that sweareth falsely by my name: and it shall remain in the midst of his house, and shall consume it with the timber thereof and the stones thereof.
>
> Zechariah 5:3-4

5.   THE CURSE ON LYING AND SWEARING.

> Then said he unto me, THIS IS THE CURSE that goeth forth over the face of the whole earth: for every one that stealeth shall be cut off as on this side according to it; and every one that sweareth shall be cut off as on that side according to it. I will bring it forth, saith the LORD of hosts, and it shall enter into the house of the thief, and into the house OF HIM THAT SWEARETH FALSELY by my name: and it shall remain in the midst of his house, and shall consume it with the timber thereof and the stones thereof.
>
> Zechariah 5:3-4

Most people tell lies and think nothing of it. But there is a curse on all liars. You must have a proper fear of telling lies. There is a curse on all liars. You must avoid telling lies if you want to avoid curses. Many democratic politicians tell lies to the people. They go on television defending things they do not even believe themselves. They know that what they are saying is untrue but they persist in it in order to be politically correct. Lying politicians must keep looking out of the window to see if the curse is arriving at their gates. The curse will surely come to those who live their lives by peddling deception.

6.   THE CURSE ON ARMED ROBBERS.

THE MURDERER RISING WITH THE LIGHT KILLETH THE POOR AND NEEDY, AND IN THE NIGHT IS AS A THIEF.

The eye also of the adulterer waiteth for the twilight, saying, No eye shall see me: and disguiseth his face. In the dark THEY DIG THROUGH HOUSES, WHICH THEY HAD MARKED FOR THEMSELVES IN THE DAYTIME: they know not the light.

For the morning is to them even as the shadow of death: if one know them, they are in the terrors of the shadow of death. He is swift as the waters; THEIR PORTION IS CURSED IN THE EARTH: he beholdeth not the way of the vineyards.

Job 24:14-18

There is a curse on armed thieves who go around from house to house, killing and stealing. The curse multiplies in every nation as the number of armed thieves multiplies. In many nations there are no walls around the house. People dwell in safety and have no need of walls. In many places, however, there is a need for high walls, security cameras, fierce dogs and electric fencing. Surely, the wrath of God is on all armed robbers and they are cursed in every mission they undertake.

7.   THE CURSE ON NON-TITHERS.

Will a man rob God? Yet ye have robbed me. But ye say,
Wherein have we robbed thee? In tithes and offerings. YE
ARE CURSED WITH A CURSE: for ye have robbed me,
even this whole nation.

Bring ye all the tithes into the storehouse, that there may
be meat in mine house, and prove me now herewith, saith
the LORD of hosts, if I will not open you the windows of
heaven, and pour you out a blessing, that there shall not be
room enough to receive it.

Malachi 3:8-10

There is a curse on non-tithers. My book on tithing[1] has a
list of curses that belong to people that do not pay tithes. These
curses include frustration, poverty, war, crop failure, harvest
failure, sickness, misery and death.

8.   THE CURSES ON DISOBEDIENT PEOPLE.

But it shall come to pass, IF THOU WILT NOT HEARKEN
unto the voice of the Lord thy God, to observe to do all
his commandments and his statutes which I command
thee this day; that ALL THESE CURSES SHALL COME
UPON THEE, and overtake thee:

Deuteronomy 28:15

The curses for disobedience are horrific. You do not want
to know the curses that are lined up for people who disobey the
Word. If we knew how powerful the Word of God was, we would
make the best efforts to obey it. Decide to be an obedient person
so that the curse that follows disobedience will pass over you and
not harm you.

---

[1] *Why Non-Tithing Christians Become Poor and How Tithing Christians Can Become
Rich*

9. THE CURSE ON THOSE WHO MISTREAT THE HANDICAPPED.

CURSED IS HE WHO MISLEADS A BLIND PERSON on the road … Cursed is he who distorts the justice due an alien, orphan, and widow…

Deuteronomy 27:18-19 (NASB)

10. THE CURSE ON THOSE WHO NEGLECT THE WEAK AND THE VULNERABLE IN OUR SOCIETY.

Then shall he say also unto them on the left hand, depart from me, YE CURSED, into everlasting fire, prepared for the devil and his angels:

FOR I WAS AN HUNGRED, AND YE GAVE ME NO MEAT: I WAS THIRSTY, AND YE GAVE ME NO DRINK:

I WAS A STRANGER, AND YE TOOK ME NOT IN: NAKED, AND YE CLOTHED ME NOT: SICK, AND IN PRISON, AND YE VISITED ME NOT.

Matthew 25:41-43

The handicapped and the weak are special people to the Lord. God is on the side of those who are weak and handicapped in any way. Anyone who misleads a blind person is cursed. Anyone who distorts justice due foreigners is cursed. Anyone who mistreats orphans is cursed. Anyone who mishandles a widow is cursed. Watch out in your dealings with any of these groups of people. There are many problems in this world. You do not need to compound the problems of your life by mistreating any of these groups of people. If you do not want to give them anything, just pass on and leave them alone. But do not mishandle them, for God will protect them and smite you with the sword of His angel.

Be especially careful with foreigners who do not understand your language. Foreigners are often mistreated and cheated. As they say, "a visitor has eyes but does not see". Visitors, strangers, foreigners and aliens have a grace over their lives that will provoke divine judgment if you mishandle them.

11. THE CURSE ON THOSE WHO TRUST IN MAN.

There is a curse for those who trust in man instead of trusting God. Place your trust in God and have faith that He will take care of you.

> Thus saith the LORD; CURSED BE THE MAN THAT TRUSTETH IN MAN, and maketh flesh his arm, and whose heart departeth from the LORD.
>
> For he shall be like the heath in the desert, and shall not see when good cometh; but shall inhabit the parched places in the wilderness, in a salt land and not inhabited.
>
> Jeremiah 17:5-6

12. THE CURSE ON FALSE PREACHERS.

There is a curse for preachers who do not preach the truth. All pastors should take note of the need to speak the truth and preach the right things. Failure to preach the right things does not only result in your church not growing but also attracts a curse.

> But though we, or an angel from heaven, PREACH ANY OTHER GOSPEL unto you than that which we have preached unto you, LET HIM BE ACCURSED.
>
> Galatians 1:8

13. THE CURSE ON FALSE PRIESTS.

> And now this commandment is for you, O PRIESTS. "If you do not listen, and if you do not take it to heart to give honor to my name," says the Lord of hosts, "THEN I WILL SEND THE CURSE upon you and I will curse your blessings; and indeed, I have cursed them already, because you are not taking it to heart."
>
> Malachi 2:1-2 (NASB)

14. THE CURSE ON THOSE WHO DO NOT LISTEN TO THE PROPHETS.

Because ye have said, The Lord hath raised us up prophets in Babylon; Know that thus saith the Lord of the king that sitteth upon the throne of David, and of all the people that dwelleth in this city, and of your brethren that are not gone forth with you into captivity;

Thus saith the Lord of hosts; Behold, I will send upon them the sword, the famine, and the pestilence, and will make them like vile figs, that cannot be eaten, they are so evil.

AND I WILL PERSECUTE THEM WITH THE SWORD, WITH THE FAMINE, AND WITH THE PESTILENCE, AND WILL DELIVER THEM TO BE REMOVED TO ALL THE KINGDOMS OF THE EARTH, TO BE A CURSE, AND AN ASTONISHMENT, and an hissing, and a reproach, among all the nations whither I have driven them: BECAUSE THEY HAVE NOT HEARKENED TO MY WORDS, SAITH THE LORD, WHICH I SENT UNTO THEM BY MY SERVANTS THE PROPHETS, rising up early and sending them; but ye would not hear, saith the Lord.

                                                            Jeremiah 29:15-19

15. THE CURSE FOR WICKEDNESS.

Wicked people are cursed. When you are wicked to someone expect a curse to follow you or to happen to you one day. All the wicked rulers of the world who have mercilessly murdered and tortured people are cursed. Their curses are multiplied because the people they hurt also spoke curses on them. This is why the frustration in the world is multiplied. Many families are connected to wicked people, liars and thieves. It is difficult to come into this world without encountering a curse somewhere close by.

THE CURSE OF THE LORD IS IN THE HOUSE OF THE WICKED: but he blesseth the habitation of the just.

Proverbs 3:33

16. THE CURSE FOR THOSE WHO DO NOT HELP THE LORD'S WORK.

Curse ye Meroz, said the angel of the LORD, CURSE YE BITTERLY THE INHABITANTS THEREOF; BECAUSE THEY CAME NOT TO THE HELP OF THE LORD, to the help of the LORD against the mighty.

Judges 5:23

Avoid the curse on those who do not come to help the work of the Lord. It is a curse to see the work of the Lord needing help and to close your heart to those needs. You must rise up and get involved. Do not hold back your life, your money or your time. It is a curse to hide yourself when souls are perishing. Perhaps this explains the frustration that people feel as they live their lives in guilt, knowing every day that they should have served the Lord instead of building their own personal empires.

17. THE CURSE ON LEADERS WHO MAKE THE PEOPLE GO INTO DIFFICULTY AND HUNGER.

HE THAT WITHHOLDETH CORN, THE PEOPLE SHALL CURSE HIM: but blessing shall be upon the head of him that selleth it.

Proverbs 11:26

18. THE CURSE ON THOSE WHO IGNORE THE PLIGHT OF THE POOR.

He that giveth unto the poor shall not lack: BUT HE THAT HIDETH HIS EYES SHALL HAVE MANY A CURSE.

Proverbs 28:27

19. THE CURSE FOR THOSE WHO MISLEAD THE PUBLIC.

This is another warning for politicians who specialize in deception. There are those who can deceptively explain on television that the green colour you are looking at is actually red.

HE THAT SAITH UNTO THE WICKED, THOU ARE RIGHTEOUS; HIM SHALL THE PEOPLE CURSE, nations shall abhor him:

Proverbs 24:24

20. THE CURSE ON THOSE WHO COMMIT ADULTERY.

The EYE ALSO OF THE ADULTERER waiteth for the twilight, saying, No eye shall see me: and disguiseth his face.

He is swift as the waters; THEIR PORTION IS CURSED in the earth: he beholdeth not the way of the vineyards.

Job 24:15,18

21. THE CURSE ON POSSESSING ACCURSED OBJECTS.

And ye, in any wise KEEP YOURSELVES FROM THE ACCURSED THING, lest ye make yourselves accursed, when ye take of the accursed thing, and make the camp of Israel a curse, and trouble it.

Joshua 6:18

Those who possess accursed things can draw curses into their lives. It is important not to bring charms, curios, images and idols into your house, lest you create a home for an evil spirit and a curse. Since there are things that are accursed but hidden from us, it is important to pray general prayers to bind the influence of any cursed object in your life.

I take authority over every accursed object that may have entered your house accidentally. Be free from every curse and lurking evil spirit. It will have no effect over you. We return to sender all wickedness. We undo the spells, incantations, charms and evil plans that are determined against you in the name of Jesus. Today marks the end of the power of darkness in your life. You are set free from this very moment.

22. THE CURSE ON THOSE WHO HAVE SEX WITH FAMILY MEMBERS.

CURSED BE HE THAT LIETH WITH HIS SISTER, the daughter of his father, or the daughter of his mother. And all the people shall say, Amen.

Deuteronomy 27:22

Do not have sex with your sister or brother. Some of the problems we pray about have no solutions because there are fixed curses that have come about from the sin of incest. In our different evangelistic campaigns, I have travelled to places where incest is common. Brothers and sisters are made to have sex with each other and even marry each other.

The curse for these practices was also evident. These cities had unusual and frightening diseases. The most debasing and humiliating conditions any human being could ever have were prevalent in towns where incest was also common.

Watch out for your life as you play around with these curses!

23. THE CURSE ON THOSE WHO HAVE SEX WITH ANIMALS.

Cursed be he that lieth with any manner of beast. And all the people shall say, Amen.

Deuteronomy 27:21

Beware of having sex with animals. It brings on you a curse. Do not joke or toy with these divine laws. There is no need to end your life or bring upon yourself a great difficulty by having sex with a dog or a cat. It may seem like a joke to you but a frightening curse may be your portion because of this. Some Western nations are seeking to legalize these actions as well as to be able to marry an animal. The end of all this will be fire and brimstone.

24.   THE CURSE ON CERTAIN LOCATIONS.

Call now, if there be any that will answer thee; and to which of the saints wilt thou turn? For wrath killeth the foolish man, and envy slayeth the silly one. I have seen the foolish taking root: BUT SUDDENLY I CURSED HIS HABITATION.

His children are far from safety, and they are crushed in the gate, neither is there any to deliver them. Whose harvest the hungry eateth up, and taketh it even out of the thorns, and the robber swalloweth up their substance.

Job 5:1-5

And David lamented with this lamentation over Saul and over Jonathan his son:

(Also he bade them teach the children of Judah the use of the bow: behold, it is written in the book of Jasher.)

The beauty of Israel is slain upon thy high places: how are the mighty fallen!

Tell it not in Gath, publish it not in the streets of Askelon; lest the daughters of the Philistines rejoice, lest the daughters of the uncircumcised triumph.

Ye MOUNTAINS OF GILBOA, LET THERE BE NO DEW, NEITHER LET THERE BE RAIN, UPON YOU, NOR FIELDS OF OFFERINGS: for there the shield of the mighty is vilely cast away, the shield of Saul, as though he had not been anointed with oil.

From the blood of the slain, from the fat of the mighty, the bow of Jonathan turned not back, and the sword of Saul returned not empty.

Saul and Jonathan were lovely and pleasant in their lives, and in their death they were not divided: they were swifter than eagles, they were stronger than lions.

Ye daughters of Israel, weep over Saul, who clothed you in scarlet, with other delights, who put on ornaments of gold upon your apparel.

How are the mighty fallen in the midst of the battle! O Jonathan, thou was slain in thine high places. I am distressed for thee, my brother Jonathan: very pleasant hast thou been unto me: thy love to me was wonderful, passing the love of women. How are the mighty fallen, and the weapons of war perished!

2 Samuel 1:17-27

25. THE CURSE ON PEOPLE WHO DESTROY THE EARTH.

The earth mourns and withers, the world fades and withers, the exalted of the people of the earth fade away.

THE EARTH IS ALSO POLLUTED BY ITS INHABITANTS, for they transgressed laws, violated statutes, broke the everlasting covenant.

THEREFORE, A CURSE DEVOURS THE EARTH, AND THOSE WHO LIVE IN IT ARE HELD GUILTY. Therefore, the inhabitants of the earth are burned, and few men are left.

Isaiah 24:4-6 (NASB)

The people who destroy the earth through deforestation, pollution, war, nuclear waste, chemical waste, industrialization and many other human inventions are cursed for destroying the earth. The ozone layer is destroyed, our rivers are polluted, the earth is over-heating and the climate is modified, all leading to the destruction of the earth.

And the nations were angry, and thy wrath is come, and the time of the dead, that they should be judged, and that thou shouldest give reward unto thy servants the prophets, and to the saints, and them that fear thy name, small and great; AND SHOULDEST DESTROY THEM WHICH DESTROY THE EARTH.

Revelation 11:18

God does not take lightly the destruction of this beautiful planet that He has created. The the bombs, the guns, the missiles, the experiments, the chemicals and even the viruses that man has created, are destroying the earth and are bringing a curse on mankind.

CHAPTER 5

Custom-Made Curses

As the bird by wandering, as the swallow by flying,
SO THE CURSE CAUSELESS SHALL NOT
COME.

Proverbs 26:2

A custom-made curse is spoken and designed for someone in particular. For instance, Joshua spoke a custom-made curse for anyone who attempted to rebuild Jericho. This type of curse is different from the top Bible curses that affect everyone.

I once declared a curse on anyone who attempted to turn our Bible school into a secular educational institute. It is an important curse because many Bible schools intended for training ministers have been turned into ordinary secular institutions. That is an example of a custom-made curse. It is specially targeted at backslidden leaders who would want to turn a spiritual institution into a secular and unspiritual school. Today, many secular institutions do not tolerate or encourage churches on their campuses. They consider churches to be a nuisance. Why should a church allow itself to be turned into a secular institution?

1. The curse issued by Joshua for anyone who rebuilt Jericho.

There is a curse on developing projects that God does not want. Do not build accursed places like nightclubs, drinking bars, brothels and drug centres. Do not build places that increase sin and release diseases, curses and destruction. Joshua released a curse for anyone who would take up the project of re-building Jericho. Indeed, this curse happened practically when Hiel the Bethelite attempted to re-build Jericho. When Hiel the Bethelite was laying the foundation of a new Jericho, his first son died. When the project was completed and they were setting the gates of the city, his youngest son also died. Such is the power of custom-made curses. You must study history and enquire if there are any custom-made curses lurking around.

And Joshua adjured them at that time, saying, Cursed be the man before the Lord, that riseth up and buildeth this city Jericho: he shall lay the foundation thereof in his firstborn, and in his youngest son shall he set up the gates of it.

Joshua 6:26

In his days did Hiel the Bethelite build Jericho: HE LAID THE FOUNDATION thereof IN ABIRAM HIS FIRSTBORN, AND SET UP THE GATES thereof IN HIS YOUNGEST SON SEGUB, according to the word of the Lord, which he spake by Joshua the son of Nun.

1 Kings 16:34

2.   The curse issued by David for Joab's family and descendants.

There are families that are cursed because someone spoke a legitimate curse over them for a crime committed. Being in such a family will make you a part of that curse. Many families have curses of hypertension, diabetes, asthma, sickle-cell disease, madness, epilepsy and other inherited diseases. These illnesses come only because you are a part of a family. These diseases do not come to you because you contracted a germ. Your membership of the family is all that you need to qualify for the curse. Notice how David declared that Joab and his entire family would be cursed forever because of what Joab did to Abner.

And afterward when David heard it, he said, I and my kingdom are guiltless before the Lord for ever from the blood of Abner the son of Ner:

LET IT REST ON THE HEAD OF JOAB, AND ON ALL HIS FATHER'S HOUSE; and let there not fail from the house of Joab one that hath an issue, or that is a leper, or that leaneth on a staff, or that falleth on the sword, or that lacketh bread.

2 Samuel 3:28-29

3.   The curse issued by Saul for those who broke the fast.

Unfortunately, there are people who issue curses haphazardly and indiscriminately. When you curse too frequently, you can easily curse yourself. You may curse all the enemies of your friend, but end up becoming one of his enemies. In so doing, you end up cursing yourself.

Curses are things that must be spoken carefully and infrequently. Saul spoke a curse, which turned on him because it was his own son who fell into the curse.

> And the men of Israel were distressed that day: for Saul had adjured the people, saying, CURSED BE THE MAN THAT EATETH ANY FOOD UNTIL EVENING, that I may be avenged on mine enemies. So none of the people tasted any food.
>
> And all they of the land came to a wood; and there was honey upon the ground.
>
> And when the people were come into the wood, behold, the honey dropped; but no man put his hand to his mouth: for the people feared the oath. But Jonathan heard not when his father charged the people with the oath: wherefore he put forth the end of the rod that was in his hand, and dipped it in an honeycomb, and put his hand to his mouth; and his eyes were enlightened. Then answered one of the people, and said, Thy father straitly charged the people with an oath, saying, CURSED BE THE MAN THAT EATETH ANY FOOD THIS DAY. And the people were faint.
>
> Then said Jonathan, My father hath troubled the land: see, I pray you, how mine eyes have been enlightened, because I tasted a little of this honey.

1 Samuel 14:24-29

CHAPTER 6

The Causes of Curses

As the bird by wandering, as the swallow by flying, so
THE CURSE CAUSELESS SHALL NOT COME.

Proverbs 26:2

A curse is a proclamation that is made against you. These words have great power to effect a series of happenings in your life. One of the reasons why curses have such power is because they are legal declarations that are often punishments or judgments for genuine errors, mistakes or sins you have committed.

A punishment is something that you deserve. A curse does not come without a good reason or a good cause. You will see that the list of curses below have a legitimate cause. And because every curse has a good reason to be there, it also requires a good reason to be removed.

A curse is a declaration which affects you mightily. When a declaration is made by a judge, it will affect you greatly. I have a friend who was tried in court for various offences. Eventually, the judge told my friend, "You will go to prison for nine years." That declaration was so powerful that it changed the life of my friend forever. Instead of going home to his wife and children, he was carried away to live with criminals. The judge's words were enforced by the police, the army, the prison service, the secret service, the special forces, the immigration service, the military police and Interpol.

The curse of going to prison for nine years was declared by the judge and enforced by all these powers. But there was a reason, a cause for which this declaration was made. My friend had done something that made a judge declare this curse. The curse always has a cause. This is how a curse comes about. It does not come out of a vacuum. It comes for a reason. It has a legal basis. It is enforced by many unseen powers. Let's have a look at some of the causes of the curses in the Bible.

Causes of Curses

1. **The curse of Adam was caused by him listening to his wife's voice instead of God's voice.** Many men experience curses today because they listen to their wives more than they listen to God.

And unto Adam he said, BECAUSE THOU HAST HEARKENED UNTO THE VOICE OF THY WIFE, and hast eaten of the tree, of which I commanded thee, saying, Thou shalt not eat of it: cursed is the ground for thy sake; in sorrow shalt thou eat of it all the days of thy life;

Thorns also and thistles shall it bring forth to thee; and thou shalt eat the herb of the field;

In the sweat of thy face shalt thou eat bread, till thou return unto the ground; for out of it wast thou taken: for dust thou art, and unto dust shalt thou return.

Genesis 3:17-19

2. **The curse on Eve came about because she influenced her husband wrongly.** Many women experience curses today because they manipulate, misdirect and influence their husbands into doing the wrong things.

And the man said, The woman whom thou gavest to be with me, SHE GAVE ME OF THE TREE, and I did eat. And the Lord God said unto the woman, WHAT IS THIS THAT THOU HAST DONE? And the woman said, The serpent beguiled me, and I did eat.

Unto the woman he said, I will greatly multiply thy sorrow and thy conception; in sorrow thou shalt bring forth children; and thy desire shall be to thy husband, and he shall rule over thee.

Genesis 3:12-13, 16

3. **The curse on the nations came about because they had no compassion for the hungry, the thirsty, the strangers, the naked, the sick and the prisoners.** Having no mercy for the people whom God loves carries a curse.

Then shall he say also unto them on the left hand, Depart from me, ye cursed, into everlasting fire, prepared for the devil and his angels: For I was an hungred, and ye gave me no meat: I was thirsty, and ye gave me no drink: I was a stranger, and ye took me not in: naked, and ye clothed me not: sick, and in prison, and ye visited me not.

Matthew 25:41-43

4. The curse on Israelites was caused by their not following the voice of God.

But it shall come to pass, IF THOU WILT NOT HEARKEN UNTO THE VOICE of the Lord thy God, to observe to do all his commandments and his statutes which I command thee this day; that all these curses shall come upon thee, and overtake thee:

Deuteronomy 28:15

5. The curse of Noah was caused by his son dishonouring him.

And Noah awoke from his wine, and knew WHAT HIS YOUNGER SON HAD DONE unto him. And he said, CURSED BE CANAAN; A servant of servants shall he be unto his brethren.

Genesis 9:24-25

6. The curse on the Israelites was caused by their not paying tithes.

Will a man rob God? Yet ye have robbed me. But ye say, Wherein have we robbed thee? In tithes and offerings. YE ARE CURSED WITH A CURSE: FOR YE HAVE ROBBED ME, even this whole nation.

Malachi 3:8-9

7. The curse on Hiel in which his two sons died during the construction of Jericho was caused by ignoring the curse of Joshua.

In his days did Hiel the Bethelite build Jericho: he laid the foundation thereof in Abiram his firstborn, and set up the gates thereof in his youngest son Segub, according to the word of the Lord, which he spake by Joshua the son of Nun.

1 Kings 16:34

CHAPTER 7

Why Are Curses so Powerful?

For verily I say unto you, That whosoever shall say unto this mountain, Be thou removed, and be thou cast into the sea; and shall not doubt in his heart, but shall believe that those things which he saith shall come to pass; he shall have whatsoever he saith.

Mark 11:23

1.   Curses are powerful because Jesus taught us that we can have what we say.

J esus said, "You can have what you say" (Mark 11:23). This principle teaches that when a person speaks out words of faith; whether to a mountain, a hill, a valley or a river, there will be a response to the declarations. Even the inanimate, non-living object will respond to words spoken.

Throughout the Bible, men of authority have spoken curses and blessings over people, individuals and nations. The years have gone by and proven that their words were not idle words but powerful creative words that determined the outcome of lives.

The words that Almighty God spoke over Adam and Eve have determined the course of the human race. The futility experienced by all of us is something we cannot shake off. Death looms ahead of every human being and stands as a thief of everything we do here.

Faith works by making declarations that come to pass. Faith is a real force that is activated every time you speak, even when you are joking. You must be careful of what you say.

2.   Curses are powerful because they are a manifestation of faith.

Through faith we understand that the worlds were framed by the word of God, so that things which are seen were not made of things which do appear.

Hebrews 11:3

Faith is a very powerful force because it is the force that was deployed in the creation of the planets, the stars, the sun and the moon. Our sun is one of many stars in the universe. We are taught that the world was created by faith. God spoke the world into existence when He said, "*Let there be light.*" Spoken words are the reason for Jupiter and its sixty-two moons, Saturn with its fifty-three named moons and Neptune and its fourteen moons.

The fantastic planet, Saturn, with its amazing rings of colour is a favourite for those who study the planets and the stars. These wonders were all created by faith. We understand that the worlds were created by the word of God through faith. Faith is a great force that can create a life of blessings or a life of curses. When a man of faith speaks words, they can create a world of blessings or a world of curses. Watch out for authority figures that speak words of faith. Watch out for these people, for they speak words that can change your life forever.

3.   Curses are powerful because death and life are in the power of the tongue.

Death and life are in the power of the tongue: and they that love it shall eat the fruit thereof.

Proverbs 18:21

Life and death are truly in the power of the tongue. The Bible says, "The tongue is a little member…" (James 3:5), but it is through the words we speak that life and death are released. I remember a mother who angrily told her daughter, "*You will sell beans.*" Her daughter was on her way to university. This young girl felt she was a twentieth century modern high-flyer. She felt she was now superior to her mother and the entire family who had been selling beans in the market for years. Her mother declared over this university student; "*You will sell beans*".

It was amazing to see this young lady finish studying Information Technology at the university, and return to sell beans at the exact same spot where her mother had been selling beans for years. Watch out for an authority figure when they make declarations, because life and death is in the power of the tongue.

4.   Curses are powerful because snares are released through the power of the spoken word.

Thou art snared with the words of thy mouth, thou art taken with the words of thy mouth.

Proverbs 6:2

Curses are powerful because they trap you and tie you down. When Noah discovered that Ham had dishonoured him, he spoke curses that tied down the descendants of Ham forever.

He said, *"A servant of servants shall thou be."* Across the globe today, perhaps, six thousand years later, the majority of the black race are tied down in a state of deep servant-hood. They are caught, ensnared and trapped by the words of Noah. Words are powerful! You must not joke about things you do not mean.

Even your jokes can turn against you. There are girls who have jokingly said, "I don't want to marry." Today, they are still unable to marry even though they are beautiful and now desire to be married. There are people who said, "I can't pass this exam." Today, they are tied down by their constant failures.

There are people who joke with their children, calling one a devil and the other an angel. As the years went by, one of them grew to be an angel while the other turned into a veritable devil.

Indeed, you are snared by the words of your mouth! This is why spoken blessings and spoken curses are so powerful. You are snared by what you say. A word spoken creates snares and traps, preventing people from ever escaping. Life and death are released when words are spoken. Worlds are created when faith words are spoken! You can have what you say and you will have what you say when you speak forth blessings or curses!

CHAPTER 8

Despise Not Prophesyings

Despise not prophesyings.

1 Thessalonians 5:20

Despise not prophesying! Despise not the prophesying of curses! Despise not the prophesying of blessings! Be particularly careful when an authority figure is prophesying blessings or curses. Prophesying means to speak forth by divine inspiration, to foretell future events and to declare a thing that can only come to pass by divine authority. Prophesying is to speak words under the inspiration of the Holy Spirit. In the Bible, prophesying does not only stand for predictions but also for words spoken under the inspiration and direction of the Holy Spirit.

Many people despise prophecies, predictions and declarations of faith that come from the mouth of authority figures. That is a spiritual mistake. The Bible teaches us not to despise or look down on such declarations. God inspires His servants to speak forth words that you must only say "Amen" to. When Elisha prophesied about a twenty-four hour miracle, the servant of the king despised him and paid for it with his life.

Then Elisha said, Hear ye the word of the Lord; Thus saith the Lord, To morrow about this time shall a measure of fine flour be sold for a shekel, and two measures of barley for a shekel, in the gate of Samaria.

Then a lord on whose hand the king leaned answered the man of God, and said, Behold, if the Lord would make windows in heaven, might this thing be? And he said, Behold, thou shalt see it with thine eyes, but shalt not eat thereof.

2 Kings 7:1-2

It is a Mistake to Despise Prophesying

Do not think to yourself that a word that is spoken by an authority figure is powerless and will not happen. Some years ago, a man of God destroyed his spiritual father's church and took over the property that belonged to this father. The spiritual father then sent a message to him saying, "The day you mount the pulpit in that church you will die." There had been great commotion during that church crisis and the day came for this local pastor to mount the pulpit. It was a Sunday and the pastor stood behind the pulpit and preached his Sunday sermon. On the Monday following and the weeks after, he boasted, "You see, I am still alive. I did not die. He said that I would die if I ever preached from that pulpit again. But here I am."

Such boasting is ill advised. When Adam and Eve lived in the Garden of Eden they were given a solemn warning, "In the day that you eat of this tree, you will surely die." Did they actually die on the day that they ate of the tree of the knowledge of good and evil? No, they did not die physically in twenty-four hours. They lived to a good old age of over nine hundred years. Adam died just short of a thousand years. With God, a thousand years is as a day and a day is as a thousand years. In actual fact they died within the day that they ate the tree. According to God's calculation, they actually did die in the day they ate of the tree.

Be careful when you despise or make fun of a prophecy. Sometimes the meaning of a prophecy is not clear.

When the prophet Elisha prophesied that there would be abundance of food and prosperity within a few hours, the king's adviser could not see how this would be possible. He unfortunately made a wrong remark about Elisha's prophecy. He asked, "How could that be?" He paid with his life because he mocked at the prophecy. He was trampled to death because he despised the prophecy of Elisha.

Elisha replied, "Listen to this message from the Lord! This is what the Lord says: By this time tomorrow in the markets of Samaria, six quarts of choice flour will cost only one piece of silver, and twelve quarts of barley grain will cost only one piece of silver.

The officer assisting the king said to the man of God, "THAT COULDN'T HAPPEN EVEN IF THE LORD OPENED THE WINDOWS OF HEAVEN!

Then the people of Samaria rushed out and plundered the Aramean camp. So it was true that six quarts of choice flour were sold that day for one piece of silver, and ten quarts of barley grain were sold for one piece of silver, just as the Lord had promised. The king appointed his officer to control the traffic at the gate, but he was knocked down and trampled to death as the people rushed out.

So everything happened exactly as the man of God had predicted when the king came to his house. The man of God had said to the king, "By this time tomorrow in the markets of Samaria, six quarts of choice flour will cost one piece of silver, and twelve quarts of barley grain will cost one piece of silver."

The king's officer had replied, "That couldn't happen even if the Lord opened the windows of heaven!" And the man of God had said, "You will see it happen with your own eyes, but you won't be able to eat any of it!"

And so it was, for THE PEOPLE TRAMPLED HIM TO DEATH AT THE GATE" (2 Kings 7:1-2, 16-20 NLT)

Prophesying also means to speak words that edify, exhort and comfort. There may not be any prediction of events when you prophesy to edify, exhort and comfort.

It is important to know all the different types of speaking which are actually prophesying. To "despise not prophesyings" is to not despise any of the different types of prophesying that the Bible speaks of. The prophecy you doubt is the prophecy that **will not** happen for you. The prophecy you believe, is the one that **will** work in your favour.

But he that prophesieth speaketh unto men to edification, and exhortation, and comfort.

1 Corinthians 14:3

1.   **"Despise not prophesying" means you must respect the prophecies of the scripture.**

Knowing this first, that no PROPHECY OF THE SCRIPTURE is of any private interpretation.

For the prophecy came not in old time by the will of man: but holy men of God spake as they were moved by the Holy Ghost.

2 Peter 1:20-21

The whole Bible is a collection of prophecies. It is called "the prophecy of the scripture". This is why the prophecy that you believe is the one that comes to pass. The whole Bible is a prophecy but it is not everything in the Bible that comes to pass in your life. It is the sections you believe that happen in your life.

When a whole section of the church took the scripture "*you must be born again*" seriously and believed in that prophecy, the charismatic movement was created where people could only join the church by being born again. The scripture about being born again had been there for years. A group of Christians decided to believe in it literally and emphasize it. Their belief in that portion of scripture is what generated the evangelical and charismatic movements we have today.

2.   **"Despise not prophesying" means you must scream "Amen" to the prophecies spoken over your life.**

And I will bless them that bless thee, and curse him that curseth thee: and in thee shall all families of the earth be blessed.

Genesis 12:3

Even the prophet Jeremiah said, Amen: the Lord do so: the Lord perform thy words which thou hast prophesied...

Jeremiah 28:6

When someone speaks a blessing over you, it is important for you not to sit there like a deaf and dumb doll. Shout "Amen" when you hear a blessing coming your way. "Amen" means "so be it". Scream "Amen" when you hear a blessing coming your way. Decide to be the one with the loudest "Amen" always. When you say "Amen" you secure the blessing for yourself and make it a reality.

3. **"Despise not prophesying" means you must block negative words and encourage positive words spoken in your direction.**

In the sweat of thy face shalt thou eat bread, till thou return unto the ground; for out of it wast thou taken: for dust thou art, and unto dust shalt thou return.

Genesis 3:19

And he said, Cursed be Canaan; a servant of servants shall he be unto his brethren.

Genesis 9:25

When someone speaks a curse, do not take it lightly. It is important to fight negative words that are spoken against your life with counter curses and blocking prayers. It is a mistake to despise prophesying and take words, thoughts and intentions that people have said against you lightly.

4. **"Despise not prophesying" means you must respect the prophecies and proverbs that come from fathers.**

Amazingly, sections of the book of Proverbs are described as prophecies. Many wisdom nuggets are actually prophecies for your life.

The words of Agur the son of Jakeh, even the prophecy: the man spake unto Ithiel, even unto Ithiel and Ucal,

Surely I am more brutish than any man, and have not the understanding of a man.

Proverbs 30:1-2

5.   "Despise not prophesying" means you must respect the prophecies of your mothers.

The teachings of your mother may be prophecies. Despising these words may bring a curse on your life.

The words of king Lemuel, the prophecy that his mother taught him.

Proverbs 31:1

6.   "Despise not prophesying" means you must receive the prophecies in books.

Many times you receive prophecies whilst reading a book.

And he saith unto me, Seal not the sayings of the prophecy of this book: for the time is at hand.

For I testify unto every man that heareth the words of THE PROPHECY OF THIS BOOK, If any man shall add unto these things, God shall add unto him the plagues that are written in this book:

Revelation 22:10, 18,

7.   "Despise not prophesying" means you must receive the impartation of gifts that come through the spoken word.

Many people receive impartations through prophecies.

Till I come, give attendance to reading, to exhortation, to doctrine.

Neglect not the gift that is in thee, which WAS GIVEN THEE BY PROPHECY, with the laying on of the hands of the presbytery.

1 Timothy 4:13-14

CHAPTER 9

A Proper Respect for Curses

And he shewed me a pure river of water of life, clear as crystal, proceeding out of the throne of God and of the Lamb.

In the midst of the street of it, and on either side of the river, was there the tree of life, which bare twelve manner of fruits, and yielded her fruit every month: and the leaves of the tree were for the healing of the nations.

AND THERE SHALL BE NO MORE CURSE: but the throne of God and of the Lamb shall be in it; and his servants shall serve him: And they shall see his face; and his name shall be in their foreheads.

AND THERE SHALL BE NO NIGHT THERE; and they need no candle, neither light of the sun; for the Lord God giveth them light: and they shall reign for ever and ever.

Revelation 22:1-5

Today, there are curses in operation on the earth. The curses in the earth run so deep and so wide that no one is able to escape from its reality. Curses abound on every continent and on all kinds of people. There is no human being - rich or poor, black or white - who can escape the power of the thick curses on earth. Frustration, disappointments and disillusionment mark almost every aspect of life on this earth. There are few people who can say they have escaped the sorrows on this earth.

One of the amazing characteristics of Heaven will be the absence of curses. On the other hand a key characteristic of life on this earth is the presence of curses. There are curses everywhere. You may be sleeping on an accursed bed. You may be living in a house that was built with accursed money. The land on which you build your house may be cursed land on which blood has been shed. Even if there are no specific curses on you, there may be curses in your life because of what your parents did. Even if your parents did not do anything that warrants a curse, your ancestors may have. The global curses spoken over Adam, Eve and Noah obviously affect the human race. The curses of Adam, Eve and Noah will affect everyone.

A Proper Respect For A Black Mamba

Anyone who does not have a proper respect for curses is like someone who does not understand the power and danger of snakes. I remember watching a documentary on a British lady who came to Africa with her boyfriend to study to become a wildlife game warden.

One afternoon, they were in a classroom when somebody spotted a black mamba outside on the corridor. As they were wildlife specialists, they had no intention of killing the black mamba. Rather, they decided to encourage it to go away.

This British lady's boyfriend was excited about it all and got involved in catching the black mamba. In the process however, the young man had the tiniest scratch from the black mamba. He was not actually bitten by the black mamba but had only received the slightest nick. Everyone, including the lecturer, did not consider this to be of any danger to anyone, and they continued with the class as normal. Twenty minutes into the lecture, the young man fell out of his seat in the classroom, staring silently into outer space through glazed eyes. He was pronounced dead within an hour.

Even the slightest nick from a black mamba, without any bleeding, is enough to kill a grown man. Indeed, you must have a proper respect for a black mamba.

A Proper Respect for a Curse

So it is with a curse! You must have a proper respect for curses. The slightest abrasion, the slightest cut, or the slightest scratch of a curse on your life can have far-reaching consequences. To take the bite, the scratch, the nick of a black mamba lightly, is to disrespect the potential that it carries to kill you within a few minutes.

This is the kind of respect you must have for curses. It may be a brief word or statement. It may seem inconsequential. The one speaking the curse may seem weak and powerless to harm you, but you must be careful "not to despise prophesyings".

If you do not have a proper respect for curses spoken, you will live to fulfil them beyond your wildest imagination. I pray that you will see and respect the power that resides within the smallest spoken word of a curse. When you have a proper respect for curses, you will be afraid to steal, cheat, lie or do anything that may activate a curse in your life.

CHAPTER 10

The Wonders of a Curse

And thou shalt become an astonishment, a proverb, and a byword, among all nations whither the Lord shall lead thee.

Deuteronomy 28:37

A curse is a wonderful thing in the sense that it makes you wonder! How a brief statement made to someone can profoundly affect him, and even future generations after him, is sometimes unfathomable. Anyone who studies the concept of curses will only come to the conclusion that a curse is an astonishing thing. Its power knows no bounds.

A curse is usually a set of brief words brought on by mysterious causes that result in an equally mysterious fulfilment. The pervading influence of a curse seems to be endless and boundless. It is as though there are invisible beings ensuring that the words spoken certainly come to pass, no matter how long it takes. There are nine things that make a curse stand out uniquely.

A Curse Creates an Unmistakeable Picture

A curse creates a picture!

Every curse creates an unmistakable picture!

To recognize a curse you must know the picture it creates!

The curse on man creates the unmistakeable picture of toil and sweat that yields little fruit.

The curse on women creates the unmistakeable picture of sorrow, disappointment and struggles with husbands and children.

The curse on Jews creates the unmistakeable picture of worldwide inexplicable hatred, scattering and persecution.

The curse on Jew haters creates the picture of inexplicable ultimate defeat and humiliation.

The curse on black people creates the inexplicable picture of servanthood, poor leadership, poverty and insignificance.

A trained medical doctor will notice certain symptoms and signs because he is trained to recognize the picture of a disease. It is an unmistakeable picture to him because he is trained to see it.

This book is being written to train your eyes to recognize the picture each curse creates.

In the same way, you will now recognize the picture of the curse when you see it. Your trained eyes will pick out the unmistakeable picture that shows that a curse is working.

The Nine Wonders of a Curse

1. A CURSE IS A WONDER BECAUSE IT IS MADE UP OF BRIEF WORDS AND BRIEF STATEMENTS.

Here are examples of brief statements spoken long ago, which are still having an effect on our lives.

"In the sweat of thy face shalt thou eat bread".

"Blessed are those who bless you and cursed are those who curse you".

"A servant of servants shall thou be…".

2. A CURSE IS A WONDER BECAUSE IT HAS MYSTERIOUS AND REMOTE CAUSES.

…A servant of servants shall he be…

Genesis 9:25

The curse on the sons of Ham is very severe, affecting a third of the earth's population. Yet it is related to an event that happened six thousand years ago. Its fulfilment is mystically related to an event that took place between a father and his son. Someone may have considered what transpired between Noah and his son Ham, as a childish prank. Yet, the rebuke spoken by Noah ("a servant of servants shall thou be") is determining the outcome of huge populations on this earth.

As the bird by wandering, as the swallow by flying, so the curse causeless shall not come.

Proverbs 26:2

3. A CURSE IS A WONDER BECAUSE IT IS ALWAYS FULFILLED NO MATTER HOW LONG IT TAKES.

It has been over six thousand years since Adam heard the words, "*Cursed is the ground for thy sake*". It has been thousands of years since Eve heard the words, "*Your desire shall be for your husband*". The weariness that I feel as I write this book is evidence of the words "*in the sweat of thy face shalt thou eat bread*". How mysteriously these words have been fulfilled.

"*A servant of servants shall thou be.*" It has been six thousand years since Noah spoke those words. Yet, they still seem to be holding the sons of Ham in bondage. This is why a curse is a wonder. No matter how long and no matter how far, it is always fulfilled.

4. A CURSE IS A WONDER BECAUSE IT RESULTS IN ASTONISHMENT, AMAZEMENT AND CONSTERNATION.

And thou shalt become an astonishment, a proverb, and a byword, among all nations whither the Lord shall lead thee.

Deuteronomy 28:37

The words that define a curse are: "an astonishment", "a proverb", "a byword", and "an amazement".

It is simply amazing to see the curse on Adam and Eve being fulfilled in every person, no matter the country, the profession or the education of the individual.

It is simply astonishing to see the curses that were bestowed on Jew-haters coming to pass in great detail.

It is just wonderful to see how a nation can become a proverb and a byword because of some statements made by a prophet five thousand years ago.

It is important to have a proper respect for curses because they can turn you into "an astonishment, an amazement, a proverb and a byword".

5.   A CURSE IS A WONDER BECAUSE IT IS A WRITTEN PRESCRIPTION.

Then I lifted up my eyes again and looked, and behold, there was a flying scroll. And he said to me, "What do you see?" And I answered, "I see a flying SCROLL; its length is twenty cubits and its width ten cubits." Then he said to me, "THIS IS THE CURSE that is going forth over the face of the whole land; surely everyone who steals will be purged away ACCORDING TO THE WRITING on one side, and everyone who swears will be purged away according to the writing on the other side.

Zechariah 5:1-3 (NASB)

The curse of Zechariah was written on a scroll that was flying through the air. The written curse is specific. Likewise, things that are happening are specific and are prescribed. The demons see the prescription of poverty, disease, sickness and frustration and are thereby empowered to implement them on all those for whom it has been prescribed. This is why curses follow certain patterns that do not vary.

6.   A CURSE IS A WONDER BECAUSE CURSES CAN AND DO FLY.

Then I turned, and lifted up mine eyes, and looked, and behold a FLYING roll. And he said unto me, What seest thou? And I answered, I see a flying roll; the length thereof is twenty cubits, and the breadth thereof ten cubits. Then said he unto me,

This is the curse that goeth forth over the face of the whole earth: for every one that stealeth shall be cut off as on this side according to it; and every one that sweareth shall be cut off as on that side according to it.

Zechariah 5:1-3

The curse is not walking, but flying! This speaks of the speed with which curses attach themselves to people that are cursed.

7. A CURSE IS A WONDER BECAUSE CURSES ARE WORLDWIDE.

Then said he unto me, This is THE CURSE THAT GOETH FORTH OVER THE FACE OF THE WHOLE EARTH: for every one that stealeth shall be cut off as on this side according to it; and every one that sweareth shall be cut off as on that side according to it.

Zechariah 5:3

Curses are worldwide in their effect. They go across the face of the whole earth. If there is a curse on white men or black men, you will find out that it will work wherever white men or black men are found on the earth.

8. A CURSE IS A WONDER BECAUSE CURSES ARE SPECIFIC, ENTERING PARTICULAR HOUSES.

Then I turned, and lifted up mine eyes, and looked, and behold a flying roll. And he said unto me, What seest thou? And I answered, I see a flying roll; the length thereof is twenty cubits, and the breadth thereof ten cubits. Then said he unto me,

THIS IS THE CURSE that goeth forth over the face of the whole earth: for every one that stealeth shall be cut off as on this side according to it; and every one that sweareth shall be cut off as on that side according to it.

I will bring it forth, saith the Lord of hosts, and IT SHALL ENTER INTO THE HOUSE OF THE THIEF, AND INTO THE HOUSE OF HIM THAT SWEARETH FALSELY BY MY NAME: and it shall remain in the midst of his house, and shall consume it with the timber thereof and the stones thereof.

Zechariah 5:1-4

This curse of the thief enters only the houses of thieves. There were many houses in those days, but only the house of the thief was selected by the flying curse.

9. A CURSE IS A WONDER BECAUSE CURSES ARE MERCILESS, CONSUMING EVERYTHING, DOMINATING EVERYTHING.

Then I turned, and lifted up mine eyes, and looked, and behold a flying roll. And he said unto me, What seest thou? And I answered, I see a flying roll; the length thereof is twenty cubits, and the breadth thereof ten cubits. Then said he unto me,

THIS IS THE CURSE that goeth forth over the face of the whole earth: for every one that stealeth shall be cut off as on this side according to it; and every one that sweareth shall be cut off as on that side according to it.

I will bring it forth, saith the Lord of hosts, and it shall enter into the house of the thief, and into the house of him that sweareth falsely by my name: and it shall remain in the midst of his house, and SHALL CONSUME IT WITH THE TIMBER THEREOF AND THE STONES THEREOF.

Zechariah 5:1-4

Curses consume everything that they encounter. This curse will consume the timber and the stones of the building. When a curse is in operation, it consumes your background, your education, your efforts and your investments. This is why people who live under curses are dominated by the curse. You will notice the lives of all men and women are completely dominated by the words spoken in the book of Genesis. You will notice that Jews and the sons of Ham are completely dominated by the curses spoken many years ago. Such is the nature of a curse! It is consuming, dominating and merciless in its very nature!

SECTION 2

THE EVIDENCE OF CURSES

CHAPTER 11

The Curse on Adam

THE CURSE

And unto Adam he said, Because thou hast hearkened unto the voice of thy wife, and hast eaten of the tree, of which I commanded thee, saying, Thou shalt not eat of it: cursed is the ground for thy sake; in sorrow shalt thou eat of it all the days of thy life;

Thorns also and thistles shall it bring forth to thee; and thou shalt eat the herb of the field;

In the sweat of thy face shalt thou eat bread, till thou return unto the ground; for out of it wast thou taken: for dust thou art, and unto dust shalt thou return.

Genesis 3:17-19

The Implications of the Curse on Adam

1. *"Unto dust shall thou return"*:   Death came to Adam, bringing an end to all his activities and achievements on this earth. Adam was cursed to turn back into dust.

2. *"Cursed is the ground for thy sake"*: Work was going to be hard labour. The ground was cursed and every job was to be difficult henceforth.

3. *"In sorrow shalt thou eat of it all the days of thy life"*: Sorrow was to now be a part of life on this earth. Sadness, sorrow, crying, grief, misery are all manifestations of the curse on this earth. Adam and his descendants would now eat, drink and live on earth, in sorrow.

4. *"Thorns and thistles shall it bring to thee"*: Pain, hurt and brokenness were to be a part of Adam's life. Thorns would prick him, and thistles would hurt him continually as he worked on the field.

5. *"In the sweat of thy face shalt thou eat bread"*: Every job was to come with intense labour and sweat. No career, no work would come without a struggle, hustle, suffering, labour and toil. There would be no prosperity without sweat.

A Curse Creates a Picture

The curse on Adam was a curse that affected all men. All men are cursed to sweat and toil with little fruit. A curse creates a picture!

Every curse creates an unmistakable picture!

To recognize a curse you must know the picture it creates!

The curse on man creates the unmistakeable picture of toil and sweat that yields little fruit.

The curse on women creates the unmistakeable picture of sorrow, disappointment and struggles with husbands and children.

The curse on Jews creates the unmistakeable picture of worldwide inexplicable hatred, scattering and persecution.

The curse on Jew haters creates the picture of inexplicable ultimate defeat and humiliation.

The curse on black people creates the inexplicable picture of servanthood, poor leadership, poverty and insignificance.

A trained medical doctor will notice certain symptoms and signs because he is trained to recognize the picture of a disease. It is an unmistakeable picture to him because he is trained to see it. In the same way, you will now recognize the picture of the curse when you see it. Your trained eyes will pick out the unmistakeable picture that shows that a curse is working.

The Fulfilment of the Curse of Adam

Adam was cursed by God for his disobedience and his allegiance to the devil. The curse turned the earth into a place of frustration, producing a lot of labour, pain, frustration and disappointment. Listen carefully to the words spoken in this curse. "In the sweat of thy face shall thou eat bread." This curse means there is going to be a lot of labour that will produce little fruit. Also, there is going to be frustration, as the ground will need so much effort in order to make it yield anything.

The next thing guaranteed by the curse was pain and disappointment. How disappointing and frustrating it is to produce thorns and thistles instead of apples and oranges. This is why frustration, disappointments and futility characterise all human activity and work on this earth. All men will discover the disappointing nature of work in this life. This is what Solomon discovered for himself. Even he, the richest man on earth, was unable to escape the network of disappointments, frustration, hard labour and pain that is found on this earth.

This is why parents want their children to be educated. Parents know that life on earth is very difficult; and it is even more difficult without education. Even with an education life is not easy at all, no matter where you live. Solomon described life on earth as an experience in futility and a continuous grasping. This endless futility, accompanied by endless searching, is a curse.

Please notice the writings of Solomon and how he rightly diagnosed the existence of a curse in this world.

THE FULFILMENT OF THE CURSE ON ADAM AS DESCRIBED BY SOLOMON

1. **Solomon said that THE LIFE of man was full of grasping and futility.**

   I have seen all the works which have been done under the sun, and, behold, ALL IS VANITY and STRIVING AFTER WIND.

   Ecclesiastes 1:14 (NASB)

2. **Solomon said that THE ACHIEVEMENTS of men were actually useless.**

   Then I looked on all THE WORKS THAT MY HANDS HAD WROUGHT, and on the labour that I had laboured to do: and, behold, ALL WAS VANITY and vexation of spirit, and there was no profit under the sun.

   Ecclesiastes 2:11

3. **Solomon said that anyone who had analysed what life on this earth actually was, would HATE LIFE itself.**

   THEREFORE I HATED LIFE; because the work that is wrought under the sun is grievous unto me: for all is vanity and vexation of spirit.

   Ecclesiastes 2:17

4.   **Solomon said that life on earth was terrible because death will eventually take you away and all YOUR ACHIEVEMENTS WILL BE HANDED OVER to someone else.**

Yea, I hated all my labour which I had taken under the sun: BECAUSE I SHOULD LEAVE IT UNTO THE MAN THAT SHALL BE AFTER ME. And who knoweth whether he shall be a wise man or a fool? Yet shall he have rule over all my labour wherein I have laboured, and wherein I have shewed myself wise under the sun. This is also vanity.

Ecclesiastes 2:18-19

5.   **Solomon described life on earth as FULL OF SORROW and grief. This is exactly what God said to Adam. "In sorrow shalt thou eat of it."**

For all HIS DAYS ARE SORROWS, and his travail grief; yea, his heart taketh not rest in the night. This is also vanity.

Ecclesiastes 2:23

6.   **Solomon said that life on earth was full of sadness because ALL THAT MEN GET FOR THEIR HARD WORK IS ENVY.**

Again, I considered all travail, and every right work, that FOR THIS A MAN IS ENVIED of his neighbour. This is also vanity and vexation of spirit.

Ecclesiastes 4:4

7.   **Solomon said life was evil because people just worked and WORKED WITHOUT KNOWING WHY they were working. Even those who did not have relatives worked anyway, because there was nothing else to do.**

There is one alone, and there is not a second; yea, he hath neither child nor brother: yet is there no end of all his labour; neither is his eye satisfied with riches; NEITHER

SAITH HE, FOR WHOM DO I LABOUR, and bereave my soul of good? This is also vanity, yea, it is a sore travail.

Ecclesiastes 4:8

8. **Solomon said life on earth was cursed and futile because no matter how much you earned or had you were STILL NOT SATISFIED.**

HE THAT LOVETH SILVER SHALL NOT BE SATISFIED with silver; nor he that loveth abundance with increase: this is also vanity.

Ecclesiastes 5:10

9. **Solomon described life on earth as cursed and futile because many people who had worked hard to obtain everything they could possibly dream of, NEVER EVEN HAD A CHANCE TO ENJOY IT.**

A man to whom God hath given riches, wealth, and honour, so that he wanteth nothing for his soul of all that he desireth, YET GOD GIVETH HIM NOT POWER TO EAT THEREOF, but a stranger eateth it: this is vanity, and it is an evil disease.

Ecclesiastes 6:2

10. **Solomon described life on earth as cursed and futile because many times BOTH GOOD AND BAD PEOPLE seem to have THE SAME EXPERIENCES in this life.**

There is a futility which is done on the earth; that is, THERE BE RIGHTEOUS MEN TO WHOM IT HAPPENS ACCORDING TO THE DEEDS OF THE WICKED. On the other hand, there are evil men to whom it happens according to the deeds of the righteous: I say that this too is futility.

Ecclesiastes 8:14 (NASB)

CHAPTER 12

How the Curse on Adam is Working Out

In the sweat of thy face shalt thou eat bread, till thou return unto the ground;...

Genesis 3:19

Whoever you are, upon the face of this earth, you will be faced with the reality of the curse on Adam. "In the sweat of thy face shalt thou eat bread". There is no job or work on this earth that does not have this characteristic. The description, "sweating" speaks of toiling, struggling, labouring and suffering.

All things are full of labour; man cannot utter it: the eye is not satisfied with seeing, nor the ear filled with hearing.

Ecclesiastes 1:8

And he called his name Noah, saying, this same shall comfort us concerning our work and toil of our hands, because of the ground which the Lord hath cursed.

Genesis 5:29

Work in this world can be classified in many ways: executive jobs, political jobs, construction jobs, architectural jobs, computer related jobs, spiritual jobs, administrative jobs and low-skill jobs. Whatever the classification and whatever the job, all work has the characteristics of toiling, suffering, struggling and labouring. If you look at the classification of jobs listed below, you will discover that no category of work has escaped the curse.

HOW THE CURSE HAS AFFECTED TWENTY TYPES OF WORK THAT EXIST TODAY

1. **Managerial work:** Presidents, Chief Executives, Managing Directors, Administrative Managers.

"In the sweat of thy face shall thou be a manager...."

Presidents, chief executives, managing directors are in so many meetings and involved in so many discussions that they soon realize they have lost control of their own time. Indeed, chief executives can become bottlenecks in their own organizations because they are unable to find the time to take needed decisions.

Managers are often isolated people with few friends in the organisation they work for. Most managers spend all their time and their life running these organisations that depend extensively on them. Managers and chief executives have so much stress that they have their own set of "executive illnesses". For instance, diseases like stomach ulcers, high blood pressure, heart attacks are more associated with highly stressed executives.

2.   **Medical work:** Doctors, dentists, pharmacists, nurses, paramedical staff, laboratory, radiology, computer and medical engineers.

"In the sweat of thy face shall thou be a doctor, dentist, pharmacist, nurse …"

Medical workers are perhaps those who sweat more than anyone else. Medical doctors go to school for many years. They lose their friends whilst they are at school because they are glued to their books and have to pass many exams. After qualifying as doctors, they may study for another ten years in order to become specialists. After qualifying, they work for such long hours that they hardly get to go home to enjoy their salaries. Many doctors are forced to deal with death, bad news, sadness and sorrow on a daily basis. The other medical professions are equally stressful. All medical workers are in danger of contracting dangerous diseases like yellow fever, dengue fever, HIV, bird flu, hepatitis, Ebola and Zika virus. Truly, it is only in the sweat, struggle, toil, suffering, and labour of their lives that medical workers are eating bread!

3.   **Scientific work:**   Inventors, researchers, developers, astrophysicists, nuclear scientists.

"In the sweat of thy face shall thou be a researcher, developer, scientist…"

Scientists are greatly stressed individuals because of the momentous value of the work they do. Thousands of hours go into research that often yields nothing. Many hours, many days are spent in fruitless research whose value may be seen only after the death of the researcher. There are many dangers of infections, explosions and accidents that threaten scientists.

4.   Legal work: Judges, lawyers, paralegal workers.

"In the sweat of thy face shall thou be a lawyer...."

Lawyers go to school for many years. They study, toil, struggle and suffer for years in school. They have to have very high grades in school. Many people who study Law are unable to qualify for the Bar, because they do not make the grade. After graduating, a lawyer struggles to develop a good reputation as a lawyer so that he can have a successful practice.

Many lawyers work in their firms till very late. Many young lawyers do not sleep much as they strive to climb the ladder in their law firm. There are many unsuccessful lawyers. Many lawyers have to do other jobs in order to survive. In the sweat of their face the lawyers are eating bread!

5.   Educational work: Teachers, professors, lecturers, administrators of schools.

"In the sweat of thy face shall thou be a teacher, professor, lecturer and administrator..."

Teachers work hard and for long hours. You may not have to give your life for your teaching job but you might lose many other things. Disrespectful students, unappreciative parents, endless assignments, taking work home, low salaries and poverty are among the great difficulties that teachers face. In the sweat of their face teachers are earning low salaries and struggling to survive in this life.

6.   Finance work: Bankers, traders, stockbrokers, actuaries.

"In the sweat of thy face shall thou be a banker, trader, stockbroker and bank worker..."

Bank workers are known to struggle, toil and suffer with long hours of stressful work. They also have a lot of negative internal politics to deal with. There are many risks, debts, financial scandals and financial crises that stress bank workers out. Many bank workers are up to their necks in loans and mortgages. They are bound to their jobs and can never be free from their debts. In the sweat of their faces, these bank workers are earning high salaries and swimming in debt! How paradoxical!

7.   **Construction work:** Architects, engineers, quantity surveyors, contractors, project managers.

"In the sweat of thy face shall thou be an architect, engineer, quantity surveyor, contractor and project manager..."

The sweat in architecture starts in university where the students often have longer hours of work than others. Contractors and construction workers have some of the highest stress levels because of the need to meet targets. Other dangers of financial mismanagement and losses during construction give rise to much stress in the construction world. Construction work is one of the most stressful and expensive jobs. In the sweat of their faces, contractors and engineers are eating bread and breaking down under the stress involved.

8.   **Administrative work:** Administrators, secretaries, data officers.

"In the sweat of thy face shall thou be an administrator..."

Many administrative workers, data officers, secretaries and personal assistants struggle through life. Many of them are not appreciated for their hard work. Those who have good jobs have to work very hard to earn their living. Others while away their time and have to spend long hours doing nothing, and waiting for their bosses to come or go. Many are also forced to give sexual favours at work in order to rise to the next level. Indeed, there is a lot of sweating just to eat some bread. Administrators and secretaries are truly sweating to eat a little bread.

9. **Entrepreneurial work:** Investors, business entrepreneurs, market women, merchants, retail traders, street vendors.

"In the sweat of thy face shall thou be an entrepreneur..."

Many entrepreneurs and businessmen fail because their businesses are unable to become genuinely established. Many businessmen struggle under the burden of debts they have contracted. Many entrepreneurs and businessmen struggle, toil, labour and suffer from a lack of financing for their businesses. The lack of good ideas for their businesses, the competition in their field of business, the lack of customers for their products and the lack of a steady income are just a few of the problems of business people! Indeed, the struggle of businessmen proves the curse on all men is still real today in spite of the different kinds of modern jobs that exist. Many businessmen are great hustlers with a good presentation. Behind their suits and their sharp talk is nothing but emptiness, vanity and sweat!

10. **Information technology work:** Hardware developers, programmers, web designers, App developers.

"In the sweat of thy face shall thou be a computer scientist..."

Today, there are many people who work in the computer world. They develop software, hardware and invent many useful computer systems. The stress, struggle and toil of this large group of people are related to the sector that they are developing. Computers are used in every field of work. The stress, struggle and toil of every field of work are transposed into the computer scientist's life. Many computer scientists are wearing out their eyes as they sit before their computers day and night. They are becoming millionaires and sacrificing their families in the process. Leaving the farms and moving to computers has not removed the curse of "in the sweat of thy face shall thou eat bread". In spite of the air-conditioned and modern offices, our computer scientists are equally sweating it out on earth. The curse is a wonder! It is happening practically!

11. **Agricultural and fishing, mining workers:** Farmers, fishermen, miners, animal husbandry workers.

"In the sweat of thy face thou shall be a farmer, fisherman or miner..."

The toiling, the sweating, the struggling and the suffering are very easy to see in the lives of farmers, fishermen and miners. Farming still employs the largest group of people in the world. A lot of farmers are poor. Most farmers get very little for all their farming efforts. This is why European and American farmers are greatly subsidized. Famines generally occur most where people only specialize in farming.

One of the most dangerous jobs is mining. It is a dirty job and underground mines are cold, noisy, dark, damp and scary. Breathing in the dust in a mine can lead to many lung diseases. There is a real danger of accidents occurring underground where miners can be trapped and die.

Many fishermen drown or some get lost at sea; and many of them get very little after fishing all night.

Apostle Peter almost drowned in the Sea of Galilee. He met Jesus Christ after he had toiled all night and caught nothing for all his hard work. The great apostle was equally labouring under the curse "in the sweat of thy face shall thou eat bread".

12. **Artisan work:** Tailors, beauticians, hairdressers, mechanics, masons, carpenters, plumbers, electricians, tilers.

"In the sweat of thy face shall thou be an artisan..."

Tailors, hairdressers, carpenters, masons and labourers work very hard and get very little for all their efforts. The curse that has been placed on all forms of work on this earth is alive and is working against them. Many artisans are constantly lying to their customers about one thing or the other. In spite of all the extra jobs they take, they struggle to make ends meet.

13. **Machines, equipment, factory work:** Inventors, manufacturers, assemblers, operators of machines, factory workers.

"In the sweat of thy face shall thou be a factory worker..."

The suffering, toil and struggle of a factory worker are known all over the world. Whether it is a factory that makes cars, tinned fish, clothes or shoes, factory work is no easy thing. Many factory hands are underpaid and work under dangerous conditions. The business world is always looking for places to set up factories where labour is cheap. People who work in factories are often seen as dispensable workers who are mere tools for creating real wealth for the owners of the factory. Have you ever wondered why factory workers are always going on strike? It is because they are frustrated, sweating and labouring under the curse.

14. **Unskilled labourers:** Cleaners, labourers, assistants, attendants, waiters, helpers, cooks, cashiers, refuse collectors.

"In the sweat of thy face shall thou be a cleaner, a labourer, a waiter, a helper, a cook, a cashier, a waste disposal officer, refuse collector..."

Unskilled labourers are those who prove this scripture very easily. Labourers, assistants, helpers and unskilled workers sweat from morning to evening with very little to show for it. For instance, waste disposal officers may have to clear up human waste and put their lives at risk while doing so.

In many cases there is no safety gear and they are exposed to sewage waste without any protection. These workers suffer because they are exposed to human waste, dangerous gases and dangerous chemicals. I once watched a waste disposal worker wading barefoot through faeces as he worked all night. I could not believe my eyes. This is the work he had to do every day. Indeed, the curse is real and frightening.

15. **Military and security services work:** Soldiers, police, air force pilots, army officers, prison officers, commandos, military staff, spies, security officers, personal bodyguards, navy officers, fire officers.

"In the sweat of thy face shall thou be in the military..."

Being in the military or security services is a sad and difficult job. A soldier often has to fight foolish fights based on the whims and fancies of political leaders who are too proud to accept peace. Soldiers often die for foolish causes. Soldiers often die because of the decisions proud and wicked politicians take.

Being in the military is extremely hazardous, because you will have to go to some of the most dangerous places in the world. You will have to interact, and fight with some of the most dangerous people in the world.

Being a soldier requires lots of time away from home. Being a military man is a struggle. It is full of painful toiling under uncomfortable conditions. The constant threat of death multiplies the stress of a soldier's work. Soldiers wear a chain around their neck with an inscription of their name and address on it in case they are killed suddenly. The nameplate is used to identify them in case their bodies are dismembered and disfigured. What a job!

16. **Religious work:** Pastors, apostles, religious leaders, church workers.

"In the sweat of thy face shall thou be a religious worker..."

Pastors are also labouring on earth under the same conditions as everyone else! Pastors are under a lot of stress. Being a minister of the gospel is more difficult than being a doctor, a lawyer or a politician. Pastors struggle and toil as much as anyone else on this earth. Being in the ministry and serving the Lord does not mean that you are exempt from eating bread through the sweat of your face.

I remember when my wife's friends would say to her, "Your husband doesn't work any more." I can understand how another person's job looks easy from the outside. Sleep all week and deliver one sermon on Sunday! How easy that sounds!

I also remember when I had previous employees of a top international firm coming to work in the ministry. They were shocked at the amount of work they had to do in the ministry. Several people have come out of top international banks to work in our church. Every single one of them has said without exception that they have never worked that much in their lives. Truly, "In the sweat of thy face shall thou eat bread", applies to pastors as well.

17. **Sports work:** Sportsmen, sports workers, soccer players, golfers, tennis players, track and field athletes.

"In the sweat of thy face shall thou be a sportsman ..."

Sportsmen are just like labourers, attendants and artisans in the sense that they also labour, struggle, toil and suffer to earn a living. Most sportsmen have to train very hard and have to spend many hours in private toil, suffering and labour.

We all know sportsmen who have become millionaires through their particular sport whether it is golf, tennis or soccer.

The reality is that there are many others who spent their lives trying but never amounted to anything.

Sportsmen are under great pressure to perform or lose their position and their income. Even when sportsmen become rich, they hardly know how to use their money and their riches often dissipate into thin air. Unfortunately, most sportsmen cannot continue their sport beyond a certain youthful age. Their earnings come to an abrupt end at a tender age. When I began to play golf, I realised how hard professional golfers have worked to eat bread. Everything looks easy from the outside, but the curse is real. "In the sweat of thy face shall thou eat bread."

18. Entertainment work: Actors, models, film producers, directors, musicians, photographers.

"In the sweat of thy face shall thou be an entertainer..."

Entertainers are just like any other workers on earth in the sense that they will also labour, struggle, toil and suffer to earn a living. Most singers, dancers, models and actors have had to train very hard and have had to spend many hours in private toil, suffering and labour.

We all know singers who became millionaires through a song they made.

The reality is that there are many others who spent their lives trying to sing a nice song but never amounted to anything.

Singers and actors are under great pressure to perform or lose their fame. Most singers hardly know how to use their money and their riches often turn into rags. Unfortunately, most singers, dancers, models and actors have a short period in which they shine. After this, most of them disappear into oblivion. Amazingly, most singers have only one famous song. It is very difficult for singers to come up with two songs that really hit the mark. Indeed, singers, stars, actors, photographers are fulfilling the curse; "in the sweat of thy face shall thou eat bread".

19. Political workers: Presidents, parliamentarians, ministers of state, congressmen, government workers.

"In the sweat of thy face shall thou be a politician..."

Presidents and politicians have very difficult lives. Many politicians campaign all their lives to have a job that lasts for just four years.

Democratic politicians have to please everyone in order to be chosen in the next election. It is not easy to please everyone! It is not easy to participate in every type of religious service and pretend to worship elsewhere.

Many politicians are insecure because everyone wants to replace them and take over their position. It is a very difficult thing to rule over millions of greedy, selfish, forgetful and ungrateful people.

You can virtually see a president's hair turn grey as he struggles through his term of office.

20.   Creative workers: Artists, authors, poets, composers, inventors.

"In the sweat of thy face shall thou be a creative worker ... "

Artists are just like any other workers on earth in the sense that they will also labour, struggle, toil and suffer to earn a living. Most authors, inventors and composers have had to spend many hours in private toil, suffering and labour.

We all know authors who became millionaires through some books they wrote.

The reality is that there are many others like them who spent their lives writing but never amounted to anything.

Many artists, composers and inventors are not appreciated in their lifetime and often die in poverty. Unfortunately, most authors, composers and poets also have a short period during which they can shine.

You can pick and choose from any of the jobs that exist in the world today. Whatever the job, no matter how unsavoury it is, you will find that the pattern remains the same. There is sweat, there is toil, there is struggle, there is futility, there is suffering and there is vanity!

From being a miner to being a president, a crab fisherman, a mercenary, a journalist, a cleaner, a negotiator, a lumber logger, a prison warden, a mountain rescue worker, a school teacher, a disposer of refuse, an undertaker, a model, a guard, a vet, an oil rig worker, a protocol officer, an electrician, a tower builder, a welder, a fire fighter, a driver, a foreman, a personal bodyguard, a painter, a laundry worker, a night security officer, a nurse, a dancer, a surgeon, a pilot, a flight engineer, an ambulance driver, a fire engine driver, a policeman, a health worker, a broadcaster, a nursery school teacher, a mental health nurse, a marijuana seller, a groundnut seller, a plantain seller, a physician specialist, a chief executive, a midwife, a soccer player, a referee, a businessman, an event organizer, a market woman, a trader, a school principal, a mechanic, a traffic warden, a politician, a weatherman, a tax collector, a lawyer, a used car dealer, a pimp, a prostitute, a pornographer, a banker, a dentist, a soldier, a naval officer, a submarine commander, a hundred-metre sprinter, a boxer, a bus conductor, a long jump and high jump specialist, an astronaut, a civil engineer, a captain of a ship, a tipper truck driver, a cremator, a latrine worker, a sexton, a maintenance worker, a grounds worker, an advisor, an orthodontist, a computer hardware engineer, an astronomer, a political scientist, a mathematician, a chemistry teacher, an app developer, a physicist, a law professor, an actuary, an optometrist, a statistician, a computer and systems manager, a web developer, a jockey, an aircraft mechanic, an apostle or a pastor, you will only eat bread in the sweat of your face according to the word of the Lord that came to Adam.

The Curse of Death

Through this same curse man is doomed to die. No matter which country you come from and no matter what medicines you take, your destiny is death. This is the nature of a curse. *It is astonishing in its invariability. It is marvellous in its unrelenting outcome.*

... for in the day that thou eatest thereof thou shalt surely die.

Genesis 2:17

The curse on Adam is a wonder because whichever direction you turn, wherever you go, death will meet you one day or another. How has this curse of death been implemented in the earth? The curse of Adam is ensured by a multitude of death-causing agents that release death in the earth and ensure that the word of the Lord comes to pass.

This list of death-causing agents ensures that everybody on earth dies. Whatever the case, whatever your age, whatever your nationality, one of these listed agents may definitely lead to the fulfilment of the curse on Adam in your life.

Wisdom, carefulness and the grace of God, can cause you to elude some of these agents of death for many years. Understand that wisdom is your master key to overcoming a curse!

In the natural, this is a list of death-causing agents. However, the real cause of death is what God said to Adam *"in the day that thou eatest thereof thou shalt surely die."*

The List of Death-Causing Agents

1. Heart disease (1 in 5)

2. Cancer (1 in 7)

3. Smoking-related deaths (1 in 9)

4. Falling down a staircase   (1 in 20)

5. Stroke (1 in 23)

6. Obesity-related (1 in 35)

7. Accidental injury (1 in 36)

8. Heavy drinking (1 in 49)

9. Breast cancer (1 in 95)

10. Motor vehicle accident (1 in 100)

11. Suicide, Intentional self-harm (1 in 121)

12. Prostate cancer (1 in 133)

13. Internal Revenue Service audit (1 in 250)

14. Accidental poisoning (drug, alcohol & vapours) (1 in 281)

15. Fall involving bed, chair or other furniture (1 in 184)

16. Having identity stolen (1 in 200)

17. Victim of assault (1 in 211)

18. Death by falling down (1 in 246)

19. Brain tumour (1 in 298)

20. Gunshots (1 in 325)

21. Death by being murdered (1 in 300)

22. Pedestrian accident (1 in 649)

23. Motorcycle accident (1 in 770)

24. Exposure to smoke, fire and flames (1 in 1,116)

25. Complications from medical or surgical care (1 in 1,170)

26. Natural forces (1 in 3,357)

27. Injury while mowing lawn (1 in 3,623)

28. Bicycle accident (1 in 4,717)

29. Gun accidents (1 in 6309)

30. Drowning (1 in 8,942)

31. Flu (1 in 9,410)

32. Electrocution (1 in 9,943)

33. Heat exposure (1 in 12,517)

34. Air-travel accidents (1 in 20,000)

35. Floods (1 in 30,000)

36. Cataclysmic storm (1 in 46,044)

37. Legal execution – electric chair (1 in 58,618)

38. Tornadoes (1 in 60,000)

39. Lightning strikes (1 in 83,930)

40. Bees (1 in 100,000)

41. Snake or other venomous bite or sting (1 in 100,000)

42. Earthquakes (1 in 131,890)

43. Spousal murder (1 in 135,000)

44. Dog attacks (1 in 147,717)

45. Death by choking on food (1 in 370,000)

46. Fireworks (1 in 386,766)

47. Tsunami (1 in 500,000)

48. Fireworks discharge (1 in 615,488)

49. Death by meteorite (1 in 700,000)

50. Spider's bite (1 in 716,010)

51. Food poisoning (1 in 3,000,000)

52. Mad cow disease (1 in 40,000,000)

53. Shark attack (1 in 3,943,110)

54. Death by hayflick limit (125 years)

CHAPTER 13

The Curse on Eve

Unto the woman he said, I will greatly multiply thy sorrow and thy conception; in sorrow thou shalt bring forth children; and thy desire shall be to thy husband, and he shall rule over thee.

Genesis 3:16

This chapter deals with the curse on Eve. It is a curse that affects all women because all women are descendants of Eve.

A curse creates a picture!

Every curse creates an unmistakable picture!

To recognize a curse you must know the picture it creates!

The curse on man creates the unmistakeable picture of toil and sweat that yields little fruit.

The curse on women creates the unmistakeable picture of sorrow, disappointment and struggles with husbands and children.

The curse on Jews creates the unmistakeable picture of worldwide inexplicable hatred, scattering and persecution.

The curse on Jew haters creates the picture of inexplicable ultimate defeat and humiliation.

The curse on black people creates the inexplicable picture of servanthood, poor leadership, poverty and insignificance.

A trained medical doctor will notice certain symptoms and signs because he is trained to recognize the picture of a disease. It is an unmistakeable picture to him because he is trained to see it. In the same way, you will now recognize the picture of the curse on Eve when you see it. Your trained eyes will pick out the unmistakeable picture that shows that a curse is working.

The Implications of the Curse on Eve

1. *"I will greatly multiply thy sorrow"*: Through this curse, women were cursed to have great sorrow in this life. Apart from the sorrows of men, women are given an extra dose of sorrow by this curse.

2. *"In sorrow shalt thou bring forth children"*: Through this curse, women were cursed to suffer whilst trying to conceive and have children. Great pain and suffering awaits the female race as they try to have children in this life.

3. *"Thy desire shall be to thy husband"*: Through this curse, a great inexplicable attraction for men has descended on all women. This great attraction is actually a punishment for the disobedience in the Garden of Eden. Through their inexorable attraction to boys, girls have had many inconceivable sorrows and hardships.

4. *"He shall rule over thee"*: Men dominate women in school, at work and in every kind of business. Through this curse, great hardships have descended on women. Men have dominated women and caused a lot of suffering to women. Many women have suffered intolerable hardships at the hands of men through marriage.

The Fulfilment of the Curse of Eve

1. *"I will greatly multiply thy sorrow"*: Today, women suffer more from anxiety, depression and fear than men. Indeed, their sorrows and fears are greatly multiplied.

   Anxiety disorders are a category of mental disorders characterized by feelings of anxiety and fear. From the time a girl reaches puberty until about the age of 50, she is twice as likely to suffer from anxiety and fear than a man.

   Women are also more likely to have multiple psychiatric disorders during their lifetime than men. Women also suffer more from depression than men.

   Indeed, depression is the most common women's mental health problem. Depression is also far more persistent in women than in men. All these facts are a fulfilment of the curse "I will greatly multiply thy sorrow!"

2. *"In sorrow shalt thou bring forth children"*: Many women do not find suitable husbands to marry them. Women greatly outnumber men. The curse begins to manifest from the time a girl needs to find a husband. The struggle begins from when a woman has to find a suitor. That is why many

pastors constantly pray for their church members to find husbands. A lot of women have children with men they are not married to.

The next part of the curse is fulfilled when a woman struggles to conceive. Many women struggle to have children. Thousands of hospitals exist to help women become pregnant. When women do become pregnant, the curse continues to hound them as they try to deliver these children into the world safely.

When children are born safely into the world, another phase of the curse kicks in as they bring up these children with great hardship and sorrow. Many women struggle all their lives just to bring up their children. Many children are a great source of concern to their mothers until the very end of the mother's lives. Indeed, how true is the curse "In sorrow shalt thou bring forth children".

3. *"Thy desire shall be to thy husband"*: Young girls are drawn to boys and their hearts are broken over and over. Today, millions of girls are attracted to boys as part of their punishment.

The inexplicable attraction of girls like Eva Braun to a man like Adolf Hitler remains a mystery that can only be explained by a curse. Many women end up as disappointed wives who ask themselves why they even bothered to marry.

Women, irrespective of social standing, economic background, education levels and financial status are in one relationship or another. Most of the tears women shed comes from the pain of their relationships with men. No matter how old a woman is, she seems to want to get married. Sometimes the curse is manifested in the pain of not getting married or in the pain of not being chosen.

4. *"He shall rule over thee"*: Historically, women have been through a lot of difficulty under the domination of men. Women all over the world have been ruled and dominated by men. Even today, men continually dominate women.

Women have been forbidden to vote or participate in elections in many countries for many years.

All over the world, even where democracy flourished, women were initially not allowed to vote. Even in the most advanced countries, women were not seen as people who could choose a leader. Their vote simply did not count. For instance, before 1970, women in Switzerland, Bangladesh, Jordan, Cape Verde, Portugal, Samoa, Namibia, Moldova, South Africa, Kuwait and Liechtenstein were not allowed to vote or stand for election.

Many societies today claim that women are the property of their fathers or husbands. Women are not permitted to wear clothing of their own choosing or to go anywhere without permission from a man. Fathers decide whom their daughters will marry and wives must obey their husbands.

In Ancient Greece, Athenian women were given no education and were married at puberty to grown men. They remained forever the property of their fathers, who could cause them to divorce and make them marry another. They lived in segregation and could not leave the house without a chaperone. They could not buy or sell land.

Under Roman Law, the power of the husband was absolute; he could chastise his wife (even until the later Roman period) to the point of killing her.

Under English Common Law a woman's legal identity disappeared upon marriage, she was a woman eclipsed, covered by her husband. She could no longer contract, sue or be sued in her own right. All her property, her dowry or portion, and anything she earned or inherited during the marriage belonged automatically to her husband, with the exception of paraphernalia (clothes, jewels, bed linen and plates).

During the Renaissance women were generally excluded from education, because it was considered unnecessary, and even folly by most people, to teach girls to read and write. A woman who was exceptionally accomplished risked being labelled as "mannish" or even accused of being a witch.

The first legislation against witchcraft was established around A.D. 670. It wasn't until the 14th century that thousands (the lowest estimate is 100,000) of people across Europe, 75% of them women, began to be killed for this "crime". Henry VIII made witchcraft a felony in 1541; this was later repealed but reintroduced by Elizabeth I in 1563 and the first Englishwoman was hanged for the "crime" in 1566. A 120-year witch-killing craze began in earnest and it saw over 5,000 British women accused. The last trial in England was in 1712, but persecution continued until the end of the 18th century.

The sufferings of women in history are indeed a fulfilment of the words *"He shall rule over thee!"*

CHAPTER 14

The Curse of Isaac

The Curse

Therefore God give thee of the dew of heaven, and the fatness of the earth, and plenty of corn and wine:

Let people serve thee, and nations bow down to thee: be lord over thy brethren, and let thy mother's sons bow down to thee: CURSED BE EVERY ONE THAT CURSETH THEE, and blessed be he that blesseth thee.

Genesis 27:28-29

The Implications of the Curse of Isaac

" *C**ursed be everyone that curseth thee"*: There shall be a frustration, difficulty, poverty and defeat for all those who take up arms against Jacob and who rise in hatred against Jews. This is a curse against anti-semitism and has been fulfilled many times throughout history.

It is therefore of interest to note what has happened to all the mighty nations and empires which persecuted and murdered Jews in the past. All Jew haters will come to the same end, as did Rome, the Crusaders, Nazi Germany, the Soviet Union and so many others that do not even exist today. Let us look at these examples, one by one, and see the common pattern. A curse is a wonder! It is a wonder because it always comes to pass no matter how long it takes. The words spoken by authority figures have carried through the centuries and worked out an amazing pattern that is difficult to ignore.

Each Curse Has a Picture

Each curse creates a picture!

Every curse creates an unmistakable picture!

To recognize a curse you must know the picture it creates!

The curse on man creates the unmistakeable picture of toil and sweat that yields little fruit.

The curse on women creates the unmistakeable picture of sorrow, disappointment and struggles with husbands and children.

The curse on Jews creates the unmistakeable picture of worldwide inexplicable hatred, scattering and persecution.

The curse on Jew haters creates the picture of inexplicable ultimate defeat and humiliation.

The curse on black people creates the inexplicable picture of servanthood, poor leadership, poverty and insignificance.

A trained medical doctor will notice certain symptoms and signs because he is trained to recognize the picture of a disease. It is an unmistakeable picture to him because he is trained to see it. In the same way, you will now recognize the picture of the curse when you see it. Your trained eyes will pick out the unmistakeable picture that shows that a curse is working.

The Fulfilment of the Curse of Isaac

1. The fulfilment of the curse on the Roman Empire: "Cursed be everyone that curseth thee".

The mighty Roman Empire once dominated the world. Every nation was subject to its great and spreading power. Unfortunately for this great empire, it took on an enemy which was protected by a great and mighty curse. There were a number of military campaigns between the Jews and the Roman Empire.

From the year 63 BC, General Pompey subdued Judea. From then on, the Jewish kingdom was subject to the Roman Empire. A serious rebellion against the Roman Empire began in AD 66 and ended with the destruction of the Jewish Temple in AD 70.

It was the 14th of April, AD 70 during the Passover, when Titus, commander of the Roman Army laid siege to Jerusalem. He eventually overcame the city and burnt down the holy Temple of the Jews.

During the four years of war, the Romans took 97,000 Jews as prisoners. Thousands of them were forced to become gladiators and were killed in the arena, fighting wild animals or fellow gladiators. Some, who were considered criminals, were burned alive. Others were employed at Seleucia, where they were put to digging a tunnel. But most of these prisoners were brought to Rome, where they were forced to build the Forum of Peace (a park in the heart of Rome) and the Colosseum.

The boundless riches from the Temple treasury were used to strike coins with the legend JUDAEA CAPTA ("Judaea defeated"). The Menorah and the Table from the Holy Temple were exhibited in the Temple of Peace. The Romans then destroyed Jerusalem and annexed Judaea as a Roman province. As a punishment for their rebellion, the Romans systematically forced all Jews to leave Palestine.

Three years later, in 73 AD, a small Jewish force still held out against the mighty Roman Empire in a mountain fortress called Masada. The Romans had besieged the fort for two years, and the 1,000 Jewish men, women, and children inside were beginning to starve. In desperation, the Jewish revolutionaries decided to kill themselves rather than surrender to the Romans.

After 73 AD, the Jews were scattered all over the world in Europe, Africa and Asia. Many Jews migrated to areas throughout the Mediterranean region and to other parts of the world.

"Cursed be everyone that curseth thee": There shall be a frustration, difficulty, poverty and defeat for all those who take up arms against Jacob and who rise in hatred against Jews.

The Roman Empire, which destroyed the Jews in Jerusalem, experienced the curse of Isaac that protects Israel. That ancient curse declares "cursed be those who curse you" and is mysteriously fulfilled today because the Roman Empire has now been destroyed and wiped out completely.

Astonishingly today, two thousand years later, there is no Roman Empire but there is a Jewish state of Israel with its capital in Jerusalem.

2. The fulfilment of the curse in the Empire of the Tsars: "Cursed be everyone that curseth thee".

The Russian Empire existed from 1721 until it was overthrown during the February Revolution in 1917. The Russian Empire was one of the largest empires in world history, stretching over three continents. It was surpassed in landmass only by the British and Mongol empires. The Russian Empire at one time hosted the largest population of Jews in the world. Within these territories the Jewish community flourished and developed. The Russian

Empire was ruled by the Boyars and then by emperors called Tsars.

A large-scale wave of anti-Jewish demonstrations swept over Ukraine in 1881, after Jews were wrongly blamed for the assassination of Alexander II. Thousands of Jewish homes were destroyed, many families reduced to extremes of poverty; large numbers of men, women, and children were injured and some killed.

Tsar Alexander III was a staunch reactionary and an anti-Semite. He escalated anti-Jewish policies and sought to ignite "Popular anti-Semitism", which portrayed the Jews as "Christ-killers".

The tsarist government implemented programs that ensured the Jews remained isolated. As a result of these attacks on Jews, many of them migrated to the United States.

But soon after these events, the almighty Russian empire mysteriously came to an end following a revolution.

A communist revolution arose in 1917 and wiped out the Tsars forever. Lenin and communism replaced Tsar Nicholas, who was murdered. Lenin's government carried out "the Red Terror" in the nation that resulted in millions of deaths.

The Jews, who had been persecuted a few years earlier, had migrated, survived and prospered in America. A few of them even migrated to Israel and revitalized the Holy Land. "Cursed be those who curse you" was fulfilled against the Russian Empire that was ruled by tsars. Today, the empire of the tsars is no more but the Jewish state of Israel exists and flourishes.

3.   The fulfilment of the curse in the Spanish Empire: "Cursed be everyone that curseth thee".

The Spanish Empire was one of the largest empires in world history and one of the first with a global extent.

The Spanish Empire became the foremost global power of its time, and was the first to be called *the empire on which the sun never sets*. The empire, administered from Madrid by the Spanish Crown, comprised territories and colonies in Europe, America, Africa, Asia and Oceania.

A large number of Jews settled in Spain when the Romans destroyed their home in Israel. The Jews lived happily in Spain for a thousand years until the Queen of Spain, Isabella and King Ferdinand decided to expel all Jews from Spain. The Jews were asked to convert to the state religion, Christianity, or leave Spain. Some 300,000 Jews had to convert to Catholicism. Those who did not convert had to either flee Spain or were killed in the Spanish Inquisition.

A turning-point in the history of the Jews of Spain was reached under Ferdinand II who ordered the expulsion of Jews from Spain. At that time, the Spanish Jews, like the Jews of France, were compelled to distinguish themselves from Catholics by wearing a yellow badge on their clothing.

During the expulsion of Jews from Spain, tens of thousands of refugees died trying to reach safety. In some instances, Spanish ship captains charged Jewish passengers exorbitant sums, then dumped them overboard in the middle of the ocean. In the last days before the expulsion, rumours spread throughout Spain that the fleeing refugees had swallowed gold and diamonds, and many Jews were knifed to death by brigands hoping to find treasures in their stomachs.

Christopher Columbus, who discovered America, set sail on August 3, 1492, a day after the expulsion of the Jews from Spain began. Many Jews are said to have left Spain for the expedition to the Americas.

A few years later, the Spanish began to decline as a world power. By 1588, the Spanish navy had been completely destroyed. The Spanish Empire that persecuted the Jews so bitterly does not exist today. The curse "cursed be those that curse you" began to work against the Spanish Empire. The downfall and disappearance of the mighty Spanish Empire can be attributed to the fulfilment of "cursed be everyone that curseth thee." As I write this book in the year 2016, there is nothing like a Spanish Empire. However, today in the year 2016, Israel exists as a nation with its capital in Jerusalem.

4. The fulfilment of the curse on Nazi Germany: "Cursed be everyone that curseth thee".

Hitler embarked on a program to persecute the Jews. The Nazi political party, which was responsible for killing so many Jews, does not exist any more.

When Adolf Hitler took control of Germany in 1933, persecution of the Jews became an active policy.

On April 1, 1933, Jewish doctors, lawyers and shops were boycotted. Jews were then banned from being employed in government.

In May 1935, Jews were forbidden from joining the German Armed Forces.

That same year, anti-Jewish propaganda appeared in Nazi German shops and restaurants. On September 15, 1935, a law preventing sexual relations and marriages between Germans and Jews was enacted.

At the same time another law stating that all Jews, even quarter and half-Jews, were no longer citizens of Germany.

In 1936, Jews were banned from all professional jobs in the country.

Beginning August 17, 1938, Jews with first names of non-Jewish origin had to add Israel (males) or Sarah (females) to their names, and a large J was to be imprinted on their passports beginning October 5.

On November 15, Jewish children were banned from going to normal schools.

By April 1939, nearly all Jewish companies had collapsed under financial pressure.

Overall, of the 522,000 Jews living in Germany in January 1933, only 214,000 were left by the eve of World War II.

On May 19, 1943, Germany was declared clean of Jews and free of Jews.

The Nazi persecution of the Jews culminated in the Holocaust, in which approximately 6 million European Jews were deported or murdered during World War II.

Of the 214,000 Jews still living in Germany at the outbreak of World War II, 90% died during the persecution.

When the Soviet army took over Berlin in 1945, only 8,000 Jews remained in the city, all of them either in hiding or married to non-Jews.

Additionally, approximately 15,000 German Jews survived the concentration camps or survived by going into hiding.

The Jews survived the intense persecution of the Nazis from 1933 to 1945. Today, Nazi Germany is no more and the nationalist socialist party (Nazi) is an outlawed and non-existent group. Most of those who perpetrated these acts of hatred were either killed or committed suicide. Today, the Jewish nation thrives in spite of all Nazi Germany's attempts to exterminate an entire people. "Cursed are those that curse you" has been fulfilled again.

5. The fulfilment of the curse on the British Empire: "Cursed be everyone that curseth thee".

Britain was not a little island in Europe as it is today. Britain was the centre of the worldwide British Empire, which stretched from Australia, through Africa to Asia. The collapse of this vast British Empire can be traced directly to the end of the Second World War when Britain became a virtual enemy to the Jews.

The tensions between the Jews and the British Empire rose from 1938 and intensified with the publication of the MacDonald White Paper in 1939.

The MacDonald White Paper was the official stance of the British government and it proposed to prevent Jews from migrating to Israel.

The British government proposed that the Land of Israel be given to Arabs instead of Jews. The Jews were shocked because they had been persecuted so much during the Second World War and had nowhere to go.

The Jewish Agency for Palestine issued a scathing response to the White Paper, saying the British were denying the Jewish people their rights in the "darkest hour of Jewish history".

From the time the British Empire turned against the Jews, it began to decline until it no longer exists today. Today, Israel exists as a nation but the British Empire does not exist.

Although Britain was one of the victorious allies in the Second World War, the British world empire disintegrated into nothingness shortly after that.

The British Empire began to disintegrate as follows: The British Empire was forced to withdraw from India in 1947. It then began to lose its colonies. Ghana and Malaysia were lost to the empire in 1957. Throughout the 1960s, Britain lost all its colonies until Rhodesia finally gained its independence in the 1970s. Britain also lost Hong Kong and was only able to fight to gain control of the tiny Falkland Islands. Today, the British Empire is a thing of the past and has become more the focus of historians. "Cursed be those that curse you" is fulfilled again. Those who turned against Israel have disappeared and do not exist any more.

6. The Fate of the Non-Jewish Neighbours: "Cursed be everyone that curseth thee".

Israel is surrounded by nations that hate it. A stamp in your passport showing that you visited Israel will automatically prevent you from entering most Arab nations. Israel is a nation of thirteen million people and is surrounded by states that make up over two hundred and fifty million brothers and neighbours. There is constant war and hatred in the Middle East, and the entire region is in a state of constant tension. In spite of being the minority, the Jews, have flourished in an amazing way.

The Jews have become the richest religious group in American society. Though they are only 2% of the population of the United States, the Jews make up 25% of 400 wealthiest Americans. Most of them reside in rich cities: Miami, Los Angeles, Philadelphia and Boston, and mainly New York.

In the US: Forty-six percent of Jews earn more than $100,000 a year, whereas only 19% of all Americans earn over $100,000 a year.

More than 100 of the 400 billionaires on Forbes' list of the wealthiest people in America are Jews.

Jews are well represented in Wall Street, Silicon Valley, the US Congress and Administration, Hollywood, TV networks and the American press – way beyond their percentage in the population.

In 2009, five of Britain's ten richest people were Jews.

Other interesting facts about this prospering and flourishing group that make up only 0.2 percent of the world population are the following. They constitute:

54 percent of the world chess champions

27 percent of the Nobel physics laureates

31 percent of the medicine laureates.

Amazingly, such statistics cannot be said of their "neighbours". For example, between 1980 and 2000, in the area of inventions,

Egyptians registered 77 patents in the U.S.A

Saudis registered 171 patents in the U.S.A

Israelis registered 7,652 patents in the U.S.A

7. The fate of many nations: Curse of damnation

Then shall he say also unto them on the left hand, DEPART FROM ME, YE CURSED, INTO EVERLASTING FIRE, prepared for the devil and his angels:

Matthew 25:41

Another interesting curse is playing itself out amongst those who hate Jews. Isaac spoke a curse on those who cursed Jacob. All through history, many groups and nations have cursed Israel and fought against him. All through history, we can see two main groups of people who have persecuted, expelled, tortured, murdered and massacred Jews. The people of Europe and the people of the Middle-East.

It is interesting to note that both of these locations, Europe and the Middle East, have experienced great wealth and prosperity through the ages. European countries have become rich through their hard work and industries, while the Middle Eastern nations have become prosperous through the discovery of oil. However, one thing that is common in these two regions of the world is the absence of Christ and Christianity today.

You will notice that a great spiritual darkness has descended on these two large regions of the world. The absence of the light of the gospel brings about a deep impenetrable spiritual darkness over the regions. These two parts of the world are the places where Christ is not preached, not respected and not wanted.

And for this cause God shall send them strong delusion, that they should believe a lie: THAT THEY ALL MIGHT BE DAMNED who believed not the truth, but had pleasure in unrighteousness.

2 Thessalonians 2:11-12

European nations do not respect Christ any longer. They have thrown Him out and consider it an absurdity to even believe in God. In the Middle East, Christianity is not wanted and is virtually absent. Christian churches, evangelism and Bibles are not allowed in the Middle East. It is even illegal to be converted to Christianity in large parts of the Middle East. What is the result of this? We now have the two largest and darkest parts of the world, as far as the light of the gospel is concerned. These are the two regions that have expelled Jews and fought against them over the last few centuries.

Let us now have a look at the facts of church attendance and Christianity in Europe and the Middle East today.

European Christianity

Italy: Roman Catholic practice is apparently falling at the moment in Italy. A report suggests there may be as few as 15% of Catholics attending Mass every Sunday.

Spain: Most Spaniards do not participate regularly in religious worship. Only about 9% of the Spanish people attend church.

The Netherlands: Approximately 60% of the population has no religious affiliation. There are more atheists than theists for the first time in the Netherlands.

The majority of the population is agnostic. Religion in the Netherlands is generally considered a personal matter which is not supposed to be propagated in public.

Denmark: Denmark has one of Europe's lowest proportions of churchgoers, at about 2.5%.

Sweden: Very low percentages of the population attend church in Sweden. It is believed that only about 2% of the population goes to church.

Norway: Norway also has about 2% of the population attending church.

England: Only about 10% of UK citizens attend church, many of whom are immigrants. Christianity is expected to be non-existent in England by the year 2067.

Wales: Churchgoing across the denominations in Wales is also expected to decline by 75% over the next 40 years.

France: Less than 15% of French citizens attend church regularly.

Germany: Of the 82 million Germans, only 8.7% attend any type of church.

Austria: Only 9% of the population attends church.

Portugal: Only about 15% of the people in Portugal attend church.

Malta: Only a quarter of the Catholic population attend church.

Estonia: Only about 3.9% of the population attend church.

Greece: The Greek Orthodox Church was reckoned to obtain a Sunday attendance of only 20-25% of its members in Greece in 1994.

Middle-East Christianity

Christianity in Qatar: There are no local Christians in Qatar; all Christians are foreign expatriates. No foreign missionary groups operate openly in the country.

Christianity in Saudi Arabia: Saudi Arabia does not allow Catholics and Christians of other denominations to practise their faith openly, and as a result Catholics and Christians of other denominations generally only worship in secret within private homes. Items and articles belonging to religions other than Islam are prohibited. These include Bibles, crucifixes, statues, carvings, items with religious symbols, and others, although the Government's stated policy is that such items were allowed for private religious purposes.

Christianity in Kuwait: Christianity in Kuwait is a minority religion. The Christians who are native Kuwaitis number approximately 200 people.

Christianity in Oman: Almost all Christians in Oman are from other countries.

Christianity in Iran: Around 90–95% of Iranians associate themselves with the Shi'a branch of Islam, the official state religion, and about 5–10% with the Sunni and Sufi branches of Islam. The remaining 0.6% associate themselves with non-Islamic religious minorities, including Bahá'ís, Mandeans, Yarsanis, Zoroastrians, Jews, and Christians.

Christianity in Iraq: In Iraq, Christians numbered about 1,500,000 in 2003. After the Iraq War, it was estimated that the number of Christians in Iraq had dropped to as low as 450,000. Current estimates of Christians are as low as 200,000. Christians in Iraq are not allowed to evangelize. People who change their faith to Christianity are subject to societal and official pressure, which may lead to the death penalty. However, there are cases in which someone will adopt the Christian faith, secretly declaring his/her apostasy.

Christianity in UAE: The Christian population in the UAE is exclusively made up of foreign expatriate workers; there are no Christian Emirati citizens.

Christianity in Syria: Damascus was one of the first regions to receive Christianity during the ministry of Peter.

There were more Christians in Damascus than anywhere else. Christians constituted about 30% of the Syrian population in the 1920s. Today, they make up about 7.8% (using the last census) of Syria's people.

Christianity in Egypt: The Coptic Church is based on the teachings of Saint Mark who brought Christianity to Egypt during the reign of the Roman emperor Nero in the first century, a dozen of years after the Lord's ascension. Nearly all Egyptian Christians are Copts. Now, Christians most likely account for about 10% of the country's population.

How to avoid the Curse of Isaac

1. Beware of anti-Semitism

2. Support Israel always

3. Pray for Israel always

Pray for the peace of Jerusalem: they shall prosper that love thee.

Psalm 122:6

CHAPTER 15

The Curse of Moses

But it shall come to pass, if thou wilt not hearken unto the voice of the Lord thy God, to observe to do all his commandments and his statutes which I command thee this day; that ALL THESE CURSES SHALL COME upon thee, and overtake thee:

Deuteronomy 28:15

I will camp against you encircling you, and I will set siegeworks against you, and I will raise up battle towers against you.

Isaiah 29:3 (NASB)

Unlike the curse of Adam and the curse on Eve that were brief, heavyweight statements, the curse of Moses was delivered in great detail. It is interesting to see how these detailed curses have played out in the life of the nation of Israel. Let's look at the details of the curse. The curses of Moses were directed at the Jews. These curses were to come upon them because of their disobedience.

What Picture Has the Curse of Moses Created?

A curse creates a picture!

Every curse creates an unmistakable picture!

To recognize a curse you must know the picture it creates!

The curse on man creates the unmistakeable picture of toil and sweat that yields little fruit.

The curse on women creates the unmistakeable picture of sorrow, disappointment and struggles with husbands and children.

The curse on Jews creates the unmistakeable picture of worldwide inexplicable hatred, scattering and persecution.

The curse on Jew haters creates the picture of inexplicable ultimate defeat and humiliation.

The curse on black people creates the inexplicable picture of servanthood, poor leadership, poverty and insignificance.

A trained medical doctor will notice certain symptoms and signs because he is trained to recognize the picture of a disease. It is an unmistakeable picture to him because he is trained to see it. In the same way, you will now recognize the picture of the curse when you see it. Your trained eyes will pick out the unmistakeable picture that shows that a curse is working.

The Details of the Curse

1. **The curse on everything you do:**

   The Lord shall send upon thee cursing, vexation, and rebuke, IN ALL THAT THOU SETTEST THINE HAND UNTO for to do, until thou be destroyed, and until thou perish quickly; because of the wickedness of thy doings, whereby thou hast forsaken me. The Lord shall make the pestilence cleave unto thee, until he have consumed thee from off the land, whither thou goest to possess it.

   Deuteronomy 28:20-21

2. **The curse of strange diseases that wipe out the population:**

   The Lord shall make THE PESTILENCE CLEAVE UNTO THEE, UNTIL HE HAVE CONSUMED THEE from off the land, whither thou goest to possess it. The Lord shall smite thee with a consumption, and with a fever, and with an inflammation, and with an extreme burning, and with the sword, and with blasting, and with mildew; and they shall pursue thee until thou perish.

   Deuteronomy 28:21-22

A pestilence is an epidemic that sweeps through the population and affects many people. The Ebola virus, the HIV virus and the bird flu virus are well known to have produced modern epidemics (pestilence).

Epidemics wiped out thousands of Jews during the Second World War. The Germans established more than 400 ghettos for the purpose of isolating and controlling Jews. These ghettos were overcrowded unhealthy quarters in which as many as one thousand Jews could be found living in one building. This led to the outbreak of epidemics of cholera and typhus among the Jews. Two thousand Jews died every month in the Warsaw ghetto from epidemics of cholera and typhus.

In one ghetto, sanitary stations were established to bathe and disinfect the Jews to contain the epidemic. Jews were refused permission to leave the ghetto unless they were certified as disinfected and clean. The penalty for leaving the ghetto, where these epidemics were raging, was being shot on sight! Indeed, the curse of the pestilence was happening practically.

3.　　**The curse of being driven into every nation of the world:**

The Lord shall cause thee to be smitten before thine enemies: thou shalt go out one way against them, and flee seven ways before them: and SHALT BE REMOVED INTO ALL THE KINGDOMS OF THE EARTH.

Deuteronomy 28:25

Indeed, the curse of being driven into every nation of the world has happened practically to the people of Israel. Jews have mysteriously been driven from place to place. This repeated persecution, recurring expulsion and migration has never happened to any other group of people on earth.

In AD 70 Jerusalem was burnt down and the Jews were scattered all over the world.

Again, in AD 629 the entire Jewish population of GALILEE was massacred or expelled from Judea.

Between the twelfth and fourteenth centuries the Jews living in FRANCE were expelled.

In 1290 King Edward I of England issued a decree to expel Jews from ENGLAND. This remained in force for 365 years.

In the fourteenth century, Jews were expelled from EUROPE because of the Plague.

Jews were expelled from SPAIN in 1492, from SICILY IN 1493 and from ITALY in 1554.

Between 1648 and 1654, Jews were not allowed in RUSSIA and UKRAINE.

The Jews were expelled from the MIDDLE EAST and NORTH AFRICA between 1947 and 1972.

From the 1960s till 1989, thousands of Jews were forced by the authorities to leave POLAND.

In the 1970s, tens of thousands of Soviet Jews were forced out of the SOVIET UNION. Some migrated to Israel whilst others went to the United States.

4. The curse of bodies lying outside and being eaten by birds:

And thy carcase shall be meat unto all fowls of the air, and unto the beasts of the earth, and no man shall fray them away.

Deuteronomy 28:26

This curse of dead bodies lying in the open and without being buried was fulfilled practically in AD 70.

In the year AD 66 the Jews of Judea rebelled against their Roman masters. In response, the Emperor Nero dispatched an army under the generalship of Vespasian to restore order. Vespasian landed in Antioch and took command. Vespasian's son, Titus, marched up from Egypt, and after linking up with his father, the Romans now moved inland into the region of Galilee. Battles were fought on both land and on the lake of Galilee.

During the battle, the hill on which the Temple stood was covered in flames. The blood that poured from those who were slain was so much that the ground was no more visible.

The streets were covered with corpses; with soldiers pursuing fugitives over the piles of dead bodies.

5. **The curse of your wife being taken away from you:**

Thou shalt betroth a wife, and another man shall lie with her: thou shalt build an house, and thou shalt not dwell therein: thou shalt plant a vineyard, and shalt not gather the grapes thereof.

Deuteronomy 28:30

The curse of wives being taken away from their husbands was fulfilled practically during the Second World War. Males and females were always separated at the concentration camps.

Many parents chose to hide their children, claiming that they were non-Jewish orphans of war.

Families began to be forced apart from each other and many families vowed to find each other after the war.

Some families' desire to remain together often left them with the only option of going into hiding. During the war, it was extremely difficult to hide from the Germans. Indeed, some Jewish families were forced to live cut off from the world for long periods of time, sometimes years.

6. **The curse of being robbed openly and violently – the curse of having your wealth stolen:**

The fruit of thy land, and all thy labours, shall A NATION WHICH THOU KNOWEST NOT EAT UP; and thou shalt be only oppressed and crushed alway.

Deuteronomy 28:33

Thine ox shall be slain before thine eyes, and thou shalt not eat thereof: THINE ASS SHALL BE VIOLENTLY TAKEN AWAY FROM BEFORE THY FACE, AND

SHALL NOT BE RESTORED TO THEE: thy sheep shall be given unto thine enemies, and thou shalt have none to rescue them.

Deuteronomy 28:31

And he shall eat the fruit of thy cattle, and the fruit of thy land, until thou be destroyed: which also shall not leave thee either corn, wine, or oil, or the increase of thy kine, or flocks of thy sheep, until he have destroyed thee.

Deuteronomy 28:51

The curse of being robbed openly has happened practically to the Jews on many occasions.

The Jews in Europe were robbed of so much wealth by the Germans that their money financed thirty percent of the German war effort.

Nazi German officials also plundered more than £12 billion by looting and by enacting special confiscation laws. German tax authorities "actively worked to destroy Jews financially". Tax laws discriminated against Jews from 1934, while some who managed to leave Germany before the Holocaust had much of their wealth confiscated through an "exit tax".

German officials would seize and sell the property of Jews who left or were sent to extermination camps, both in Germany and in the nations conquered during the Second World War.

7.   **The curse of your children being taken away from you:**

THY SONS AND THY DAUGHTERS SHALL BE GIVEN UNTO ANOTHER people, and thine eyes shall look, and fail with longing for them all the day long: and there shall be no might in thine hand.

Thou shalt beget sons and daughters, but thou shalt not enjoy them; for they shall go into captivity. All thy trees and fruit of thy land shall the locust consume.

Deuteronomy 28:32, 41-42

The curse of your children being taken away from you has also been fulfilled many times in the life of the people of Israel.

Many Jewish children were taken away from their parents during the Second World War. One of my mother's friends was such a Jewish child who was separated from her parents during the Second World War. She was a toddler when her parents put her on a train and sent her away to safety. She never saw her parents again. Her parents probably died on a concentration camp.

In the fulfilment of this curse, the children of Jews suffered various things during the Second World War. Some children were killed immediately on arrival at the German concentration camps and killing centres.

Other Jewish children were slaughtered by the Germans shortly after birth. (For example, 870 infants born in the Ravensbrück concentration camp between 1943 and 1945, largely to Jewish and Gypsy women, were slaughtered).

Yet others, usually above the age of 10, were imprisoned or used as labourers. Finally, some children were used as subjects for German medical experiments.

Indeed, Jewish children, separated from their parents, were hidden for their own safety. In France, almost everyone in Le Chambon-sur-Lignon, hid Jewish children in the town from 1942 to 1944. In Italy and Belgium, many Jewish children survived only by being sent into hiding. Truly, the words of Moses were being carried out to the letter! There is a need to have a proper respect for curses spoken by authority figures.

8.   **The curse of becoming a wonder and an amazing story of persecution and hatred in the world:**

Moreover all these curses shall come upon thee, and shall pursue thee, and overtake thee, till thou be destroyed; because thou hearkenedst not unto the voice of the Lord thy God, to keep his commandments and his statutes which he commanded thee: and they shall be upon thee for a sign and for a wonder, and upon thy seed for ever.

Deuteronomy 28:45-46

The curse of Moses that the nation of Israel would be a sign and a wonder has come to pass literally. For centuries, the Jews had to survive as a nation without a country. Wherever they went they were hated, treated as an inferior race and made to live in ghettoes.

At different times over several centuries, the exiled Jews have been persecuted, massacred, or forced to flee for their lives from one country to another.

Thousands of Jews have been forced to flee from their homes, from England, from Spain, from Russia and from Germany. It is as though a special hand was driving them from place to place like flocks of birds with no resting place.

For example, in England, in 1190 there was a fearful wave of massacres spreading from city to city, wiping out Jewish men, women and children.

Then again in 1290, the king of England (Edward I) expelled all the Jews from Britain.

Later on in 1492 all the Jews were expelled from Spain. In other countries their treatment was even worse.

In the 1880s Jews had to flee for their lives from Russia.

In the 1930s the Jews had to flee from Germany.

9.   **The curse of great weakness and great destruction before the enemy:**

Therefore shalt thou serve thine enemies which the Lord shall send against thee, in hunger, and in thirst, and in nakedness, and in want of all things: and HE SHALL PUT A YOKE OF IRON UPON THY NECK, UNTIL HE HAVE DESTROYED THEE.

Deuteronomy 28:48

During the Second World War, the Jews were very weak before their German enemies. The German enemies placed a yoke of iron on their necks with the intention of destroying them. A yoke of destruction called "Final Solution" was placed on the neck of Israel.

In December 1941, the Germans began the "Final Solution". The "Final Solution" was the Nazi policy of wiping out all Jews. The policy resulted in the murder of 6 million Jews in concentration camps between 1941 and 1945. Adolf Hitler, Himmler and Eichmann were the key implementers of this yoke. Indeed, the Jews did not have the strength to resist this onslaught of mass murder.

Throughout the war, Jews were kept in concentration camps where long-term survival was rare. Most of those selected to work died of exhaustion and disease. The conditions were so extreme that even the fittest people rarely survived more than a few months in the camps.

10.   **The curse of warring nations besieging and capturing Israel.**

And thou shalt eat the fruit of thine own body, the flesh of thy sons and of thy daughters, which the Lord thy God hath given thee, IN THE SIEGE, AND IN THE STRAITNESS, WHEREWITH THINE ENEMIES SHALL DISTRESS THEE.

Deuteronomy 28:53

The curse of Moses that they would be besieged has occurred an astonishing twenty-three times. How many cities in the world have been besieged twenty-three times and still exist? Jerusalem has been captured and re-captured forty-four times by different people.

In the history of Jerusalem, it has been destroyed twice, besieged 23 times, attacked 52 times, captured and recaptured 44 times.

11.   The curse of women eating their own children in the siege.

The tender and delicate woman among you, which would not adventure to set the sole of her foot upon the ground for delicateness and tenderness, her eye shall be evil toward the husband of her bosom, and toward her son, and toward her daughter, and toward her young one that cometh out from between her feet, and toward her children which she shall bear: for SHE SHALL EAT THEM for want of all things secretly in the siege and straitness, wherewith thine enemy shall distress thee in thy gates.

Deuteronomy 28:56-57

This amazing curse also came to pass practically. In AD 70, Josephus, a famous historian described the horrors he witnessed in the siege of AD 70. This is what he said:

"Throughout the city people were dying of hunger in large numbers, and enduring unspeakable sufferings. In every house the merest hint of food sparked violence, and close relatives fell to blows, snatching from one another the pitiful supports of life. Need drove the starving to gnaw at anything.

Rubbish which even animals would reject, was collected and turned into food. In the end they were eating belts and shoes, and the leather stripped off their shields. Tufts of withered grass were devoured, and sold in little bundles for four drachmas.

Among the residents of the region beyond Jordan was a woman called Mary, daughter of Eleazar, of the village of Bethezuba (the name means "House of Hyssop"). She was well off, and of good family, and had fled to Jerusalem with her relatives, where she became involved with the siege. Most of her belongings which she had packed up and brought from Peraea had been plundered as well as the rest of her treasure, together with such foods.

In her bitter resentment this poor woman cursed the extortioners and this angered them. However, no one put her to death. She grew weary of trying to find food for her kinsfolk. So, driven by anger and want, she seized her child, an infant at the breast, and cried,

"My poor baby, why should I keep you alive in this world of war and famine? Even if we live till the Romans come, they will make slaves of us; and anyway, hunger will get us before slavery does; and the rebels are crueler than both. Come, be food for me, and an avenging fury to the rebels, and a tale of cold horror to the world to complete the monstrous agony of the Jews."

With these words she killed her son, roasted the body, swallowed half of it, and stored the rest in a safe place. But the rebels were on her at once, smelling roasted meat, and threatening to kill her instantly if she did not produce it. She assured them she had saved them a share, and revealed the remains of her child. Seized with horror and stupefaction, they stood paralyzed at the sight. But she said, *"This is my own child, and my own handiwork. Eat, for I have eaten already. Do not show yourselves weaker than a woman, or more pitiful than a mother. But if you have pious scruples, and shrink away from human sacrifice, then what I have eaten can count as your share, and I will eat what is left as well."*

At that they slunk away, trembling, not daring to eat, although they were reluctant to yield even this food to the mother. The whole city soon heard of this abomination. When people heard of it, they shuddered, as though they had done it themselves.

122

12.   The curse of a shrunken population:

Then the Lord will make thy plagues wonderful, and the plagues of thy seed, even great plagues, and of long continuance, and sore sicknesses, and of long continuance.   Moreover he will bring upon thee all the diseases of Egypt, which thou wast afraid of; and they shall cleave unto thee.   Also every sickness, and every plague, which is not written in the book of this law, them will the Lord bring upon thee, until thou be destroyed.   And YE SHALL BE LEFT FEW IN NUMBER, whereas ye were as the stars of heaven for multitude; because thou wouldest not obey the voice of the Lord thy God.

Deuteronomy 28:59-62

The curse of a shrinking population happened practically to the Jews during the Second World War.   Most populations increase every year.   But according to the words of Moses, Jews were left fewer in number.

In 1933 the world's Jewish population was 15.3 million.

In 1939, the world population of Jews was 17 million.

By 1945 the Jewish population in the world had shrunk to 11 million.

By 2014, the Jewish population was 14.2 million making up only 0.2 percent of the world population.

13.   The curse of being scattered throughout the whole world:

And the Lord shall SCATTER THEE AMONG ALL PEOPLE, FROM THE ONE END OF THE EARTH EVEN UNTO THE OTHER; and there thou shalt serve other gods, which neither thou nor thy fathers

have known, even wood and stone. And among these nations shalt thou find no ease, neither shall the sole of thy foot have rest: but the Lord shall give thee there a trembling heart, and failing of eyes, and sorrow of mind:

Deuteronomy 28:64-65

The curse of being scattered throughout the world has come to pass with astonishing accuracy. The Jews have been dispersed into the world on three major occasions.

The first dispersion of Jews occurred when the Assyrians conquered Israel in 722 BC. Then, the Jews were scattered all over the Middle East.

The second dispersion of Jews occurred when Nebuchadnezzar conquered and deported Jews in 597 and 586 BC and allowed them to remain in a unified community in Babylon.

The third major dispersion came about after 70 AD when the Romans destroyed Jerusalem and annexed Judaea as a Roman province.

The Israelites, as had been foretold in the Old Testament, became wandering Jews, to be found in practically every country of the world, despised, reviled and hounded by persecution from city to city and nation to nation.

Note the statistics of returning Jews according to the Israel Central Bureau of Statistics: Between 1948 and 2013, the following numbers of Jews returned to Israel from the respective countries of the world to which they had been scattered:

Country	No. of Jews Returning to Jerusalem
Russia/Ukraine (former USSR)	1,231,003
Morocco, Algeria & Tunisia	354,852
Romania	276,586

Poland	173,591
Iraq	131,138
United States of America	101,592
Ethiopia	92,730
France	81,885
Iran	76,934
Argentina	66,916
Turkey	62,837
Yemen	50,731
Bulgaria	44,372
Egypt and Sudan	37,763
Libya	35,844
United Kingdom	35,164
Hungary	32,022
India	28,702
Czechoslovakia (former)	24,468
South Africa	20,038
Germany	19,905
Yugoslavia (former)	10,768
Syria	9,547

14.   The curse of being forced to change their religion:

And the Lord shall scatter thee among all people, from the one end of the earth even unto the other; and THERE THOU SHALT SERVE OTHER GODS,

**which neither thou nor thy fathers have known, even
wood and stone.**

Deuteronomy 28:64

On several occasions, Jews have been forced to convert from
their faith to other religions or be killed.

For example, at the end of the 11th century, Ashkenazi Jews
in Germany were forced to convert from Judaism.

In the fifteenth century there were mass forced conversions of
Sephardi Jews in Spain and Portugal.

During the Spanish Inquisition, tens of thousands of Jews
were forcibly converted to Christianity on the threat of death.
The chief rabbi, Simon Maimi, was one of those who refused
to convert. He was kept buried in earth up to his neck for seven
days until he died.

CHAPTER 16

The Curses of Moses Fulfilled

And thou shalt grope at noonday, as the blind gropeth in darkness, and thou shalt not prosper in thy ways: and thou shalt be only oppressed and spoiled evermore, and no man shall save thee. Thou shalt betroth a wife, and another man shall lie with her: thou shalt build an house, and thou shalt not dwell therein: thou shalt plant a vineyard, and shalt not gather the grapes thereof.

Thine ox shall be slain before thine eyes, and thou shalt not eat thereof: thine ass shall be violently taken away from before thy face, and shall not be restored to thee: thy sheep shall be given unto thine enemies, and thou shalt have none to rescue them. Thy sons and thy daughters shall be given unto another people, and thine eyes shall look, and fail with longing for them all the day long: and there shall be no might in thine hand.

The fruit of thy land, and all thy labours, shall a nation which thou knowest not eat up; and thou shalt be only oppressed and crushed alway: So that thou shalt be mad for the sight of thine eyes which thou shalt see.

Deuteronomy 28:29-34

The sufferings of Jews throughout the centuries show the effect of the curses spoken by their founding leader, Moses. Moses proclaimed serious curses against anyone who would turn away from the living God to idols.

The Unmistakeable Picture of a Curse

A curse creates a picture!

Every curse creates an unmistakable picture!

To recognize a curse you must know the picture it creates!

The curse on man creates the unmistakeable picture of toil and sweat that yields little fruit.

The curse on women creates the unmistakeable picture of sorrow, disappointment and struggles with husbands and children.

The curse on Jews creates the unmistakeable picture of worldwide inexplicable hatred, scattering and persecution.

The curse on Jew haters creates the picture of inexplicable ultimate defeat and humiliation.

The curse on black people creates the inexplicable picture of servanthood, poor leadership, poverty and insignificance.

A trained medical doctor will notice certain symptoms and signs because he is trained to recognize the picture of a disease. It is an unmistakeable picture to him because he is trained to see it. In the same way, you will now recognize the picture of the curse when you see it. Your trained eyes will pick out the unmistakeable picture that shows that a curse is working.

It is a wonder to see how the curses and warnings of Moses have played out through the centuries. As you go through the list of unique, recurring and astonishing sufferings that the Jews have been through for thousands of years, you will only trust more in God's Word.

You will discover that there is a real God and that the Jews are His people. The blessing of God on Jacob caused them to greatly prosper in every nation they found themselves in. The monies and properties of the Jews have been stolen from them so often and yet they continue to rise and become rich and uniquely prosperous. Throughout the centuries, Jews have been the moneylenders and the top businessmen of the countries they lived in. After some years, many people in the city would find themselves owing their very lives to the Jews. Even when Joseph was prime minister of Egypt, he conducted the business of Egypt so well that the people owed their very lives to Pharaoh.

And they brought their cattle unto Joseph: and Joseph gave them bread in exchange for horses, and for the flocks, and for the cattle of the herds, and for the asses: and he fed them with bread for all their cattle for that year. When that year was ended, they came unto him the second year, and said unto him, We will not hide it from my lord, how that our money is spent; my lord also hath our herds of cattle; THERE IS NOT OUGHT LEFT IN THE SIGHT OF MY LORD, BUT OUR BODIES, AND OUR LANDS:

Wherefore shall we die before thine eyes, both we and our land? BUY US AND OUR LAND FOR BREAD, AND WE AND OUR LAND WILL BE SERVANTS UNTO PHARAOH: and give us seed, that we may live, and not die, that the land be not desolate. And Joseph bought all the land of Egypt for Pharaoh; for the Egyptians sold every man his field, because the famine prevailed over them: so the land became Pharaoh's.

Genesis 47:17-20

The supernatural history of the Jews is enough to prove to you that there is a God who rules in the affairs of men. Even as He has punished His people, He has always preserved a remnant. Even as He has scattered them, He has turned around to gather them. Even as they were destroyed, He has turned around to supernaturally bless and prosper them.

But now thus saith the Lord that created thee, O Jacob, and he that formed thee, O Israel,

Fear not: for I have redeemed thee, I have called thee by thy name; thou art mine.

When thou passest through the waters, I will be with thee; and through the rivers, they shall not overflow thee: when thou walkest through the fire, thou shalt not be burned; neither shall the flame kindle upon thee. For I am the Lord thy God, the Holy One of Israel, thy Saviour: I gave Egypt for thy ransom, Ethiopia and Seba for thee. Since thou wast precious in my sight, thou hast been honourable, and I have loved thee: therefore will I give men for thee, and people for thy life. Fear not: for I am with thee: I will bring thy seed from the east, and gather thee from the west; I will say to the north, Give up; and to the south, Keep not back: bring my sons from far, and my daughters from the ends of the earth

Isaiah 43:1-6

Let us now have a look at this amazing history of recurrent persecution, expulsion, migration and survival of the Jews. This will help you to believe in the power of the supernatural and real God.

356 BC: The attempt of Haman to wipe out Jews:

Haman, the Prime Minister of King Ahaserus attempted to wipe out the Jewish nation as reported in the book of Esther.

586 BC: The temple in Jerusalem destroyed by Nebuchadnezzar and the Babylonian Empire:

The Babylonian Empire destroyed the temple in Jerusalem, and captured over 10,000 Jewish families.

187 BC: King Antiochus III attempts to force Jews in Jerusalem to abandon their God:

Antiochus III, a Greek King, incorporated Judea into his empire. He continued to allow the Jews autonomy, but later began a program to force the Jews to abandon their God. Antiochus backed down in the face of Jewish opposition to his effort to introduce idols in their temples.

176 BC: Antiochus IV, defiles the temple and sacrifices pigs in it.

Antiochus IV, another Greek king who inherited the throne in 176 BC resumed his father's original policy of harassing the Jews. A brief Jewish rebellion only hardened his views and led him to outlaw central tenets of Judaism such as the Sabbath and circumcision, and defile the holy Temple by erecting an altar to the god Zeus. King Anthiochus IV also allowed the sacrifice of pigs in the temple.

167 BC: A priest and his family called the Maccabees fight against Antiochus IV:

The extreme measures adopted by Antiochus helped unite the Jews against him. When a Greek official tried to force a priest named Mattathias to make a sacrifice to a pagan god, the Jews murdered the official. Predictably, Antiochus retaliated; but in 167 BC the Jews rose up behind Mattathias and his five sons and fought against Anthiochus IV for their liberation.

The family of Mattathias became known as the Maccabees, from the Hebrew word for "hammer", because they were said to strike hammer blows against their enemies.

Like other rulers before him, Antiochus underestimated the will and strength of the Jews. He sent a small force to put down the rebellion but they were defeated. Again, Anthiochus led an even more powerful army into battle only to be defeated.

164 BC: The Maccabees finally recapture Jerusalem:

Jerusalem was recaptured by the Maccabees and the Temple purified and dedicated, an event that gave birth to the holiday of

Hannukah. It took more than two decades of fighting before the Maccabees forced the enemy to retreat from the Land of Israel. Antiochus had by this time died, and his successor agreed to the Jews' demand for independence.

When Mattathias died, the revolt was led by his son Judas, or Judah Maccabee, as he is often called. By the end of the war, Simon was the only one of the five sons of Mattathias to survive and he ushered in an 80-year period of Jewish independence in Judea, as the Land of Israel was now called. During that period, the kingdom of Israel regained and enlarged its boundaries almost to the extent of Solomon's reign and Jewish life flourished.

AD 19: The Expulsion of Jews living in Rome:

Roman Emperor Tiberius became angry over various issues that arose in his empire. He laid the matter before the senate and consequently 4,000 Jewish residents of military age were drafted into service to undertake duties on the island of Sardinia. Many who could not comply were killed and all other Jews were made to depart from Italy.

AD 37–41: The killing of thousands of Jews by mobs in Alexandria, Egypt:

The wealth and influence of the Alexandrian Jews was a thorn in the flesh of the non-Jewish inhabitants. Jealousy and religious intolerance combined to create a climate of hatred against the Jews. All that was lacking was a spark to make the hatred burst into the open.

When it came, the hatred exploded with frightening fury and cruelty. The first occasion was when Agrippa I passed though Alexandria on his way from Rome to Jerusalem. The Jews of Alexandria received him with great joy and honour because he was a Jewish king. The happiness of the Jews aroused jealousy among the people who publicly ridiculed the Jews and their Jewish king, Agrippa.

They incited the masses, who promptly broke into the synagogues and set up statues of their idols. Responding to the mood of the mob, the government decreed that the Jews were no longer full and equal citizens of Egypt.

This was a signal to the Jew haters that they had the approval of the government. They then expelled the Jews from their living quarters and forced them into the first ever ghetto. They then ransacked the Jewish residences and shops. Jews were also stoned and beaten to death.

AD 50: Another expulsion of Jews from Rome:

Jews were ordered by Roman Emperor Claudius "not to hold meetings" and later expelled from Rome. This is confirmed in Apostle Paul's account in Acts 18:2 "And found a certain Jew named Aquila, born in Pontus, lately come from Italy, with his wife Priscilla; (because that Claudius had commanded all Jews to depart from Rome:) and came unto them."

AD 66–73: Two Roman Emperors, Vespasian and his son Titus, destroy Jerusalem and scatter the Jews all over the world:

A Jewish revolt against the Romans, referred to in history as The Great Revolt, was crushed by two Roman Generals, Vespasian and his biological son, Titus.

The Great Revolt began in the year AD 66. The crisis escalated due to anti-taxation protests and attacks carried out on Roman citizens. The Romans responded by plundering the Jewish Temple and executing up to 6,000 Jews in Jerusalem, prompting a full-scale rebellion.

The Jews quickly overran the Roman military garrison of Judaea, whilst the pro-Roman King Agrippa II, together with Roman officials, fled Jerusalem. As it became clear the rebellion was getting out of control, Cestius Gallus, the legate of Syria, brought in the Syrian army, to restore order and quell the revolt.

Despite initial advances, the Syrian Legion was ambushed and defeated by Jewish rebels at the Battle of Beth Horon in which 6,000 Romans were massacred – a result that shocked the Roman leadership. This war went on for four years and eventually Jerusalem was besieged for seven months.

The Roman armies established a permanent camp just outside the city, digging a trench around the circumference of its walls and building a wall as high as the city walls themselves around Jerusalem. Anyone caught in the trench, attempting to flee the city would be captured, crucified, and placed in lines on top of the dirt wall facing into Jerusalem. Those attempting to escape the city were crucified, with as many as five hundred crucifixions conducted in a day.

During the fighting, a stockpiled supply of dry food was intentionally burned by Zealots to induce the 600,000 defenders to fight against the siege, instead of negotiating peace. As a result many city dwellers and soldiers died of starvation during the siege.

The defeat of the Jews caused many of the Jews to be scattered or sold into slavery. Josephus the historian claims that 1,100,000 people were killed during the siege. 97,000 Jews were captured and enslaved and many others fled to areas around the Mediterranean.

The emperor, Titus, refused to accept a wreath of victory, claiming that there is "no merit in vanquishing people forsaken by their own God."

AD 119: The Banning of Circumcision in Rome:

Roman emperor Hadrian banned circumcision and made Judaism an illegal religion in Rome.

When Hadrian first became the Roman emperor in AD 118 he was sympathetic to the Jews. He allowed them to return to Jerusalem and granted permission for the rebuilding of their Holy Temple. Unfortunately Emperor Hadrian quickly went back on his word, and requested that the site of the Temple be moved from its original location. He also began deporting Jews to North Africa. The Jews prepared to rebel until Rabbi Joshua ben Hananiah calmed them. The Jews continued preparing secretly in case a rebellion would later become necessary.

AD 132–135: The Roman Massacre of Jews in Judea in the Bar-Kokhba revolt:

There was a great devastation on the Jewish people after the war of AD 70, which destroyed Jerusalem.

However when the Romans introduced new laws against things like circumcision, a new war was started. In AD 132, under the strong leadership of Bar-Kokhba, the Jews began their rebellion on a large scale and captured approximately 50 strongholds in Judea and 985 undefended towns and villages, including Jerusalem. The Jews from other countries, and even some Gentiles, volunteered to join their crusade. The Jews minted coins with slogans such as "The freedom of Israel" written in Hebrew.

Some elements of the Jewish population organized guerilla forces and, in AD 123 began launching surprise attacks against the Romans.

Emperor Hadrian then brought an extra army legion, the "Sixth Ferrata," into Judea to deal with the Jews. The turning point of the war came when Hadrian sent into Judea one of his best generals from Britain, Julius Severus, along with former governor of Germania, Hadrianus Quintus Lollius Urbicus. Due to the large number of Jewish rebels, instead of waging open war, Severus besieged Jewish fortresses and held back food until the Jews grew weak. Only then did his attack escalate into outright war. Indeed the Romans demolished all 50 Jewish fortresses and 985 villages.

The final battle of the war took place in Bethar, Bar-Kokhba's headquarters. After a fierce battle, every Jew in Bethar was killed. Six days passed before the Romans allowed the Jews to bury their dead. Following the battle of Bethar, Jewish independence was lost.

The Romans plowed Jerusalem with a yoke of oxen! Jews were sold into slavery and many were transported to Egypt. Judean settlements were not rebuilt.

Hadrian began to establish a city in Jerusalem called Aelia Capitolina, the name being a combination of his own name and that of the Roman god Jupiter Capitolinus.

He started to build a temple to Jupiter in place of the Jewish Holy Temple.

Emperor Hadrian changed the country's name from Judea to Syria-Palestina.

In the years following the war, Hadrian made anti-religious decrees forbidding Torah study, Sabbath observance, circumcision, Jewish courts, meeting in synagogues and other ritual practices.

AD 167: The Earliest Known Accusation of Jewish Deicide:

"Jewish deicide" is a long-held belief that Jews are responsible for the death of Jesus Christ!

As early as AD 167, Melito of Sardis made assertions in his sermon entitled "Peri Pascha" that transformed the charge that Jews had killed their own Messiah into the charge that the Jews had killed God Himself.

AD 306: The Synod of Elvira in Southern Spain, imposes limitations of association on Jews:

The Synod of Elvira banned intermarriage between Christians and Jews. Other social intercourses, such as eating together, were also forbidden. Canon 16 of the Synod of Elvira stated that those unwilling to change over to the Catholic Church, were not to have Catholic girls given to them in marriage, nor should they be given to Jews or heretics. If parents acted against this, they would be kept out of the church for five years. Canon 50 stated that if any of the clergy of the Faithful ate with Jews, he would be refused communion in order that he be corrected, as he should.

AD 386: Condemnation of Judaism by John Chrysostom:

John Chrysostom was the Archbishop of Constantinople and an important Early Church Father. He is honoured as a saint in the Orthodox and Catholic churches. During his first two years as a presbyter in Antioch, (AD 386-387), Chrysostom denounced Jews and Judaizing Christians in a series of eight sermons delivered to Christians in his congregation.

One of the purposes of these sermons was to prevent Christians from participating in Jewish customs. In his sermons, entitled *Adversus Judaeos* (which means "Against the Judaizers") Chrysostom criticized "Judaizing Christians", who were participating in Jewish festivals and taking part in other Jewish observances, such as observing the Sabbath, circumcision and pilgrimage to the Holy Land.

AD 399: Confiscation by Emperor Honorius of silver and gold collected by Jews for Jerusalem:

Judaism was called an unworthy religion by the Roman Emperor, Honorius. He called Judaism *superstitio indigna* which means an "unworthy superstition" and confiscated all the gold and the silver which had been collected by the synagogues for Jerusalem.

AD 415: Expulsion of Jews from Alexandria, Egypt.

In AD 415 Bishop Cyril of Alexandria incited the Greeks to kill or expel the Jews. He forced his way into the synagogue at the head of a mob, expelled the Jews and gave their property to the crowd. The Prefect Orestes, who refused to condone this behaviour, was set upon and almost stoned to death for protesting.

AD 418: The Forced Conversion of Jews in Minorca, Spain: Convert or be expelled!

Prompted by a miraculous dream, the local Bishop Severus of Minorca, led his congregation across the island to force the conversion of Jews in Minorca to Christianity. Tensions rose greatly on that day and public arguments between Christians and Jews culminated in a riot and the burning of the local synagogue.

For several days there were further debates between Christians and Jews, and many Jews fled to the countryside. After sustained pressure, the leaders of the Jewish community converted and their fellow Jews followed.

AD 419: Destruction of synagogues throughout Palestine:

The monk Barsauma gathered a group of followers and for the next three years destroyed synagogues throughout the province of Palestine.

AD 451: Persecution of Jews by The King of Persia:

Yazdegerd, the King of Persia was known for his religious zeal in promoting a religion called Zoroastrianism. This led to the persecutions of Christians, and to a much lesser extent, Jews.

He issued decrees prohibiting Jews from observing the Sabbath openly and publicly, and ordered executions of a few Jewish leaders, which resulted in the Jewish community of Isfahan publicly retaliating by flaying two Zoroastrian priests while they were alive, leading to more persecutions against the Jews.

AD 519: Burning of synagogues by Italians:

Local synagogues were burnt down by a mob in Ravenna, Italy. The Ostrogothic King Theodoric the Great ordered the town to rebuild the synagogues at their own expense.

AD 529–559: Denying of citizenship to all Jews in the Roman Empire:

A Roman Emperor called Justinian the Great published a set of laws restricting Roman citizenship to Christians. These laws were called *Corpus Juris Civilis*.

The Jewish civil rights were restricted: "They shall enjoy no honors".

The principle of *Servitus Judaeorum* (Servitude of the Jews) was established: the Jews could testify against Christians.

The use of the Hebrew language in worship was forbidden.

Shema Yisrael ("Hear, O Israel, the Lord is One"), sometimes considered the most important prayer in Judaism, was banned as a denial of the Trinity.

Some Jewish communities were converted by force into Christianity and their synagogues turned into churches.

These new regulations by Justinian determined the status of Jews throughout the Roman Empire for hundreds of years.

AD 538: The Forbidding of Jews to employ Christian servants:

The Third Council of Orleans in Gaul (present day France) forbade Jews to employ Christian servants or possess Christian slaves. Jews were prohibited from appearing in the streets during Easter: It was stated that "Their appearance is an insult to Christianity".

AD 576: The expulsion of Jews from Clermont, France:

In Clermont, France, Bishop Avitus offered Jews a choice: accept Christianity or leave Clermont. Most Jews migrated to Marseilles.

AD 610–620: The lashing of Jews by the government of Spain:

King Sisebut of Spain was known for his devout piety to Chalcedonian Christianity. In AD 616, he ordered that those Jews who refused to convert to Christianity should be whipped. After many of his anti-Jewish edicts were ignored, King Sisebur prohibited Judaism. This was the first incident where the prohibition of Judaism affected an entire country.

AD 640: Expulsion from Arabia:

Jews living in Arabia were expelled.

AD 629 March 21: Massacre of Jews in Jerusalem:

The Roman Emperor Heraclius with his army marched into Jerusalem in AD 629. Jewish inhabitants supported him after his promise of amnesty. Upon his entry into Jerusalem the local priests convinced him that killing Jews was the fulfilment of a good commandment. Hundreds of Jews were massacred and thousands fled to Egypt. This brought an end to any remaining Jewish life in Galilee and Judea.

AD 682: Spanish attempt at the eradication of Jews:

King Erwig (of present day Spain) began his reign by enacting 28 anti-Jewish laws. He pressed for and decreed that all converts be registered by a parish priest, who would also issue them with travel permits".

AD 692: Persecution of Jews in Constantinople:

The church Council in Constantinople forbade Christians to bathe in public baths with Jews, to employ a Jewish doctor or to socialize with Jews. Breaking this rule resulted in excommunication.

AD 722: Forceful conversion of all Jews in the Roman Empire:

Emperor Leo III forcibly converted all Jews in the Roman empire into mainstream Christianity.

AD 820: The Archbishop's attempt at complete segregation of Jews:

Agobard, Archbishop of Lyons declared in his essays that Jews were accursed and demanded a complete segregation of Christians and Jews. In 826 he issued a series of pamphlets to convince Roman Emperor Louis the Pious to attack "Jewish insolence", but failed to convince the Emperor.

AD 898–929: Confiscation of Jewish property by France:

French King Charles the Simple, confiscated Jewish-owned property in Narbonne and donated it to the Church.

1008–1013: Mockery of Jews in Algeria:

Severe restrictions against Jews in present day Algeria were instituted. All Jews were forced to wear a heavy wooden "golden calf" around their necks. Christians also had to wear a large wooden cross and members of both groups had to wear black hats.

1012: First ever persecution of Jews in Germany:

One of the first known persecutions of Jews in Germany took place at this time. Henry II, a Holy Roman Emperor, expelled Jews from Mainz, Germany.

1016: First ever persecution of Jews in Tunisia:

The Jewish community that lived in Kairouan, Tunisia was forced to choose between conversion and expulsion.

1026: the Expulsion of Jews from French towns:

The Church of the Holy Sepulchre stands in Jerusalem at the place where Jesus Christ is believed to have been crucified and buried. In the year 1009, this church was destroyed by al-Hakim, the Caliph of Egypt. A French writer blamed the Jews for the destruction of the Church of the Holy Sepulchre. As a result, Jews were expelled from Limoges and other French towns.

1032: Massacre in Morocco:

Abul Kamal Tumin conquered the city of Fez in Morocco and destroyed the Jewish community in Fez, Morocco killing 6,000 Jews.

1066 December 30: The massacre of the Granada Jews in Spain:

A mob stormed the royal palace in Granada (a city in Spain), and crucified a Jew named Joseph ibn Nagrela who was an adviser to the king. Most of the Jewish population of the city were killed. More than 1,500 Jewish families, numbering 4,000 persons, died in one day.

1096: Massive Attacks on Jews in German cities:

Three hosts of crusaders passed through several Central European cities. The third, group of crusaders led by Count Eimicho decided to attack the Jewish communities, most notably in Germany, under the slogan: "Why fight Christ's enemies abroad when they are living among us?" Eimicho's host attacked the synagogue at Speyer, Germany and killed all its defenders. 800 were killed in the city of Worms, Germany. Another 1,200 Jews committed suicide in Mainz, Germany to escape his attempt to forcibly convert them. In all, 5,000 Jews were murdered.

1143: Killing of Jews in Ham, France:

During the first crusade, Christians intent on penitence assaulted Jews in many centres where they had long been established. More than 150 Jews were killed in Ham, near Orleans in central France and countless more in Normandy, Cologne and Worms.

1171: Killing of Jews in Blois, France:

31 Jews were burned at the stake for blood libel. Blood libel (also blood accusation) is an accusation that Jews kidnapped and murdered the children of Christians to use their blood as part of their religious rituals during Jewish holidays.

1180: Imprisonment of all Jews in France:

Philip Augustus of France, after four months in power, imprisoned all the Jews in his lands and demanded a ransom for their release.

1181: Cancellation of all loans given by Jews in France:

Philip Augustus cancelled all loans made by Jews to Christians and took a percentage for himself. A year later, he confiscated all Jewish property and expelled the Jews from Paris.

1190: February 6: Slaughter of Jews in Norwich, England:

Resentment against the Jewish community in England continued to grow over their perceived wealth and belief that they killed Jesus (deicide). They were also accused of the ritual murder of Christian children. On 6 February 1190, following riots in Norwich, England, all the Jews of Norwich, England, who were found in their houses were slaughtered, except a few who took refuge in the castle.

1190 March 16: Massacre of Jews and burning of records of loans owed to Jews in York, England:

On March 16th 1190, a wave of anti-Jewish riots culminated in the massacre of an estimated 150 Jews – the entire Jewish community of York – who had taken refuge in the royal castle.

The rioters were egged on by clergymen and barons who saw the riots as an opportunity to wipe out the extensive debts they owed to Jewish money-lenders in the city. These men had borrowed heavily from Jewish money-lenders but had failed to secure lucrative royal appointments and so could not afford to repay their debts. After the massacre of the Jews, they proceeded to burn the records of their debts, absolving themselves from repayment of property and debts owed to the murdered Jews.

13th century: The first appearance of Judensau, in Germany:

"Judensau" was a folk art image of Jews involved in an obscene sexual act with a large female pig. "Judensau" involved the obscene and dehumanizing imagery of Jews, ranging from etchings to depictions on Cathedral ceilings. The popularity of this kind of picture lasted for over 600 years.

1223: Law against Recording Debts owed to Jews in France:

On 1 November 1223, Louis VIII of France issued an ordinance that prohibited his officials from recording debts owed to Jews.

Lending money with interest was illegal to practice. According to Church law it was seen as a vice in which people profited from others' misfortune and was punishable by excommunication.

1235: Jews falsely accused of ritual murder in Germany:

The Jews of Fulda, Germany were accused of ritual murder. To investigate this accusation, Emperor Frederick II held a special conference of Jewish converts to Christianity at which the converts were questioned about Jewish ritual practice. Letters inviting prominent individuals to the conference still survive.

At the conference, the converts stated unequivocally that Jews do not harm Christian children or require blood for any rituals. In 1236 the Emperor published these findings and in 1247 Pope Innocent IV, the Emperor's enemy, also denounced accusations of the ritual murder of Christian children by Jews.

1236: Slaughter of Jews in Anjou, France:

Almost nothing is known of the history of the Jews of Anjou. The first circumstantial information furnished by contemporary documents is the mention of the massacres in 1236, of which the Jews were victims. These massacres were the work of the Crusaders who began their exploits in Brittany and continued them in Poitou. Three thousand Jews in Anjou were killed and five hundred were made to submit to baptism in 1236.

1240: Cheating of Jews out of their money in France:

In 1236 many Jews in Brittany, France, were massacred by Crusaders. The remainder were expelled in April 1240 by the Duke Jean le Roux. The duke declared that payment of all debts owed to Jews should be suspended. He ordered Jews to return all real estate that had been pledged to them.

1241: Cheating of Jews out of their money in England:

In England, the first of a series of royal levies against Jewish finances, which forced the Jews to sell their debts to non-Jews at cut prices, was instituted.

1250: The Massacre of the Jews of Zaragoza, Spain:

According to the story, the Jews of Zaragoza plotted to kill every Christian in Zaragoza. The magic ritual to do so required a Christian heart. The Jews were accused of capturing an innocent boy called Dominguito on Good Friday, re-enacting Jesus's trial with Dominguito as Jesus, then murdering him by crucifixion. According to the legend, the Jews were found with the boy's heart and confessed to the crime. All the Jews of Zaragoza were executed for the alleged murder of Dominguito.

1253: The Extortion of Money from Jews in England:

During King Henry's early years, the Jewish community flourished and became one of the most prosperous in Europe.

In 1239, King Henry introduced new policies, trying to reduce the financial power of Jews.

Jewish leaders across England were imprisoned and forced to pay fines equivalent to a third of their goods. All outstanding loans owed to the Jews were to be released.

Large amounts of cash were demanded from the Jews. By robbing them in this way, the Jews were rendered incapable of lending money commercially.

King Henry built a building called the *Domus Conversorum* in London in 1232 to help convert Jews to Christianity. His efforts to convert Jews intensified after 1239 and as many as 10 percent of the Jews in England had been converted by the late 1250s.

Anti-Jewish stories involving tales of child sacrifice flourished in the 1250s and, in response, Henry passed the *Statute of Jewry* in 1253, which attempted to segregate Jews and enforce the wearing of Jewish badges. It remains unclear to what extent this statute was actually implemented by King Henry.

1254: The Illegal seizing of Jewish Property in France:

King Louis IX expelled Jews from France and confiscated their properties and synagogues. Most Jews moved to Germany and further east, however, after a couple of years, some were readmitted back into France.

1263: Official Disputations (debates) between Christians and Jews take place:

During the Middle Ages, there were numerous ordered disputations between Christians and Jews. They were connected with burnings of the Talmud and violence against Jews. Both Jews and Christians were given absolute freedom to speak their arguments how they wanted, making this unique among disputations.

The Disputation of Barcelona (July 20–24, 1263) was a formal ordered debate between representatives of Christianity and Judaism regarding whether Jesus was the Messiah or not!

The disputation was held at the royal palace of King James I of Aragon in the presence of the king, his court, prominent ecclesiastical dignitaries and knights. Other important participants were Dominican Friar Pablo Christiani, a convert from Judaism to Christianity, and Rabbi Nahmanides (Ramban), a leading Jewish scholar, philosopher, physician and biblical commentator.

1267: The Forced Dressing of Jews with Pileum Cornutum:

In a special session, the Vienna city council forced Jews to wear *Pileum cornutum* (a cone-shaped headdress, prevalent in many medieval illustrations of Jews). This distinctive dress was an addition to the yellow badges Jews had already been forced to wear.

1267: The Creation of Ghettoes in Poland:

The word "ghetto" was originally used in Venice to describe the part of the city to which Jews were restricted and segregated.

At the Synod of Breslau in Poland, Jews were ordered to live in a segregated quarter called a ghetto. The aim of this order was to cut off contact as much as possible between Christians and Jews both socially and physically, thereby creating a ghetto.

1275: Jewish properties illegally seized and the Jews forced to wear a yellow badge in England:

King Edward I of England passed the Statute of the Jewry forcing Jews over the age of seven to wear an identifying yellow badge. The king also made it illegal for the Jews to have lent money to anyone so that he could seize their assets.

Many English Jews were arrested, 300 hanged and their property given to the Crown. In 1280, the king ordered the Jews to listen as the Dominicans preached salvation. In 1287 he arrested heads of Jewish families and demanded their communities to pay a ransom of 12,000 pounds.

1276: The Attempted Massacre of Jews in Fez, Morocco:

The entire population of Fez attempted to massacre all Jews in a city called Fez in Morocco. The Massacre in Fez was stopped by the intervention of the Emir.

1279: The Red Cloth of Jews in Hungary:

At the Synod of Ofen in Hungary, Christians were forbidden to sell or rent real estate to or from Jews. The Synod was held during the reign of King Ladislaus IV (1272-90) and decreed that every Jew must wear a red cloth on his left side. In addition, any Christian living in a house together with a Jew would be prohibited from participating in Church services.

1282: The Closure of all Synagogues in London:

The Archbishop of Canterbury, John Pectin ordered all synagogues in London to close down and prohibited Jewish doctors from practicing medicine on Christians.

1283: Forced migration of Jews from France:

Philip III of France caused a mass migration of Jews by forbidding them to live in the small rural localities.

1285: The Accusation of Blood Libel against Jews in Munich, Germany:

Generation after generation of Jews in Europe were tortured, and Jewish communities were massacred or dispersed and broken up because of the claim that they were using human blood to perform their sacrifices. This crime, as earlier on mentioned, was called "blood libel".

Popular preachers ingrained it in the minds of the common people that Jews were using human blood to perform the levitical sacrifices. It therefore became embedded in the minds and hearts of the common people that Jews were ritual murderers. This would turn the whole community against the Jews who would then be killed by the mob. In 1285, the Jews were accused of this kind of ritual murder in Munich, Germany, which resulted in the death of 68 Jews. 180 more Jews were burned alive at the synagogue.

1287: Massacre of Jews in Oberwesel, Germany:

An accusation of blood libel in Oberwesel, Germany, led to the killing of 40 Jewish men, women and children by a mob.

1289: Repeated Expulsion of Jews from Gascony and Anjou in France:

There have been Jews in Gascony, France, from at least the fourth century. The Jews were expelled, but kept coming back to settle.

A first order to expel all Jews was issued in 1289.

Another order to expel Jews was given in 1310.

Again, an order was given to expel Jews in 1313.

Yet another order was given to expel Jews 1316.

Debts owed to the Jews were confiscated and collected at half their value for the king's treasury. Royal agents were appointed to seize the Jews and their belongings.

1290: Jews driven in and out of England:

Edward I expelled all Jews from England, allowing them to take only what they could carry. All other Jewish property became the Crown's.

While King Edward ordered the Jews to leave England in 1290, Philip the Fair expelled the Jews from France in 1306.

With the Jews gone, Philip appointed royal guardians to collect the loans made by the Jews, and the money was passed to the Crown.

The scheme did not work well. The Jews were regarded to be good businessmen who satisfied their customers, while the king's collectors were universally unpopular.

Finally, in 1315, because of the "clamour of the people", the Jews were invited back with an offer of 12 years of guaranteed residence, free from government interference.

But in 1322, the Jews were expelled again by the king's successor, who did not honour the commitment.

1291: The Rejection of Jews from France:

Philip IV published an ordinance prohibiting the Jews from settling in France.

1298: The Extermination of Jews by German knight Rintfleisch:

During the civil war between Adolph of Nassau and Albrecht of Austria, German knight Rintfleisch claims to have received a mission from heaven to exterminate "the accursed race of the Jews". Under his leadership, a mob went from town to town destroying Jewish communities and massacring about 100,000 Jews, often by mass burning at the stake.

1305: The Seizure of Jewish Property in France:

Philip IV of France seized all Jewish property (except the clothes they were wearing) and expelled them from France (approx. 100,000 Jews were expelled). His successor Louis X of France allowed French Jews to return in 1315.

1320: The Pastoureaux Crusade against Jews, Southern France:

In 1320, a teenage shepherd claimed to have been visited by the Holy Spirit, which instructed him to fight the Moors in Spain. His followers then marched south attacking castles, royal officials, priests, lepers but most of all Jews. A crusade against the Jews was started and spread throughout most of southern France and northern Spain. One hundred and twenty communities were destroyed. At Verdun, 500 Jews defended themselves from within a stone tower where they killed themselves when they were about to be overrun.

1321: The Jewish Yellow badge of shame, Spain:

King Henry II of Castile forced Jews to wear a yellow badge. The yellow badge (or yellow patch) also referred to as a Jewish badge (German: *Judenstern*, lit. Jews' star), was a cloth patch that Jews were ordered to sew on their outer garments to mark them as Jews in public at certain times in certain countries. Whether intended or not, it served as a badge of shame.

1321: The Leprosy Accusation against Jews, France:

Jews in central France were accused of ordering lepers to poison wells. After the massacre of about 5,000 Jews, King Philip V admitted that they were innocent. The 1321 leper scare (also known as the "lepers' plot") was an alleged conspiracy of French lepers to spread their disease by contaminating well water with their powders and poisons. Lepers were the most abused people during the Middle Ages according to the American Jewish historian Solomon Grayzel. They were thrown out of settlements and treated as wild animals due to the widespread belief that the disease was highly contagious.

1336: Alsace Massacre of Jews, Germany:

Jews were persecuted in Franconia and Alsace by German robbers led by highwayman Arnold III von Uissigheim. Arnold III von Uissigheim, was a medieval German highwayman and a bandit of the Uissigheim family.

He was the leader of the massacres against Jewish communities throughout the Alsace in 1336.

Arnold became a wanted man in 1332 on the charge of highway robbery in the Wertheim *territorium*. He then commenced a wave of populist banditry and massacres against the Jewish population of the Alsace. Arnold and 47 of his band were taken captive in 1336, and Arnold tried and sentenced to death by the *Zentgericht* court.

1348: Jews massacred as scapegoats of the plague:

Europe was affected by the epidemic of the plague in the mid-14th century. Unfortunately, Jews were accused of spreading the disease by deliberately poisoning wells.

The populations of European cities massacred the Jews in retaliation for them "spreading" the plague.

Massacres directly related to the plague took place in April 1348 in Toulon, France. The Jewish quarter was ransacked and forty Jews were murdered in their homes.

In 1349, massacres and persecution spread across Europe, including the Erfurt massacre (1349), the Basel massacre, the Aragon massacre, and the Flanders massacre of Jews.

1349: The Valentine's Day Strasbourg Burning of Jews:

900 Jews were burnt alive on 14 February 1349 in the "Valentine's Day" Strasbourg massacre. The Jews were suspected of causing the Black Plague disease, even though it had not even affected the city of Strasbourg. Many hundreds of Jewish communities were destroyed in this period. Some members within the 510 Jewish communities destroyed in this period, killed themselves to avoid the persecutions.

1349: The Basel Massacre of Jews, Switzerland:

The guilds brought up charges against the Jews accusing them of poisoning the wells. Despite an attempted defence by the town council, 600 Jews together with their rabbi were burnt to death. One hundred and forty children were taken from their parents and forcible baptized. The victims were left unburied, the cemetery destroyed and the synagogue turned into a church. The remaining Jews were expelled and not readmitted until 1869.

1349: The Erfurt Massacre of Jews, Germany:

The massacre of the Jewish community in Erfurt, Germany, on March 21, 1349 involved the lynching of 3000 Jews. Accounts of the number of Jews killed in the massacre vary from over 100 to 3000. Some Jews set fire to their own homes and possessions and perished in the flames before they could be lynched.

1370: The Brussels Massacre of Jews:

The Brussels massacre was an anti-Semitic episode that occurred in Brussels in 1370. A number of Jews, variously given as six or about twenty, were executed or otherwise killed, while the rest of the small community was banished. This massacre led to the end of the Jewish community in Brussels.

1389: The Prague Massacre of Jews, Bohemia:

A priest, hit with pebbles on Holy Saturday by Jewish boys playing in the street, became insulted and insisted that the Jewish community purposely plotted against him. Several Jews attacked the communion wafer that the priest was carrying and scattered the pieces on the ground, whilst mocking the priest.

The priest's followers beat up the boys whose parents arrived to defend them. A mob was then incited to attack the ghetto. Approximately 900 Jews were slaughtered. The synagogue and the cemetery were destroyed, and homes were pillaged. King Wenceslaus insisted that the responsibility rested with the Jews for venturing outside during the Easter.

1391: The Barcelona Massacre of Jews, Spain:

Ferrand Martinez, Archdeacon of Ecija, began to incite mobs into attacking the Jewish quarter. The campaign soon spread throughout Spain.

The Jewish quarter in Barcelona, located for over 400 years near the castle, was totally destroyed. Over 10,000 Jews were killed, and many others chose conversion and became new Christians. Of these, many continued to practice Judaism in secret while paying lip service to the Church.

Such people became known by the Christians as *Marranos*. The Jews never used the term *Marrano* themselves although some knew of it. Many scholars have speculated that the origins of the word stemmed from Latin, Arabic and even Hebrew, but in actual fact it was the Spanish term for pig or pork, an expression of extreme disgust on the part of the Christians. The Jews referred to them as *anusim* - "those who were forced to convert".

1394: Expulsion of Jews from France by King Charles IV:

Using the pretence that a Christian, Denis Machuit, had become a Jew again, Charles IV once again expelled all Jews. The order, signed on Yom Kippur, was enforced on November 3.

1411: Twenty-four Laws against Jews, Spain:

Vincente Ferrer was a Dominican friar who threatened and forced Jews into mass conversions. Ferrer would preach in synagogues with a Torah in one hand and a cross in the other.

Together with Paul of Burgos they instituted 24 edicts against the Jews in order to drive them to Christianity. These included a ban on working in handicrafts, trading in wine, flour, meat or bread, carrying arms, shaving, leaving the country, etc. Punishment was 100 lashes and a fine.

1420: The Expulsion of Jews from Lyon, France:

All Jews were expelled from Lyon, including the refugees from Paris who were expelled 20 years earlier. The only Jews left in France remained in Provence until 1500.

1421: The Persecution of Jews in Vienna, Austria:

This persecution was also known as the Vienna Edict. It involved the confiscation of the possessions of the Jews, and the forced conversion of Jewish children.

Charges of blood libel (using the blood of children for Jewish sacrifices) and host desecration (mistreating the Holy Communion) brought about the destruction of the entire Jewish community in Vienna, Austria.

This destruction of the Jewish community in Vienna was done under the auspices of Archduke Albert V of Austria.

Many Jews were forcibly baptized whilst others took their own lives. Archduke Albert ordered the execution of 92 men and 120 women who were burned at the stake south of the Vienna city. The Jews were placed under an "eternal ban" and the synagogue was demolished.

1434: The Basel Council Against Jews:

The Basel Council Instituted new measures against the Jews throughout Europe. The council, aside from adopting many of the old measures like preventing interaction between Jews and Christians, prohibited Jews from entering universities, and forced them to listen to conversion sermons. The council encouraged Christian study of Hebrew in order to "combat Jewish heresy".

Jews were forbidden to obtain academic degrees and to act as agents in the conclusion of contracts between Christians.

1435: The Majorcan Massacre of Jews:

Majorca, a Mediterranean island under Spanish control hosted a Jewish community, possibly as early as in the 2nd century that was massacred in 1435. Over 300 Jews were killed and many others forced to undergo baptism. Jewish habitation on Majorca ebbed and flowed with the whims of the island's rulers, who were caught up in the intrigues of the Spanish crown, but among the Jews were influential merchants, money-lenders, and slave-traffickers, whose value to the ruling class of Spain often led to their protection.

1438: The Confinement of Jews in Morocco:

Establishment of *mellahs* (ghettos) in Morocco. Jewish population was confined to *mellahs* in Morocco beginning from the 15th century and especially since the early 19th century. It first was seen as a privilege and a protection against the Arabs' attacks in the region, but with the growing of the population, it then became a poor and miserable place.

1465: The Moroccan Massacre of Jews:

Riots broke out after Sultan Abd al-Haqq asked the Jews of Fez for financial help and appointed Harun (Aaron ben Batash), a local Jew, to be his prime minister. During the riots the Sultan was murdered and Aaron was executed by having his throat cut. Most of the city's Jews were killed. Some reports claim that thousands were killed with only 11 left alive. There was a massacre of the entire Jewish population of Fez.

1470: Massacre of Jewish converts, Vallidolid, Spain:

Marranos (Jews who had converted to Christianity) were attacked by a mob. Don Henry IV of Castile interceded and much damage was averted.

1473 : Massacre of Jewish Converts, Cordova, Spain:

This was partly due to the populace's jealousy of the New Christians holding many important positions in the court and society. After the massacre, a decree was issued prohibiting them from living in Cordova. This process of jealousy, accusations, massacre and decree led to the accusations of heresy and, finally, to the Inquisition.

1475: False Accusations against Jews in Spain:

A student of the preacher Giovanni da Capistrano, Franciscan Bernardine of Feltre, accused the Jews of murdering an infant called Simon. The entire Jewish community was arrested, 15 leaders were burned at the stake, the rest were expelled.

The infant Simon was considered a martyr and a saint of kidnap and torture victims for almost 500 years. In 1965, Pope Paul VI declared the episode a fraud, and decanonized Simon's sainthood.

1490: Driving out Jews from Geneva, Switzerland for 300 years:

Jews were driven out from Switzerland and not allowed to return for 300 years. Jews had lived there since their expulsion from France by Philip Augustus in 1182.

1490: Burning of Jews in Avila, La Guardia:

Some Jews were accused of killing a child for ritual purposes. Although no body was ever found, they were judged guilty on November 14, 1491. Their crimes were host desecration and the taking of the child's heart for use in sorcery. They were all burned at the stake in the town of Avila. The child became a saint known as the "Child of La Guardia". Books and plays were written and embellished about him as recently as 1943.

1492: Expulsion of Jews from Spain:

Ferdinand II and Isabella issued the *General Edict on the Expulsion of the Jews* from Spain: approximately 200,000 were expelled. Some returned to the Land of Israel. Many more localities and entire countries expelled their Jewish citizens (after robbing them of their wealth), and others denied them entrance.

1492: The Burning of Twenty-Seven Jews in Germany:

Jews in Germany were accused of stabbing a consecrated wafer. 27 Jews were burned, including two women. The spot where they were killed is still called the *Judenberg* spot.

1493: Expulsion of Jews from Sicily:

Sicily became a province of Aragon in 1412. Approximately 37,000 Jews were driven out of Sicily. Despite an invitation during the 18th century, Jews, except in extremely small numbers, never returned.

1496: Expulsion of Jews from Portugal:

Forced conversion and expulsion of Jews from Portugal. This included many who fled Spain four years earlier.

1498: Extortion of money and property from Jews in Lithuania:

Prince Alexander of Lithuania forced most of the Jews to forfeit their property or convert. The main motivation was to cancel the debts the nobles owed to the Jews. Within a short time trade grounded to a halt and the Prince invited the Jews back in.

1506: The Lisbon Massacre of Jews:

A marrano (a Jew recently converted to Christianity) expressed his doubts about miracle visions at St. Dominics Church in Lisbon, Portugal.

Following this, a crowd, led by Dominican monks, killed him, then ransacked Jewish houses and slaughtered any Jew they could find. The countrymen heard about the massacre and joined in. Over 2,000 marranos were killed in three days.

1510: Execution of Jews in Germany:

Forty Jews were executed in Brandenburg, Germany for allegedly mishandling Holy Communion. The remainder were expelled. Less-wealthy Jews were expelled from Naples and the remainder were heavily taxed. 38 Jews were also burned at the stake in Berlin.

1516: Establishment of Jewish ghetto in Venice:

The first ghetto in Italy is established on one of the islands in Venice.

1519: Martin Luther Challenges the Doctrine of Dealing Kindly with Jews:

Martin Luther led Protestant Reformation and challenged the doctrine of *Servitus Judaeorum* . He advocated that they do not deal kindly with the Jews.

1535: Enslavement of all Tunisian Jews:

After Spanish troops captured Tunis all the local Jews were sold into slavery.

1543: Martin Luther's 8-point Plan to Get Rid of All Jews:

In his pamphlet *On the Jews and Their Lies* Martin Luther advocated an eight-point plan to get rid of the Jews as a distinct group either by religious conversion or by expulsion. Some of the action points under the plan were:

1. "...set fire to their synagogues or schools..."
2. "...their houses also be razed and destroyed..."
3. "...their prayer books and Talmudic writings... be taken from them..."
4. "...their rabbis be forbidden to teach henceforth on pain of loss of life and limb..."
5. "...safe-conduct on the highways be abolished completely for the Jews..."
6. "...usury (money lending) be prohibited to them, and that all cash and treasure of silver and gold be taken from them..." and
7. "Such money should now be used in ... the following [way]... Whenever a Jew is sincerely converted, he should be handed a certain amount"
8. "...young, strong Jews and Jewesses [should]... earn their bread in the sweat of their brow..."
9. "If we wish to wash our hands of the Jews' blasphemy and not share in their guilt, we have to part company with them. They must be driven from our country" and
10. "...we must drive them out like mad dogs."

Luther got the Jews expelled from Saxony in 1537 and in the 1540s he drove them from many German towns. He tried unsuccessfully to get the elector to expel them from Brandenburg in 1543. His followers continued to agitate against the Jews and in 1573 the Jews were banned from the entire country.'

1540: Banishment of Jews from Prague:

All Jews were banished from Prague.

1546: Martin Luther Releases "Admonition Against Jews":

Martin Luther's sermon *Admonition against the Jews* contains accusations of ritual murder, black magic, and poisoning of wells. Luther recognizes no obligation to protect the Jews.

1547: Rejection of Jews from Russia:

Ivan the Terrible becomes ruler of Russia and refuses to allow Jews to live in or even enter his kingdom because they "bring about great evil".

1550: Expulsion of Jews from Genoa, Italy:

Dr. Joseph Hacohen is chased out of Genoa for practicing medicine; soon all Jews are expelled.

1554: Burning of a Franciscan Friar:

Cornelio da Montalcino, a Franciscan Friar who converted to Judaism, is burned alive in Rome.

1555: Creation of a Locked Nightly Ghetto with Yellow Hats for Jews in Rome:

Pope Paul IV wrote: "It appears utterly absurd and impermissible that the Jews, whom God has condemned to eternal slavery for their guilt, should enjoy our Christian love."

The Pope introduced anti-Jewish legislation and installed a locked nightly ghetto in Rome. The law also forced Jewish males to wear a yellow hat and females a yellow kerchief. Owning real estate or practicing medicine on Christians was forbidden. The law also limited Jewish communities to only one synagogue.

1558: Expulsion of Jews from Recanati, Italy:

A baptized Jew Joseph Paul More entered a synagogue on Yom Kippur under the protection of Pope Paul IV and tried to preach a conversion sermon. The congregation evicted him. Soon after, all Jews were expelled from Recanati.

1563 : Drowning of 300 Jews in Ice in Russia:

When Russian troops captured Polotsk from Lithuania, Jews were given an ultimatum: embrace Russian Orthodox Church or die. Around 300 Jewish men, women and children were thrown into ice holes in the Dvina river.

1593: Expulsion of Jews from Papal States:

Pope Clement VIII issued the *Caeca et obdurata* ('Blind Obstinacy'): It stated:

"All the world suffers from the money lending activities of the Jews, their monopolies and deceit. ... Then as now Jews have to be reminded intermittently anew that their ethical and moral doctrines as well as their deeds rightly deserve to be exposed to criticism in whatever country they happen to live."

1614: The New "Haman" of Frankfurt:

Vincent Fettmilch, who called himself the "new Haman of the Jews", led a raid on Frankfurt synagogue that turned into an attack which destroyed the whole Jewish community.

1615: Another Expulsion of Jews from France:

King Louis XIII of France decreed that all Jews must leave the country within one month on pain of death.

1648–1655: The Ukranian Massacre of Jews:

The Ukrainian Cossacks led by Bohdan Chmielnicki massacred about 100,000 Jews and similar number of Polish nobles. 300 Jewish communities were destroyed.

1670: Jews Driven out of Vienna, Austria:

Leopold I ordered Jews to be expelled within a few months. Although Leopold was reluctant to lose the large amount of taxes (50,000 Florins) paid by the Jews, he was persuaded to do so by Margaret, the daughter of Phillip IV, the Spanish Regent and a strong follower of the Jesuits. Margaret blamed the death of her firstborn child on the tolerance shown to the Jews. The last Jews left on the 9th of April.

Leopold I, after evicting the Jews, sold the Jewish quarter for 100,000 florins, which was then renamed Leopoldstadt in his honor. The synagogue and the *bet midrash* (talmudic study hall) were converted into St. Margaret's Church.

A tablet was placed into the foundation stating that it was now a temple dedicated to God, and not "a murderers pit".

1727: Jews driven out by Catherine of Russia:

In her words, "The Jews... who are found in Ukraine and in other Russian provinces are to be expelled at once beyond the frontiers of Russia."

1742: Jews Driven out by Elizabeth of Russia:

Elizabeth of Russia issued a decree of expulsion on all Jews to leave the Russian Empire.

1744: Frederick II The Great allows only ten families into Breslau, Poland:

Frederick the Great, limited Breslau in Poland to ten "protected" Jewish families. The reason for this was to prevent them from "transforming Poland into a complete Jerusalem". He encouraged this practice in other Prussian cities.

1744 December: Archduchess of Austria expels Jews:

Archduchess of Austria Maria Theresa orders: "... no Jew is to be tolerated in our inherited duchy of Bohemia" by the end of

February 1745. In December 1748 she reverses her position, on condition that Jews paid for readmission every ten years. This extortion was known as *malke-geld* (queen's money). In 1752 she introduced the law limiting each Jewish family to one son.

1790–1792 Destruction of Jewish communities in Morocco.

Destruction of most of the Jewish communities of Morocco.

1805: Massacre of Jews in Algeria.

1815: Establishment of Ghetto in Rome after the Defeat of Napoleon:

Pope Pius VII re-establishes the ghetto in Rome after the defeat of Napoleon.

1819: Anti-Jewish Riots of Germany:

These riots that spread to several neighbouring countries like Denmark, Latvia and Bohemia were known as Hep-Hep riots.

The Hep-Hep riots were violent demonstrations against German Jews, beginning in the Kingdom of Bavaria.

The anti-Semitic communal violence began on August 2, 1819 in Würzburg and soon reached the outer regions of the German Confederation. Many Jews were killed and much Jewish property was destroyed.

The riots took place in a period of heightened political and social tension, shortly following the end of the Napoleonic Wars in 1815 and the great famine of 1816-17.

1835: Persecution of Jews by Tsar Nicholas I of Russia:

An oppressive constitution for the Jews was issued by Tsar Nicholas I of Russia.

1840: The Accusation of Jews of Ritual Murder in Damascus:

A blood libel (accusation that Jews had killed a human being for their blood sacrifice) was started with the disappearance of Father Thomas, a Franciscan superior. After a "confession" was extracted from a Jewish barber, seven others were arrested, two of whom died under torture. The French consul Ratti Menton, accused the Jews of ritual murder and requested permission to kill the suspects. Other Jews were arrested, including sixty-three children who were starved to persuade their parents to confess. Sir Moses Montefiore, Adolphe Cremieux, and Solomon Munk intervened on behalf of the Jews and in August the charges were dropped.

1879: Anti-Semitism is promoted in intellectual circles of Germany:

Heinrich von Treitschke, a German historian and politician, justified the anti Jewish campaigns in Germany, thereby bringing the concept of anti-Semitism into learned circles.

1881–1884: Violent Demonstrations in southern Russia:

Hatred and persecution for Jews in Russia propelled the mass Jewish emigration to the United States. About 2 million Russian Jews emigrated in the period 1880–1924, many of them to the United States.

1882: Blood libel accusations against Jews in Hungary:

The Tiszaezlar blood libel accusation in Hungary, aroused public opinion throughout Europe.

1882: First International Anti-Jewish Congress convenes at Dresden, Germany.

1882: Persecution of Jews by Tsar Alexander III of Russia:

In Russia, temporary regulations regarding the Jews known as "May Laws" were proposed by minister of internal affairs

Nikolai Ignatyev and enacted on 15 May 1882, by the Emperor Alexander III of Russia.

These laws adopted a systematic policy of discrimination, with the object of removing the Jews from their economic and public positions, in order to "cause one-third of the Jews to emigrate, one-third to accept baptism and one-third to starve".

A *pogrom* (violent demonstration against Jews) left 40 dead, 170 wounded, and 1,250 dwellings destroyed. Fifteen thousand Jews were reduced to total poverty.

1887: Jews prevented from receiving education in Russia:

Russia introduced measures to limit Jews access to education, known as the *quota*.

1891: Expulsion of 20,000 Jews from Moscow, Russia:

Following the expulsion of Jews from Russia, the Congress of the United States eased immigration restrictions to allow Jews to enter the United States of America.

1893: Establishment of an anti-Semitic German political party:

Karl Lueger established an anti-Semitic *Christian Social Party* and became the Mayor of Vienna in 1897.

1903: The Kishinev Massacre, Moldova:

Riots broke out after a Christian child, Michael Ribalenko, was found murdered. Although it was clear that the boy had been killed by a relative, the government chose to call it a ritual murder plot by the Jews.

The mobs were incited by Pavolachi Krusheven, the editor of the anti Jewish newspaper *Bessarabetz*. Vyacheslav Von Plehve, the Minister of Interior, supposedly gave orders not to stop the rioters.

During three days of rioting, forty-seven Jews were killed, ninety-two severely wounded, five hundred slightly wounded and over seven hundred houses were destroyed. Despite a world-wide outcry, only two men were sentenced to seven and five years and twenty-two were sentenced for one or two years. This *pogrom* was instrumental in convincing tens of thousands of Russian Jews to leave Russia for the West and for Israel. The child's real murderer was later found.

The most popular newspaper in Kishinev, the Russian-language anti-Semitic newspaper *Bessarabetz*, (meaning 'Bessarabian'), published by Pavel Krushevan, regularly published articles with headlines such as "Death to the Jews!" and "Crusade against the Hated Race!" (referring to the Jews).

1905: Massacre of Jews in Dnipropetrovsk, Ukraine:

In 1883 and 1905 there were violent demonstrations against Jews in Yekaterinoslav. During the 1905 *pogrom* 66 Jews were killed, 125 wounded whilst Jewish homes and shops were looted. To protect the Jewish population, a self-defence organization was established in 1904 with 600 members, including several non-Jews.

1915: The Expulsion of 250,000 Jews from Russia:

The First World War prompted expulsion of 250,000 Jews from Western Russia.

Jews were attacked for being revolutionaries or counter-revolutionaries, unpatriotic pacifists, warmongers or religious zealots.

Approximately 70,000 to 250,000, were murdered in violent demonstrations.

1925: The rise of Adolf Hitler:

Adolf Hitler publishes a book called *Mein Kampf.*

Hitler stated in his book: "Hence today I believe that I am acting in accordance with the will of the Almighty Creator: *by defending myself against the Jew, I am fighting for the work of the Lord."*

1929: The Hebron Massacre:

The Hebron massacre refers to the killing of sixty-seven Jews (including 46 Yeshiva students and teachers) on 24 August 1929 in Hebron, then part of Palestine. The massacre was conducted by Arabs incited to violence by rumours that Jews were planning to seize control of the Temple Mount in Jerusalem.

Jewish homes were pillaged and synagogues were ransacked. Many of the 435 Jews who survived were hidden by local Arab families.

Soon after, all Hebron's Jews were evacuated by the British authorities.

1933–1941: The great persecution of Jews in Germany:

Persecution of Jews in Germany rises until they are stripped of their rights not only as citizens, but also as human beings. During this time anti-Semitism reached its all-time high.

1934: The Expulsion of Jews from Afghanistan:

2,000 Afghani Jews were expelled from their Afghan towns and forced to live in the wilderness.

1935: Laws against Jews in Germany enacted:

Germany introduced the new Nuremberg laws in which Jewish rights were rescinded. Jews were stripped of citizenship.

Marriages between Jews and citizens of Germany were forbidden.

Sexual relations outside marriage between Jews and nationals of Germany or kindred blood were forbidden.

Jews were not permitted to employ female citizens of Germany or kindred blood as domestic servants.

Jews were forbidden to display the German national flag or the national colours. On the other hand they were permitted to display only the Jewish colours.

1938: Concentration camps for Jews opened in Germany:

Several decrees were passed by the German government.

A decree authorizing local authorities to bar Jews from the streets on certain days was passed.

A decree empowering the Justice Ministry to void wills that offended the "sound judgment of the people" was passed.

A decree providing for the compulsory sale of Jewish real estate was passed.

A decree providing for the liquidation of Jewish real estate agencies and brokerage agencies was passed.

1938 November 9–10: The Night of the Broken Glass:

In one night most German synagogues and hundreds of Jewish-owned German businesses were destroyed. Almost 100 Jews were killed, and 10,000 were sent to concentration camps.

1938 July 6: Rejection of Jews by thirty-one countries:

The Evian Conference was convened by President Franklin D. Roosevelt to deal with the Jewish refugee problem. It was held in Evian, France, from July 6--15, 1938.

After Germany annexed Austria in March 1938, Roosevelt called for an international conference to promote the emigration of Austrian and German Jewish refugees and create an international organization whose purpose would be to deal with the general refugee problem. The president invited delegates from 32 countries, including the United States, Great Britain, France, Canada, six small European democratic nations, the Latin American nations, Australia, and New Zealand. When he proposed the conference, Roosevelt made it clear that no country would be forced to change its immigration quotas, but would instead be asked to volunteer changes.

During the conference, it became painfully obvious that *no country was willing to volunteer anything*. The British delegate claimed that Britain was already fully populated and suffering from unemployment, so it could take in no refugees. His only offer consisted of British territories in East Africa, which could take in small numbers of refugees.

The French delegate declared that France had reached "the extreme point of saturation in regards to the admission of refugees." Only the Dominican Republic, a tiny country in the West Indies, volunteered to take in refugees—in exchange for huge amounts of money.

1939: The Rejection of a ship full of Jews:

The "Voyage of the damned", *S.S. St. Louis*, carrying 907 Jewish refugees from Germany, was turned back by Canada, Cuba and the USA.

1939: February: The Rejection of Jewish children by America:

The Congress of the United States rejected the Wagner-Rogers Bill, which was an effort to receive 20,000 Jewish refugee children under the age of 14 from Nazi Germany.

The Wagner–Rogers Bill would have increased the quota of immigrants by bringing a total of 20,000 German children under the age of 14 (10,000 in 1939, and another 10,000 in 1940) to the United States from Nazi Germany. The bill was sponsored by Senator Robert F. Wagner and Rep. Edith Rogers in the wake of the 1938 Kristallnacht attacks on Jews in Germany. The bill had widespread support among religious and labour groups, but was opposed by patriotic organizations. It never came to a vote because it was blocked by Senator Robert Rice Reynolds of North Carolina, who held a powerful position because of his seniority.

1939–1945: The Mass murder of six million Jews:

About 6 million Jews, including about 1 million children, were systematically killed by Nazi Germany between 1939 and 1945 under the leadership of Adolf Hitler.

1939–1945: Systematic stealing of twelve billion pounds of Jewish money:

Over twelve billion pounds sterling at the time – was plundered from German Jews by bogus laws and looting. In an official study examining the years between 1933 and 1945, Hans-Peter Ullmann, a Cologne history professor, said the tax authorities under the Nazis actively worked to "destroy Jews financially" and to loot wealth in the nations the Germans occupied.

Even Jews who managed to escape from Germany before the Holocaust had to leave part of their wealth behind in the form of an "exit tax".

According to Prof Ullmann, "Conservatively, stolen Jewish money financed at least 30 percent of the German war effort."

1948–2001: The Jewish Exodus from Arab lands:

Jewish exodus from Arab lands. The Jewish population in the Arab Middle East and North Africa has decreased from 900,000 in 1948 to less than 8,000 in 2001.

This short history of the persecution of Jews through the centuries, outlines the fulfilment of the words spoken by Moses in a most dramatic and amazing way. Whilst the curse seems to work itself out, the blessing on the other hand, lifts up the same people to survive against all odds.

CHAPTER 17

How the Blessing of Isaac is Working Out

Therefore God give thee of the dew of heaven, and the fatness of the earth, and plenty of corn and wine:

Let people serve thee, and nations bow down to thee: be lord over thy brethren, and let thy mother's sons bow down to thee: cursed be every one that curseth thee, and blessed be he that blesseth thee.

Genesis 27:28-29

And I will bless them that bless thee, and curse him that curseth thee: and in thee shall all families of the earth be blessed.

Genesis 12:3

Isaac blessed his son Jacob and Jacob's name was changed to Israel. Jacob is the person who grew to become the nation Israel. Jacob, the nation of Israel, received the blessing of the dew of the heavens, the fatness of the earth and plenty of corn and wine. He also received the blessing of having the nations bow down to him and becoming the lord of his relatives.

These blessings have carried through the centuries and made Israel and the Jews become who they have become. There is no other explanation that can help us understand why this small group of people should be so distinguished in the earth. Even more amazing is the fact that this group of people has been persecuted, expelled, hated and murdered by so many nations and yet has continued to stand out and shine through the centuries.

Even though there are many ethnic groups of people in the world, none of them has stood out and affected the world the way this group of people has. It is worth analysing and discovering the secret behind the unusual achievements of the Jews. As usual, the Bible gives us the answers. The wonders of the blessings and the curses are working! The blessings spoken by Isaac over his son, Israel, are prevailing and counteracting the hatred that exists against Jews. Nothing but the power of a blessing can explain the success and prosperity of the Jews. Let us now look at how the blessing of Isaac is working itself out in the lives of the Jews today.

1. **The blessing of Isaac is working because *the most famous person* ever was a Jew.** Jesus Christ was the most famous person that ever lived. Jesus Christ is the Son of God. The Jews were blessed and God chose them and used them to bring His Son into the world. All the history of mankind is dated and related to when this most famous and outstanding Jew (Jesus Christ) was born into this world. The Jews are a famous nation and have been used by God to impact the whole world.

2. **The blessing of Isaac on Israel is working because many *famous people* of our world have been Jews.** There is no way to explain why so many outstanding, unique and famous people come from Israel. Apart from *the most famous person* who ever lived, many other very famous people are Jews. Indeed, many Jews changed their names to protect themselves from persecution; and so it is likely that many more famous people are actually Jews. Let's have a look at some of the famous Jews of our world.

Sigmund Freud: Sigmund Freud is one of the world's famous descendants of Jacob. Sigmund Freud explored the human mind more thoroughly than any other who came before him.

His contributions to psychology are vast. Freud was one of the most influential people of the twentieth century and his enduring legacy has not only influenced psychology, but art, literature and even the way people bring up their children.

Freud's lexicon has become embedded within the vocabulary of western society. Words introduced by Freud through his theories are now used in everyday English. They include words such as anal (personality), libido, denial, repression, cathartic, Freudian slip, and neurotic.

Freud believed that when we explain our own behaviour to ourselves or others (conscious mental activity) we rarely give a true account of our motivation. This is not because we are deliberately lying. Whilst human beings are great deceivers of others, they are even more adept at self-deception. Our rationalizations of our conduct therefore disguise the real reasons.

Freud's life work was dominated by his attempts to find ways of penetrating this often subtle and elaborate camouflage that obscures the hidden structure and processes of personality.

Freud was the founding father of psychoanalysis, a method for treating mental illness and also a theory that explains human behavior.

Karl Marx: Karl Marx was a Jew who has been both lauded and criticized. Marx has been described as one of the most influential figures in human history. Many intellectuals, labour unions and political parties worldwide have been influenced by Marx's ideas, with many variations on his groundwork. Marx is typically cited with Emile Durkheim and Max Weber as one of the three principal architects of modern social science. Marx's work in economics laid the basis for much of the current understanding of labour and its relation to capital, and subsequent economic thought. He published numerous books during his lifetime, the most notable being "The Communist Manifesto".

Albert Einstein: Perhaps, Einstein was the most intelligent descendant of Jacob. Einstein was a German-born Jewish theoretical physicist. He is best known for his theory of relativity and specifically mass–energy equivalence, $E = mc^2$, the most famous equation of the twentieth century. Einstein received the 1921 Nobel Prize in Physics, *"For his services to Theoretical Physics, and especially for his discovery of the Law of the Photoelectric Effect."* Einstein published over 300 scientific works and over 150 non-scientific works. Einstein is revered by the physics community, and in 1999, Time Magazine named him the "Person of the Century". In a wider sense the name "Einstein" has become synonymous with genius.

Siegfried Samuel Marcus 1831 –1898: The very first car was made by another descendant of Jacob. Siegfried Samuel Marcus was a German-born Austria-Hungarian inventor of Jewish descent. He was the first to use a gasoline-powered engine to propel a car, creating the first ever self-propelling vehicle. In 1870 he put an internal combustion engine on a simple handcart and this made him the first to propel a vehicle by means of gasoline. Today, this car is well known as "The first Marcus Car".

Because of Marcus' Jewish ancestry, his name and all memorabilia were removed by the German Nazis. His memorial in front of the Vienna Technical University was removed. After World War II, the monument was rebuilt.

Marcus was removed from German encyclopaedias as the inventor of the modern car, under a directive from the German Ministry for Propaganda during World War II. His name was replaced with the names of Daimler and Benz.

3. **The blessing of Isaac on Israel is working because the Jews have won a disproportionately high number of** *Nobel Prizes* **as compared to other groups of people.** The Nobel Prize is regarded by far as the most prestigious prize in the world; and is awarded to those who, during the preceding year, shall have conferred the greatest benefit on mankind.

    Since the Nobel Prize was first awarded in 1901 approximately 193 of the 855 honourees have been Jewish (22%), even though Jews make up less than 0.2% of the global population.

4. **The blessing of Isaac on Israel is working because many of the** *richest and most successful people* **on earth have been Jews as compared to other groups in humanity.** Note this list of the descendants of Jacob below and be amazed at the wonders of spoken blessing.

a. **THE FOUNDER OF GOOGLE:** Google, the world's largest Internet company, was founded by Larry Page and Sergey Brin while they were Ph.D. students at Stanford University. Sergey Brin, whose father was a Soviet mathematician economist, was born to a Jewish family in Moscow. In 1979, he and his family fled persecution and migrated to America.

b. **THE FOUNDER OF FACEBOOK:** Zuckerberg was raised Jewish and had his bar mitzvah when he turned 13. Unfortunately, he became an atheist afterwards. One of the other co-founders of Facebook, Dustin Moskovitz is also Jewish.

c. **THE FOUNDER OF VIBER:** Viber was founded by four Israeli partners: Talmon Marco, Igor Magazinnik, Sani Maroli and Ofer Smocha, with Marco as its CEO.

d. **THE CEO OF MICROSOFT:** Steve Ballmer, is Jewish.

e. **THE FOUNDER OF ORACLE:** Lawrence Joseph 'Larry' Ellison was born in New York City, to an unwed Jewish woman. He founded the world's second largest software company, Oracle, and is listed as the world's richest Jew, and by Forbes as the sixth richest person in the world.

f. **THE OWNER OF CHELSEA FOOTBALL CLUB:** Roman Abramovitch who owns the Chelsea Football Club, as well as a private investment company, Millhouse LLC, is also a Jew and a descendant of Isaac.

g. **THE FOUNDER OF TESCO STORES:** The descendants of Isaac are to be found prospering and flourishing everywhere. Tesco supermarket, the largest supermarket in England is also Jewish. Jack Cohen, the son of Jewish migrants from Poland, founded Tesco in 1919 when he began to sell war-surplus groceries from a stall at Well Street Market.

h. **THE FOUNDERS AND OWNERS OF GOLDMAN SACHS INVESTMENT BANK:** Marcus Goldman was a Jewish banker, businessman, and financier. He was born in Trappstadt, Bavaria and immigrated to the United States in 1848. He was the founder of Goldman Sachs, which has since become one of the world's largest and most influential investment banks. The Goldman Sachs CEO and Chairman: Lloyd Blankfein recalled the role of his rabbi and Jewish organizations in helping him realize he could succeed despite growing up in a working-class neighborhood. "The only person I knew who put on a suit everyday was our rabbi," Blankfein told a crowd of 1,700 fellow Wall Street insiders one night at a $26 million record-breaking fundraising dinner for UJA-Federation of New York.

i. **THE FOUNDATION OF WAL-MART:** Sam Walton, the founder of Wal-Mart, married Helen Robson an English Jew whose father was a wealthy banker, lawyer and rancher. Sam Walton's Jewish father-in-law gave him his first loan of $20,000 with which he started business.

j. **THE FOUNDER OF LEHMAN BROTHERS:** In 1844, 23-year-old Henry Lehman, the son of a Jewish cattle merchant, emigrated to the United States from Rimpar, Bavaria and opened a dry-goods store. In 1847, following the arrival of his brother Emanuel Lehman, the firm became "H. Lehman and Bro". With the arrival of their youngest brother, Mayer Lehman, in 1850, the firm changed its name again and "Lehman Brothers" was founded. It was acquired by Barclays in 2008.

k. **THE FOUNDER OF MACY'S:** Isidor Straus was a Jewish German-born American who co-founded Macy's department store with his brother Nathan. He and his wife, Ida, died when the RMS Titanic sank in 1912.

l. **THE FOUNDER OF MARKS AND SPENCER:** Marks & Spencer was founded in 1884 by Michael Marks and Thomas Spencer in Leeds, UK. Marks was a Polish Jew from Słonim. Some people even stopped shopping at Marks & Spencer because they suspected it was Jewish.

m. **THE FOUNDER OF SEAR'S:** Julius Rosenwald was born in 1862 to the clothier Samuel Rosenwald and his wife Augusta Hammerslough Rosenwald, a Jewish immigrant couple from Germany. He was born and raised just a few blocks from the Abraham Lincoln residence in Springfield, Illinois, during Lincoln's Presidency of the United States.

He is best known as a part-owner and leader of Sears, Roebuck and company, and for establishing the Rosenwald Fund which donated millions in matching funds to support the education of African American children in the rural South, as well as other philanthropic causes in the first half of the 20th century. He was the principal founder and backer for the Museum of Science and Industry in Chicago, to which he gave more than $5 million and served as President from 1927 to 1932.

n. **FOUNDER OF VOLKSWAGEN:** The all-time most popular car, the Volkswagen Beetle, was not invented by Adolf Hitler but by a Jewish engineer, Josef Ganz. With 21.5 million sales since production in Germany until its layoff in 2003, the Volkswagen Beetle was the longest running and most prolific car in history.

o. **FOUNDER OF MERCEDES BENZ:** One of the most famous cars in the world was also brought about by a descendant of Jacob. Daimler and Maybach; two Germans created the first car for the market. However, they could not sell it until Emil Jellinek an Israeli and the son of *Rabbi Aaron Jellinek,* took over the business. He convinced Maybach to build a new and improved car, to be called "Mercedes", named after his daughter Mercedes. The Mercedes quickly shattered all records, going 60 km/h and easily winning the competitive Nice races. It was branded "the car of tomorrow" and took the world by storm.

p. **FOUNDER OF CITROEN:** André-Gustave Citroen, was the 5th and last child of Jewish parents, diamond merchant Levie Citroen from the Netherlands and Masza Amelia Kleinman from Warsaw, Poland. In 1900, he visited Poland the birth land of his mother, who had recently died. During that holiday he saw a carpenter working on a set of gears with a *fish-bone* structure. These gears were less noisy and more efficient. Citroën bought the patent for very little money, leading to the invention that is credited to Citroën: double helical gears. This is also reputed to be the inspiration of the *double chevron* logo of the Citroën brand.

q. **THE CEOs of many huge companies are Jews:** Companies like Walt Disney, Time Warner, Warner Music, Warnervision, ESPN, ABC, NBC, Dreamworks, Universal

Pictures and many famous banks are all descendants of Isaac.

5. **The blessing of Isaac on Israel is working because many** *amazing scientific discoveries* **of our world have been made by Jews as compared to other groups of people.**

1. Israel developed the PillCam – the first pill that could be swallowed to record images of the digestive tract. The capsule is the size and the same shape as a pill, and contains a tiny camera. This invention is used very widely and was an extremely significant development in the field of medicine.

2. Israel was the country to develop the USB flash drive. Used by nearly everyone I know, it surely is one of the most useful modern inventions. It allows you to store all your files in a compact way, making it easier to access and work away from your computer.

3. Israeli inventions in the consumer goods market continue to thrive, as seen by the invention of the epilator. An epilator is an electrical device used to remove hair by mechanically grasping multiple hairs simultaneously and pulling them out. The first one, Epilady, was originally manufactured by a Kibbutz in Israel in 1986, and has since sold more than 30 million units.

4. Israel is "the land of milk and honey" thanks to its "super cows", which produce far more milk than cows in other countries. Israeli cows produce up to 10.5 tons of milk a year – 10% more than North American cows and almost 50% more than Germany's cows! A combination of air conditioning, constant monitoring and pedometers to tell when the animals are getting fidgety helps to keep the milk flowing, according to Bloomberg.

5. Israel developed the BabySense device, which helps prevent cot deaths by monitoring a baby's breathing and movements through the mattress while they sleep. An auditory and

visual alarm is activated if any irregularities occur during their sleep, which has helped parents prevent cot death worldwide.

6.   Viber is also an Israeli invention. It is an app that allows you to call people around the world for free. Available for download on any smart phone, the app allows you to make calls across the world for free, using Wifi. Its high speed connection and ability to keep in contact with anyone anywhere truly makes it one of Israel's best inventions.

CHAPTER 18

The Curse of Noah

And the sons of Noah, that went forth of the ark, were Shem, and Ham, and Japheth: and Ham is the father of Canaan. These are the three sons of Noah: and of them was the whole earth overspread. And Noah began to be an husbandman, and he planted a vineyard: And he drank of the wine, and was drunken; and he was uncovered within his tent.

And Ham, the father of Canaan, saw the nakedness of his father, and told his two brethren without. And Shem and Japheth took a garment, and laid it upon both their shoulders, and went backward, and covered the nakedness of their father; and their faces were backward, and they saw not their father's nakedness. And Noah awoke from his wine, and knew what his younger son had done unto him.

And he said, Cursed be Canaan; A servant of servants shall he be unto his brethren.

Genesis 9:18-25

A curse creates a picture!

Every curse creates an unmistakable picture! To recognize a curse you must know the picture it creates!

The curse on man creates the unmistakeable picture of toil and sweat that yields little fruit.

The curse on women creates the unmistakeable picture of sorrow, disappointment and struggles with husbands and children.

The curse on Jews creates the unmistakeable picture of worldwide inexplicable hatred, scattering and persecution.

The curse on Jew haters creates the picture of inexplicable ultimate defeat and humiliation.

The curse on black people creates the inexplicable picture of servanthood, poor leadership, poverty and insignificance.

A trained medical doctor will notice certain symptoms and signs because he is trained to recognize the picture of a disease. It is an unmistakeable picture to him because he is trained to see it. In the same way, you will now recognize the picture of the curse when you see it. Your trained eyes will pick out the unmistakeable picture that shows that a curse is working.

The curse of Noah is often called the "Curse of Ham". Someone would ask, "So do you believe in the curse of Ham? Do you believe that black people are cursed? The answer to that question is simple. I believe that all the curses in the bible are real. I believe the Bible is the word of God. The bible contains curses that have been spoken against different groups of people. This book contains discussions on all the different curses that affect human beings. The great promise of heaven is that there will be no curse!

The curse of Adam affected all males!

The curse of Eve affected all females!

The curse of Moses affected Jews!

The curse of Isaac affected Jew-haters!

The curse of Noah affected black people!

Unfortunately, the curse of Noah has been used by white people as a basis for despising, torturing, enslaving and cheating black people. This is a misuse of scripture. Why didn't they use the curse of Eve or Adam to make men and women suffer more terribly on this earth? It is the same way in which Jew-haters have used scriptures as the basis for maltreating Jews.

In this book, I am not giving you the basis to mistreat anybody; whether black, white or Jew. I AM SHOWING YOU THAT THE CURSE IS REAL AND I AM SHOWING YOU HOW TO NEUTRALIZE THESE CURSES BY THE WISDOM OF GOD!

This curse of Noah is the curse to be a "servant of servants" is the curse to be low and inferior. Noah cursed and said, "Cursed be Canaan; a servant of servants shall he be." Inferiority, mediocrity, shoddiness and suffering were slammed onto the descendants of Ham by the words of Noah. Ham dishonoured his father and the result was this curse. The curse was not spoken against Ham, but against Canaan. Since Ham was the one who dishonoured his father, we assume that Canaan was receiving this curse on behalf of Ham's descendants. This curse is also called the curse of Ham because Canaan had done nothing to deserve a curse. It was his father, Ham, who had dishonoured Noah. Indeed, this brief, startling curse on the descendants of Ham has worked itself out in such a way that proves a curse is indeed a wonder!

So who were the descendants of Ham? The sons of Ham were Cush, and Mizraim, Phut, and Canaan. (1 Chronicles 1:8).

Cush was the forefather of various Ethiopian tribes that settled south of Egypt and also overran Arabia, Babylonia, and India.

Mizraim was the forefather of various Egyptian tribes. Mizraim means "double." Tribes of the double Egypt (upper and lower Egypt), called the land of Ham, came from him.

Phut was the forefather of the Libyans and other tribes in northern Africa.

Canaan was the forefather of the peoples that settled mainly in Palestine, Arabia.

A servant of servants is the description of the poorest and lowest. First of all, servants are seen to be lower than their masters. A servant of servants will therefore be even poorer and lower in society. A servant of servants therefore describes someone that is very low, very poor and very deprived.

Has this picture of being very low, very poor and very deprived descended on any group of people on this planet? Is there any group of people who are very low in status, very poor and very deprived no matter where they live?

A quick look at life on earth reveals that the African nations and the African people, wherever they are found, are the poorest, and least developed community. Generally speaking, they are usually the lowest and the least on the ladder of development, in education, in wealth, in leadership, in political advancement, in governance and in health. The black communities of our world are an unmistakable pattern and picture.

What is the cause of this unmistakable global picture? It is a curse that creates an inexplicable and unmistakable picture. The picture of a servant of a servant is a portrait of lowliness, suffering, deprivation and poverty. The picture of a servant of a servant is the picture of being inferior, being under and being disregarded.

That picture reflects the same story being told about those under the curse whenever, however and wherever they may be found.

Let's have a look at the story, the picture and the history created by these powerful words of Noah spoken thousands of years ago against his son who mocked him. Below, you will find facts about the descendants of Ham.

The picture is amazing and consistent through the ages. What can explain such a pattern except the curse? Christians must grow up spiritually and respect the power of curses and blessings that are spoken by men of authority. I am presenting these details so that you will fear the power of spoken words and learn to use these spiritual forces carefully. The astonishing thing about a curse is the way it is fulfilled everywhere and all the time.

How bad is the situation on the African continent? Is Africa the lowest and the poorest continent? Is the picture of the servant of servants fulfilled in Africa? Is there something we need to pray about? Is there something we need to address?

The story of Africa is the story of the lowest, the least and the most deprived! It is the story of the suffering servant of servants, lower than the lowest. It is the story of how lowness has become the state of affairs in spite of the fact that it is the richest continent.

Let us have a look at the statistics:

## 1.	The Story of black people in the fifty-four nations of Africa

•	Seventy-five percent of the world's poorest countries are located in Africa, and that includes Zimbabwe, Liberia and Ethiopia. In 2012 and 2013, the Democratic Republic of Congo, Africa's second largest country, was also ranked the poorest in the world. According to the Gallup World Poll, in 2013, the 10 countries with the highest proportion of residents living in extreme poverty were all in sub-Saharan Africa.

•	Approximately one in three people living in sub-Saharan Africa are undernourished. The Food and Agriculture Organization (FAO) of the United Nations estimated that 239 million people (around 30 percent of the population) in sub-Saharan Africa were hungry in 2010. This is the highest percentage of any region in the world. In addition, the U.N. Millennium Project reported that over 40 percent of all Africans are unable to regularly obtain sufficient food.

- In sub-Saharan Africa, 589 million people live without electricity. As a result, a staggering 80 percent of the population relies on biomass products such as wood, charcoal and dung in order to cook.

- Of the 738 million people globally who lack access to clean water, 37 percent are living in sub-Saharan Africa. Poverty in Africa results in over 500 million people suffering from waterborne diseases. According to the U.N. Millennium Project, more than 50 percent of Africans have a water-related illness like cholera.

- 38 percent of the world's refugees are located in Africa. Due to continuing violence, conflict and widespread human rights abuses, the United Nations High Commissioner for Refugees (UNHCR) reports that 11 million people, including stateless people and returnees, exist in Africa.

- Women in sub-Saharan Africa are over 230 times more likely to die during childbirth or pregnancy than women in North America. More than one million people, mostly children under the age of five, die every year from malaria. Malarial deaths in Africa alone account for 90 percent of all malaria deaths worldwide.

    POVERTY IN AFRICA: Most African countries have remained stuck with a GDP per capita below $2000 for the past six decades. (GDP per capita of European countries is about $35,000).

- 32 of the world's 38 heavily indebted poor countries are in Africa.

- Half the population of Africa lives on less than US $1 a day. The average income level is sometimes so low that even working people live under the poverty line.

- Between 1975 and 2000 Africa was the only place on earth where poverty had intensified. Decade after decade, politicians and international organizations have failed to reduce poverty. Nor have they been able to help Africa generate growth or build basic infrastructure.

- Globalization and worldwide technological advancement have only made Africa's poverty worse. In many cases, oil-rich African countries are likely to be exploited by other countries or powerful corporations who always find a way not to pay billions of dollars in taxes.

EDUCATION IN AFRICA: Primary school enrollment in African countries is among the lowest in the world.

- 33 million primary school-aged children in Sub-Saharan Africa do not go to school.

- 40% of Africans over the age of 15, and 50% of women above the age of 25 are illiterate.

- Africa loses an estimated 20,000 skilled personnel each year to developed countries.

HEALTH IN AFRICA: Epidemics like Ebola and HIV AIDS threaten African populations. The epidemics impoverish individuals, thus further entrenching the roots of poverty in Africa.

- Average life expectancy in Africa is only 46 years.

- There are an estimated 5,500 AIDS deaths a day in Africa.

HOUSING IN AFRICA: Slums are home to 72 percent of urban Africa's citizens.

SANITATION IN AFRICA: Basic sanitation and hygienic standards, which have prevented millions of deaths across the world are yet to be instilled across Africa.

HUNGER IN AFRICA: In the past 30 years only sub-Saharan Africa saw no improvement in the fight against malnutrition and hunger in Africa. Currently there is an estimated 80 percent of Africans who suffer from hunger, 30 percent of whom are children.

WATER IN AFRICA: "All peoples, whatever their stage of development and their social and economic conditions, have the right to have access to drinking water in quantities and of a quality equal to their basic needs". (Action Plan, United Nations Water Conference, Mar del Plata, 1977).

More than 30 years after this statement, over 50% of Africans still suffer from water-related diseases such as cholera, diarrhoea.

• Although the continent is blessed with large rivers such as the Congo, the Nile, the Zambezi, the Volta and the Niger, there are sharp shortages of water in Africa.

2. *The story of black people in the Caribbean*

• For many wealthy tourists around the world, the Caribbean islands seem like the perfect vacation getaway. Spring breakers, honeymooners and retirees all flock to the golden sands to bathe in crystal clear waters and soak up some sun. However, it might be surprising to note that the murder rates in the Caribbean region are higher than in any other region of the world. At an average of 30 homicides per 100,000 inhabitants per year, the English-speaking Caribbean now has one of the highest murder rates in the world. Incidents of assaults, burglary, kidnapping and rape are also above the world average, and rising. The high incidence of crime in Trinidad and Tobago is a relatively new phenomenon: the murder rate rose from just 7.4/100,000 in 1999 to a historical high of 30.6/100,000 in 2007.

• Beyond the protected walls of the hotels, crime, violence and poverty plague the populations of these Caribbean nations. While tourism may be growing, the majority of the population continues to battle with rising rape, murder and poverty levels.

- The Dominican Republic, for example, receives the most tourists of all the Caribbean Islands, yet it ranks as the third poorest Caribbean country with a gross domestic product per capita of only $9,700.

- Jamaica similarly represents this paradox. Though Bob Marley's music resonates peace and love around the world, today, Jamaica is known for its widespread poverty and high gun crime. In fact, in 2006, 75.2% of all murders committed in Jamaica involved the use of guns.

- Social inequality and poverty in the Caribbean date back to colonialism, as the slave trade created a lasting impact on the social order and economic system of many islands. Today, the situation remains relatively unchanged, some of the largest businesses are still owned by white families who continue to reap the benefits of the plantation profits.

3. *The story of black people in Colombia*

- The main victims of violence and armed conflict in the country are people of African descent who represent almost 30% of the rural population, a proportion that has declined due to forced displacement caused by violence.

- Today, near Cartagena in Colombia, there is a province that has retained African cultural traits. The province, Palenque de san Basilio, which is a world heritage site, has the Palenquera language as the spoken language, and not Spanish. It still observes ancestral African practices. Presently, it is home to one of the poorest populations in the country.

- Today the black population in Colombia have learned to live in poverty, lack of water and sewage, labour exploitation and sexual prejudice.

- Colombia is undoubtedly one of the most important countries in the history of the trading and of enslaved

Africans in the Americas. It was a gathering place for the enslaved for distribution across the continent. Colombia is one of the places where people of African descent suffer the worst living conditions.

- The initial problem is the zero development of identity in a multi-ethnic and multicultural country. There is still denial of the African origins of most of the current population in the country.

- The level and accessibility of basic necessities is lower in the African population compared to the national average. The quality of education is the lowest in the areas of mostly African population.

- Discrimination is an issue that is not monitored or protected by any law effectively. Only in 2008 was a law drafted against racism and discrimination that raised penalties from two to five years in prison and fines between U.S. 2,700 dollars and U.S. 6,600 dollars, but so far this law has had little social impact.

4. *The story of black people in Panama*

- The story of black people in the tiny nation of Panama is still the story of the lowest and the least. The astonishing thing about a curse is the way it is fulfilled everywhere and all the time. It is the story of the servant of servants, lower than the lowest.

- Afro-Panamanians are excluded in the public sector, the education system, and within the workforce. Panamanian education isolates individuals of African descent, excluding them from academic content, ignoring discrimination when it occurs, and limiting education opportunities and advancements.

- Afro-Panamanians comprise 15 percent of the population and it is estimated that 50 percent of Panamanians have

African ancestry. The population descended from slaves brought to Panama during the colonial period.

- UNDP reports indicate that discrimination against Afro-Panamanians is an obstacle, despite their being major contributors to identity and national culture.

- The U.N. committee on the elimination of racial discrimination recognizes the continual discrimination, marginalization, impoverishment and vulnerability of indigenous peoples and those of African descent. There have been no specific courses of action proposed to improve conditions for Afro-Panamanians.

5. *The Story of black people in Argentina*

- The story of black people in Argentina is still the story of the lowest and the least. It is the story of the servant of servants, lower than the lowest.

- Tens of millions of black Africans were forcibly removed from their homelands from the 16th century to the 19th century to toil on the plantations and farms of the New World. This so-called "Middle Passage" accounted for one of the greatest forced migrations of people in human history, as well as one of the greatest tragedies the world has ever witnessed.

- Although hundreds of thousands of Africans were brought into Argentina, the black presence in Argentina has virtually vanished from the country's records and consciousness.

- According to historical accounts, Africans first arrived in Argentina in the late 16th century in the region now called the Rio de la Plata, which includes Buenos Aires, primarily to work in agriculture and as domestic servants. By the late 18th century and early 19th century, black Africans were numerous in parts of Argentina, accounting for up to half the population in some provinces, including Santiago del Estero, Catamarca, Salta and Córdoba.

- In Buenos Aires, neighbourhoods like Monserrat and San Telmo housed many black slaves, some of whom were engaged in craft-making for their masters. Indeed, black people accounted for an estimated one-third of the city's population, according to surveys taken in the early 1800s.

- Slavery was officially abolished in 1813, but the practice remained in place until about 1853. Ironically, at about this time, the black population of Argentina began to plunge.

- Many other black Argentines fled to neighbouring Brazil and Uruguay, which were viewed as somewhat more hospitable to them.

6. The Story of black people in Brazil

A curse is fulfilled everywhere and all the time. The story of black people in Brazil is once again the story of the lowest and the least in that big country. It is the story of the servant of servants, lower than the lowest.

On July 31 2015, Canadian newspaper "The Globe and Mail" released an expansive, 9000 plus word report on race in Brazil. Here are some harsh realities of being black and/or mixed in Brazil that we learn from The Globe and Mail's report:

1. Many black Brazilians hope for their children to have white skin so they do not suffer as they do.

The article opens with the story of Daniele de Araújo, a dark-skinned mixed Brazilian woman whose one prayer when she found out she was pregnant was for a white-skinned baby.

2. Many dark-skinned Brazilian women are seen as good for only domestic labour, and dark-skinned Brazilian men are seen as good for only service jobs.

It is a cornerstone of national identity that Brazil is racially mixed – more than any country on earth, Brazilians say. However, you will notice the reality of many restaurants full of white patrons and black waiters.

3. During the slave trade, Brazil imported more slaves than any other country.

20 percent of all the people abducted from Africa to be sold were brought to Brazil. Millions of these helpless Africans, an estimated five million people, washed ashore in Brazil (400,000 of the slaves went to the U.S. and Canada). Indeed, in the present day, roughly one-half of the Brazilian population trace their lineage directly to Africa. African culture has imbued Brazil permanently and profoundly, in terms of music, dance, food and in many other tangible ways.

4. Because they were cheaper to purchase and replace, Brazilian slaves were treated worse than slaves in the United States.

The journey to Brazil was cheaper than the journey to North America because of both proximity and wind patterns, which meant that the slaves were cheaper, too. Slave owners saw no point in spending money to feed their slaves well or care for them; it made more sense to work them to death and replace them. As a result, slaves in Brazil had dramatically shorter life spans than those who went to the United States. But they were essential for the development of the economy – the sugar plantations, the coffee farms and the gold mines etc.

5. Brazilian favelas (or slums) were created because former slaves were denied the right to live in cities.

6. Black and mixed Brazilians earn less than white Brazilians, and are severely under-represented in government and business.

In 2010, 51 percent of Brazilians identified themselves as black or of mixed race.

Of the 38 members of the federal cabinet, only one is black.

Of the 381 companies listed on the country's stock market, not a single one has a black or mixed-race chief executive officer.

Black and mixed-race Brazilians continue to earn 42.2 percent less than do white Brazilians.

In 2010, a São Paulo think tank analyzed the executive staff of Brazil's 500 largest companies and found that a mere 0.2 percent of executives were black, and only 5.1 percent were of mixed race.

7. **Interracial marriage in Brazil often consists of higher status blacks marrying lower status whites/morenos (brown-skinned** Brazilians) to produce lighter children.

Even interracial marriages are not the tribute to colour-blindness that they might appear to be.

8. **Blacks who do manage to succeed in society are often re-cast as moreno or white. Their success 'whitens' them.**

People with a mixed racial heritage who succeed in business or politics, such as billionaire media magnate Roberto Marinho, come to be viewed as white. For instance, soccer phenomenon Neymar da Silva Santos Jr., who presented as black when he first began to attract attention on the pitch, has, with his ascendancy, become in the popular perception, if not white, certainly not black!

9. **Brazil has little black business.**

There's no black owned radio or TV. Black people generally do not have any economic power in the country.

7. *The Story of black people in Mexico*

- Most of the afro-Mexican population live in rural villages that are notable primarily for their deep poverty and the strikingly dark skin of their inhabitants. Mexico's independence from Spain and new focus on building a national identity on the idea of mixed race, drove African Mexicans into invisibility as leaders chose not to count them or assess their needs.

- The majority of the black Mexican population work in agriculture, fishing or construction, and though some have achieved notable positions in coastal towns, most blacks have no economic power.

- Prevailing stereotypes paint the African-Mexicans as people who are happy to live the simple life apart from the rest of society, with no interest in education. The all-black shantytowns of Yanga in the Veracruz Province of Mexico, lack schools, and eager young migrants who move to bigger cities for work complain of blatant discrimination.

- A report released at the end of 2008 by Mexico's Congress said that roughly 200,000 black Mexicans who reside in the rural areas of Veracruz and Oaxaca and in tourist cities like Acapulco are out of the reach of social programs like employment support, health coverage, public education and food assistance.

8. *The Story of black people in the United States of America*

- Can you believe that the story of black people in America is the same as the story of black people in Africa? Is it not astonishing that the story of the lowest and the least applies to black people who live in the richest country in the world? The astonishing thing about a curse is the way it is fulfilled everywhere and all the time. The story of black people in the USA is still a story of people who are the least and the lowest in the land of the free and the home of the brave.

- Legally speaking, black people have the same rights as white people do in America. But they continue to reflect the picture of the typical servant. In spite of living in the richest country in the world with many opportunities that are not found elsewhere, the black Americans continue to occupy the lowest rank in the country. What is the picture of a typical servant? Low in everything. The lowest in almost every parameter!

- The imprisonment rate of black Americans is nearly six times that of white Americans.

- According to the National Association for the Advancement of Coloured People (NAACP), blacks account for about 1 million of the 2.3 million Americans currently imprisoned in the US.

- The astonishing thing about a curse is that it prevails and comes to pass no matter the circumstance. Whether America or Africa, the story is the same!

- Half the number of Black Americans who were born poor, stay poor.

- Black wealth barely exists. Race gaps in wealth, which were already wide - widened further during the Great Recession.

- Most black families are Headed by a single parent. Black children are much more likely to be raised in a single-parent household, and as research suggests, family structure can play a large role in a child's chance of success in all stages of life:

- Black students attend the worse schools.

- The unemployment rate of black Americans is more than twice the rate for whites.

- Black teenagers are more than twice as likely not to finish high school than white teens.

- In the story of the "American Dream", an education and a good job are supposed to erase the class differences into which one is born and open the door of opportunity to anyone with merit and grit, regardless of race.

- However new research is showing that getting another degree or a higher paying job may do less than it is believed do, in making good on the American Dream for families of colour.

  "The data shows that a job or an education are not the panaceas we think they are," says Darrick Hamilton, PhD, a New School economist.

  "When you look descriptively at families, we see that education does not erase the racial wealth divide," Hamilton said.

- Just as education does not erase wealth divides, racial disparities in savings and assets remain persistent even when black workers earn more.

- Growing income inequality in the United States has gained broad attention in the years since the Great Recession. Wealth – assets like homes, stocks or retirement accounts, minus debts – are heavily concentrated in the hands of a very small number of rich Americans, which largely excludes African Americans.

9. *The Story of black people in the United Kingdom*

- The amazing thing about a curse is the way it is fulfilled everywhere and all the time. The story of black people in the UK is still the story of the lowest and the least.

- The wave of black immigrants who arrived in Britain from the Caribbean in the 1950s faced significant amounts of racism. For many Caribbean immigrants, their first experience of discrimination came when trying to find private accommodation. They were generally ineligible for council housing because only people who had been resident in the UK for a minimum of five years qualified for it. At the time, there was no anti-discrimination legislation to prevent landlords from refusing to accept black tenants.

- A survey undertaken in Birmingham in 1956 found that only 15 of a total of 1,000 white people surveyed would let a room to a black tenant. As a result, many black immigrants were forced to live in slum areas of cities, where the housing was of poor quality and there were problems of crime, violence and prostitution. One of the most notorious slum landlords was Peter Rachman, who owned around 100 properties in the Notting Hill area of London. Black tenants typically paid twice the rent of white tenants, and lived in conditions of extreme overcrowding.

- The University of Maryland's Minorities at Risk (MAR) project noted in 2006 that while African-Caribbeans in the UK no longer face formal discrimination, they continue to be under-represented in politics, and to face discriminatory barriers in access to housing and in employment practices. The project also notes that the British school system "has been indicted on numerous occasions for racism, and for undermining the self-confidence of black children and maligning the culture of their parents".

- According to the 2005 UK Trade Union Congress report titled Black workers, jobs and poverty - black and minority ethnic people (bme's) were far more likely to be unemployed than the white population.

- According to the Metropolitan Police Authority, in 2002 – 2003, 10 out of the 17 deaths in police custody were black or Asian. Black convicts have a disproportionately higher rate of incarceration than other ethnicities. According to government reports, the overall number of racist incidents recorded by the police rose by 7 percent from 49,078 in 2002/3 to 52,694 in 2003/4.

- Media representation of young black British people has focused particularly on "gangs" with black members and violent crimes involving black victims and perpetrators.

- Black people, who according to government statistics make up 2 percent of the population, are the principal suspects in 11.7 percent of murders.

10. The Story of black people in Holland

- The thing about a curse is the way it is fulfilled everywhere and all the time. The story of black people in Holland is still the story of the lowest and the least.

- A visit to a refugee building in Holland will reveal several squatters who live there, seeking asylum in Europe.

- Most of these poor people are from African countries and are victims of anti-immigration policies in Europe that make obtaining a permit increasingly difficult.

- Some of the refugee buildings have been condemned because of the presence of asbestos and are extremely unhealthy to live in; but for thousands of immigrants the only other choice is living on the streets.

- Some of the refugees have stayed in as many as ten different places over the past years. Many times, the African immigrants were squatters in buildings and sometimes they lived in tents. At some point, a decision is taken to evacuate and throw them out on the streets. Many Africans have slept outside in the cold. Life for many of these black people consists of sitting around waiting, hoping and fearing. Many Africans are simply considered as worthless objects that must be gotten rid of.

- Many Africans are forced to work as prostitutes in European countries. Some become dancers in nightclubs and others are forced to sell drugs to support their families back home.

"We are here"

A visit to a community of African refugees who live in a former prison called the *Vluchthaven* will lead you to a group that calls themselves *"We Are Here"* and are considered illegal immigrants by the Dutch government. They've been very visible over the last two years, protesting the indifference that many politicians in Holland have shown towards immigrants and people seeking asylum from war-torn countries.

Those who don't live in the jail's cells are holed up in a disused garage known as the *Vluchtgarage*, a cold concrete structure on the outskirts of the city.

The *Vluchthaven*, which was originally intended to house low-risk criminal offenders, is home to some 130 stateless refugees.

11.   *The Story of black people in Spain*

- An Afro-Colombian, who came to Madrid to complete a Masters in Public Administration, said: "In the Spanish mind Black is synonymous to domestic work, poverty and lawlessness."

12.   *The Story of black people in India*

- The bewildering thing about a curse is the way it is fulfilled everywhere on this earth. The story of black people in India is perhaps one of the most astonishing stories of all black people you can find anywhere. It is still the story of the servant of servants and the story of lower than the lowest.

- The "Dalits" are of the same race as other Blacks in other parts of the world, the only difference is culture. The "Dalits" & "Dravidians" descend from the African regions of Sudan, Ethiopia and in some cases from the Bushman tribe, "Khoisan". "Dalits" were considered by the upper castes in India, to be outside the Varna or caste system. They were considered as Panchama or the fifth group, outside the proposed fourfold division of Indian people. "Dalit" means crushed and broken, and is a name that has come into prominence only within the last four decades.

- "Dalits" represent a community of 170 million in India, constituting 17% of the population. One out of every six Indians is a "Dalit".

- Due to their identity, "Dalits" regularly face discrimination and violence, and these prevent them from enjoying the basic human rights and dignity promised to all citizens of India.

- In the Hindu caste system, the "Dalit" status is associated with occupations regarded as ritually impure, such as leatherwork or butchering, rubbish removal, and animal carcasses and human waste disposal.

- "Dalits" usually work as manual labourers cleaning streets, latrines and sewers. These activities were considered to be polluting to the individual and this pollution was considered contagious.

- "Dalits" were commonly banned from full participation in Indian social life. They were physically segregated from the surrounding community.

- According to a 2014 report by The IndiaGoverns Research Institute, "Dalits" constitute nearly half of primary school dropouts. In Karnataka State, 48% of school dropouts are "Dalits".

- "Dalits" comprise a disproportionate number of India's prison inmates. While "Dalits" constitute 25% of the Indian population, they account for 33.2% of prisoners. About 94% of total Death row convicts in India are "Dalits" or from religious minorities.

The Dalit are demonstrating a rapidly expanding awareness of their African ancestry and their relationship to the struggle of Black people throughout the world. They seem particularly enamoured by African-Americans. African-Americans, in general, seem almost idolized by the "Dalit", and the Black Panther Party, in particular, is virtually revered.

13.   The Story of black people in Bangladesh

*   There are 300 million "Dalits" in South Asia. They are expected to perform only society's most unpleasant tasks such as unclogging drains, removing corpses and cleaning toilets by hand.

*   But after centuries of discrimination – of being refused access to jobs and education, of being forced to live in the most wretched neighbourhoods and of being told they cannot escape their fate – Bangladeshi "Dalits" are slowly gaining hope. Organisations have been working at a grass-roots level to educate "Dalits" and make them aware of their potential influence if they can work together.

*   "Dalit rights" is a new idea in Bangladesh, even though there are probably five million living in the country.

14.   The Story of black people in Australia

The baffling thing about a curse is the way it is fulfilled everywhere on this earth. The story of black people in Australia is one of the saddest of all. It is still the story of the servant of servants and the story of lower than the lowest.

The Aborigines were the original black occupants of the Australian continent. Unfortunately for them, Australia was invaded from the end of the eighteenth century onwards. Before the invasion, these black Aboriginal people lived throughout Australia, but mostly along the coast. The black Aborigines who lived inland in the bush and the desert survived by hunting and gathering.

The British invaded Australia at the end of the eighteenth century. This sparked off huge waves of disease that massacred thousands of these black people. In just over one hundred years from the first invasion of their land, their numbers were reduced from up to an estimated one million to only 60,000.

- When the British invaded Australia, the black Aboriginal people had their land stolen from them or destroyed. Until 1992, the Australian law regarding Aboriginal land was that of "terra nullius" – that the land was empty before the British arrived, belonged to no-one, and could legitimately be taken over.

- Most Aborigines, however, have lost their land and this has had a devastating social and physical impact on the Aboriginal people.

- Today most Aboriginal people live in terrible conditions in the outskirts of towns. Many Aborigines work as labourers on cattle ranches that were once their land.

- In the northern half of Australia, some Aborigines have managed to cling on to their land and still hunt and gather food.

- Today, Aborigines have the poorest living conditions in Australia.

- Today, the Aborigines have a far higher infant mortality rate than any other in Australia.

- Today, the Aborigines have a far higher suicide rate than any other group in Australia.

- Today, the Aborigines have the lowest life expectancy in Australia.

- Today, the Aborigines make up a high proportion of prisoners in Australia.

- An Aboriginal man is 13 times as likely to be in jail as a non-indigenous Australian, and an indigenous teenager is 28 times more likely to be in jail.

It is interesting that in far away Australia the story of a servant of servants is still prevailing. Time, distance and circumstance have not been able to wipe out the picture of the servant of servants. As you see this pattern repeat itself throughout the world and throughout the ages, it should make you have a proper respect for curses and blessings. Every Christian needs to have a proper respect for the power of spoken words.

CHAPTER 19

How the Curse of Noah is Working Out

AND NOAH AWOKE from his wine, and knew what his younger son had done unto him. And he said, Cursed be Canaan; a SERVANT OF SERVANTS SHALL HE BE unto his brethren.

And he said, blessed be the Lord God of Shem; and Canaan shall be his servant.

God shall enlarge Japheth, and he shall dwell in the tents of Shem; and Canaan shall be his servant.

Genesis 9:24-27

Noah cursed and said, "Cursed be Canaan; a servant of servants shall he be." The curse to be a servant is the curse to be low and inferior. Inferiority, mediocrity and shoddiness was slapped onto the descendants of Ham by the words of Noah. Ham dishonoured his father and the result was this curse. The curse was not spoken against Ham, but against Canaan. Since Ham was the one who dishonoured his father, we can assume that Canaan was receiving this curse on behalf of Ham's descendants. Indeed, this brief, startling curse, on the descendants of Ham has worked itself out in such a way, proving that a curse is indeed a wonder!

"The sons of Ham; Cush, and Mizraim, Phut, and Canaan" (1 Chronicles 1:8). Cush was the father of various Ethiopian tribes that settled south of Egypt and also overran Arabia, Babylonia, and India.

Mizraim was the father of various Egyptian tribes. Mizraim means "double". Tribes of the double Egypt (upper and lower Egypt), called the land of Ham, came from him.

Phut was the father of the Libyans and other tribes in northern Africa.

Canaan was the father of the peoples that settled mainly in Palestine, Arabia.

It was this group of people that were cursed to be the servants of servants. If a servant has problems, I am sure you can imagine the problems of a "servant of servants"! We can all imagine how the life of a servant will play out. Perhaps, you can then imagine how the life of a "servant of servants" will turn out to be. Also, it is important for you to imagine what it is like when a servant becomes a leader. What is it like when servants are elevated and put in charge of things? Indeed, this curse is one of the most far-reaching and devastating curses ever spoken. To be cursed into servant of servanthood is to be demoted in society below the lowest mark. Let us have a look at what it is like when such "low" servants of servants are in charge of things.

A curse creates a picture!

The curse of Noah has created an unmistakable picture of a "servant of servants".

To recognize a curse you must know the picture it creates!

The curse on man creates the unmistakeable picture of toil and sweat that yields little fruit.

The curse on women creates the unmistakeable picture of sorrow, disappointment and struggles with husbands and children.

The curse on Jews creates the unmistakeable picture of worldwide inexplicable hatred, scattering and persecution.

The curse on Jew haters creates the picture of inexplicable ultimate defeat and humiliation.

The curse on black people creates the inexplicable picture of servanthood, poor leadership, poverty and insignificance.

A trained medical doctor will notice certain symptoms and signs because he is trained to recognize the picture of a disease. It is an unmistakeable picture to him because he is trained to see it.

You will now recognize the unmistakeable and inexplicable picture of a "servant of servants". Your trained eyes will pick out the unmistakeable picture of a "servant of servants". After you pick out these signs, you can pluck them off one by one until the picture of your life and ministry do not reflect that picture.

The Picture of a Typical "Servant of Servants"

For three things THE EARTH IS DISQUIETED, and for four which it cannot bear:

For A SERVANT WHEN HE REIGNETH; and a fool when he is filled with meat;

Proverbs 30:21-22

207

When a servant rules, you can expect the world to be in confusion and in disturbance. You can expect chaos and you can expect difficulty. That is what it means for the earth to be disquieted. Obviously, a master is expected to rule. In the absence of the master, the servant will not know how to manage many things. The servant is likely to run things down and create a great deal of confusion. Please do not be angry at this message.

A "servant of servants" is an ultimate servant. He is the father of all servants. He is the mother of all servants. He manifests servanthood in a classic and unmistakeable way. Fight the curse by taking each and every descriptive point below and do the exact opposite. It is possible to neutralize this curse by understanding the pattern and picture that descends on servants of servants. You can take this picture apart by taking each item, focussing on it and preventing it specifically in your life. You may dismiss what I am saying but if you do not have a proper respect for curses, they will supernaturally envelope you and the pattern and picture will descend on you. You can neutralize this curse by taking up each and every point below and dealing with it specifically. It is my own experience in fighting this curse that I am sharing with you. Watch this:

1. **Typical servants of servants are usually very poor leaders.**

Servants are used to being led and therefore servants of servants are the poorest version of a leader you could ever have. They create poverty for everyone that is under them. If they are in charge of a country, the country will be poor, backward and two hundred years behind everyone. The lot of a servant is to receive instructions. A "servant of servants" will not know how to create a currency, manage a currency or manage an economy. Servants of servants will buy cars and toys rather than building anything useful. Where there is a "servant of servants" in charge, complicated issues like making water flow, making electricity work, making roads, creating jobs, creating wealth, creating an educational system can never be solved.

The servant of a domestic servant will not know how to manage an economy nor lead ten million people into prosperity. A typical servant does not see nor understand the problems of the masses even though he is one of them. Amazingly, many of the best leaders are products of wealthy homes who want to change the lot of the ordinary masses.

Servants are so abysmally incompetent at management and leadership that they provoke high levels of insults and complaints from everyone they lead. It is sad to see the unfortunate leadership practices of typical servants.

You must neutralize this curse by specifically becoming a different kind of leader. You must distance yourself from all patterns of "servant of servants" leadership. Isolate this particular point in your mind and determine that you can never be so described as I have done above. Let your leadership intentionally do the opposite of everything described above. Gradually, this particular feature will not be associated with you. God is giving you the wisdom to neutralize and diffuse a picture and a curse.

2. A typical "servant of servants" does not provide for others.

Where the curse of Noah is in full manifestation, you will notice a lack of provision of many things. The "servant of servants" is unable to provide the basics. It is the owner of the house who provides food and security for the household and not the maidservant. Neither does a domestic servant provide anything for the village or town where he dwells. He struggles to even cater for his own needs. Therefore, we can expect somebody who is a "servant of servants" to neglect the people that are under his care.

Pastors who are servants of servants do not provide church buildings and other nice things for their church members. They are only able to provide expensive cars and houses for their personal use. When you drive through a country that is ruled by servants of servants you will realise that there is no provision of schools, hospitals, railways, buses, water, electricity and basic roads for the people. A "servant of servants" is simply unable to arise and provide for the needs of people all around him. The people in the country will be poor and in great difficulty. That is really all you can expect if a domestic servant has been made the head of state for many years.

I know that you are not under this curse, so prove it by providing for the people you lead. Ensure that you provide all that is needed for everyone under your leadership.

3. A typical "servant of servants" does not build anything.

Where the curse of Noah is prevalent, you will notice the lack of buildings and development. A typical servant does not build anything for anyone. *Typical servants are not builders.* A servant is not likely to build anything for himself. This is why in places where this curse is prevalent, they have no skyscrapers, roads, universities, hospitals, railway lines and factories. A typical servant does not build anything. Servants of servants may receive lots of money but will simply not build or develop anything. Today, where servants of servants rule, there is gross under development. Infra structure which was built two hundred years ago in certain countries, is yet to be even thought of! The servants of servants are having parties and cannot think of such mega projects such as bridges, highways, water supply projects, hydro-electric dams and so on. The servants of servants simply say, "We have no money! We have no resources! We need a loan! We need development partner! It is not our fault! We can only buy t-shirts, make traditional cloth and buy cars to celebrate our anniversaries of independence!

To overcome the reality of this curse, you must decide to build and put aside all forms of distraction. You can neutralize this curse by not giving excuses but rather building real things. Do not be a "servant of servants" who cannot build anything. Refuse to have the stigma of a "servant of servants" attached to you. Rise up and build. Build the church. Build the roads. Build the schools. Build the hospitals. Do not sit and give excuses. Giving lame and flimsy excuses for not building is typical of people who operate under the curse of being servants of servants.

4.   Typical servants of servants cannot develop, but just loves to play with cars.

Instead of developing his nation or his church, he loves to play games with toys. A typical "servant of servants" does not know what to do about the complicated issues that surround him. He simply buys toys and enjoys them. You will notice that servants of servants buy expensive cars as their way of leading. Their first step to any kind of leadership is to buy expensive cars or fight over expensive cars.

When a pastor is a "servant of servants" his first big step is to buy an expensive car. He is so happy to drive his expensive car around whilst his church rents existing halls. You must remember that cars are almost as expensive as houses. A Land Cruiser can cost as much as one hundred and fifty thousand dollars and a completed church building seating six hundred people can cost the same amount.

5.   Typical servants of servants cannot lead but love to hold useless meetings and meaningless conferences.

A "servant of servants" is an ultimate servant. He is the father of all servants. He manifests servanthood in a classic and unmistakeable way. You will notice people who are always having numerous conferences, seminars and symposia. Because a "servant of servants" does not know what to do, he holds conferences and meetings. Speeches are given but nothing practical is done. Such people are so happy to rent hotels owned by foreigners and have their conferences and meetings there.

These typical servants of servants are so happy to wear suits and attend these programmes and give their speeches. They will never go on to the field themselves to see what is happening. They will never jump on the scaffolding and see what is happening!

211

They will never go to the actual spot where there are difficulties so as to work hard to bring things to a conclusion.

Servants are happy to be away from such hard work and are now totally confined to the air-conditioned conferences and endless deliberations without hard decisions and without ever implementing anything. Servants of servants are happy to present papers, research work and findings that will never be implemented. It is very difficult to be under such leadership because nothing substantial is ever done.

6.   A typical "servant of servants" does not do new things or create new things.

A "servant of servants" is an ultimate servant. Servants use gadgets that have been created. They do not create them. A "servant of servants" will hardly ever create anything. Rockets, phones, cars, televisions, blenders, computers, micro-waves, ovens, air conditions, drones, airplanes, helicopters, trains, buses, video cameras, cameras, rarely have the inscription, "Made in Africa". That would be quite unusual! Do not accept to be uncreative! Through the power of the Holy Spirit you can be creative and do new and powerful things.

7.   A typical "servant of servants" has unmistakeable shoddy substandard handiwork and produces shoddy inferior products.

It is the master and trained professional who produce high standard handiwork. However, servants may not know how to get things straight and perfectly done. Servants are not usually trained to the high level of professional handiwork. You can tell who built a house by looking at it. You can often tell if the house was built by black people or white people. You can tell who built a city by looking at the city. When you see shacks, poorly constructed kiosks, huts, open gutters and zinc sheet buildings you know who built it. When you see tall shiny skyscrapers made of glass and steel and concrete, you often know who built it.

You can often tell where a book was printed by just looking at it. You can tell where furniture was made by looking at the finishing. You can tell who fixed the windows and the doors by just looking at them. I once stayed in a crooked house for a few days. Honestly, this house should enter the Guinness Book of Records for its crookedness. Everything in the house was crooked. Even the floors were slanted!

Do not allow anything that you build to be crooked. Not even the smallest element should be crooked! We once owned a printing press. The manager produced thousands of twisted books and presented them to me proudly. But I refused to accept the twisted books because I pointed out that the machines, the paper, the ink and other equipment were the same ones being used in Germany to produce straight books. I instructed that all the bad books should be burnt. I refused to allow the curse to paste itself on our products. I insisted on having straight, clean, excellent products because I refused to operate under the curse of Noah.

8. A typical "servant of servants" creates a big gap between himself and the people he leads.

The curse creates an unmistakeable picture. Keep watching! Keep learning and you will recognize it wherever you go. Where the curse is prevalent, there are huge gaps between ordinary people and leaders. A typical servant tries to distance himself from other servants when he is promoted. He is so insecure that he does not want other servants to have what he has.

His mansions, his palaces, his cars and his status are so vastly different from the common man. He seems not to care for his fellow servants whom he has left far behind. When a typical "servant of servants" does build something, he builds a palace or a mansion for himself so that he will be glorified and distance himself as much as possible from other fellow servants.

9.   A typical "servant of servants" rules over poor people.

For out of prison he cometh to reign; whereas also he that is born in his kingdom becometh poor.

Ecclesiastes 4:14

It is servants of servants who preside over dusty huts and poverty-stricken masses! Good leaders, who are not operating under the curse, preside over prosperous citizens whom they have allowed to flourish under their vision and leadership. *Servants of servants are very comfortable being leaders of poor people.* They do not even notice that the people under them are suffering. They seem to be oblivious of the fact that most people are in great need and have no jobs. Servants of servants will first of all buy cars and houses for himself. He will live in luxury and wealth whilst he rules over masses of much poorer people.

Wherever servants of servants rule, people are in great difficulty and there are few jobs available. You can have a country with ninety per cent unemployment.

You can neutralize this curse by fighting specifically for the people under you to be prosperous. Do not leave them to fend for themselves! Do not leave them to struggle to make it in life! Stretch out your hand and make people under you great. Specifically do this and the picture of the curse will start to disappear.   By understanding the reality of this curse you must go in the opposite direction to ensure that the people you lead are prosperous and successful. Do not be happy to be the leader of a group of lean, hungry and poverty-stricken "have-nots.

You must neutralize this curse by specifically not being a ruler of masses of poor people. You must distance yourself from being isolated at the top. Take everyone with you to the top. Do not be unconcerned to see slums and people in difficulty. Isolate this particular point in your mind and determine that you can never be so described as I have done above. Let your leadership intentionally do the opposite of everything described above. Gradually, this particular feature will not be associated with you.

God is giving you the wisdom to neutralize and diffuse a picture and a curse.

10. A typical "servant of servants" cannot acquire land for development projects.

To buy land and to use land is a great difficulty for a servant. How many servants do you know who ever buy land and develop it?

Where the curse of Noah is in force, there is very little development. The curse of Noah prevents people from being able to acquire land and use it constructively.

Usually, servants of servants are unable to build even the smallest room for themselves. Can you imagine someone sending his maid or servant to engage in negotiations to acquire land for massive building projects?

Since you are not a "servant of servants", rise up and acquire the land that you need. Do not look bewildered and give excuses when you have to do the hard work of finding land, and solving and dealing with land issues in your country. Prove that you are not a "servant of servants" by acquiring the land necessary for projects.

Does it not sound fantastic to you that there are countries in which the government cannot acquire land to establish large commercial farms? What kind of people are at the helm of affairs in those nations?

Could it be that the Minister of Agriculture is actually a "servant of servants"? Could it be that the Minister of Finance is actually a "servant of servants"? Could it be that the overall leader of a nation is operating under the curse of Noah? Could that be why there is no progress at all in certain places no matter which government comes into power? Could it be that lowly servants of servants are struggling with complicated issues that they cannot master? It is possible to overcome this curse. Without a proper respect for the curse, the curse will envelope everyone who sits in that chair of leadership.

11. A typical "servant of servants" spends money on ceremonies, anniversaries and clothing instead of building.

Wherever the curse of Noah is manifested, you can expect ceremonies and celebrations to abound. You see, it takes much more diligence, money and intelligence to build bridges, buildings, roads and hydro-electric dams than it does to celebrate an anniversary and buy t-shirts for everybody. Servants of servants usually do not have what it takes to get into such massive, futuristic projects.

A country that is led by men who have the spirit of servants of servants, spends millions celebrating various anniversaries when they could have used the money to build houses, railway lines, schools, hospitals, bridges, hydro-electric dams or roads.

Fight against the "servant of servants" picture by setting aside anniversaries, parties and celebrations. Sit down and build something great. Use your money for development and building rather than parties and anniversaries. These poor servants of servants cannot keep themselves from spending millions on one celebration after another.

Why can you not build a road between two important cities in your country? Why don't you think about building a bridge across the most important lake in your country?

Fight the curse! Stop using tents as buildings! Stop buying t-shirts and having expensive, useless and fruitless celebrations that achieve nothing! Resist this picture! It is destroying the society! Control yourself! God is giving the wisdom to neutralize this curse! If you do not respect what I am saying, you will repeat this pattern of spending money on useless expensive celebrations which achieve nothing, instead of building the most basic infrastructure.

12. A typical "servant of servants" cannot use science and technology.

In 1977, America sent a spaceship called "Voyager" to Jupiter. That spaceship explored Jupiter, Saturn, and Neptune and is still flying into inter-stellar space. It will run out of fuel in the year 2025. It is sad to say that servants of servants cannot even *explore their own countries* and make the most out of all the resources in their nations.

Servants of servants just stare at the gadgets and facilities in the master's house, not understanding how to make them work. They are befuddled when the idea of scientific projects are brought to them. Elevators, escalators, street lights and fountains never work when a "servant of servants" is in charge.

The science and the technology involved in projects is too much for them to manage. The science and technology involved in making water and electricity flow in people's houses is beyond the managerial capacity of the "servant of servants". There are entire nations that live in total darkness because the government is unable to provide electricity for its people. I once visited a country in which the entire nation uses torch lights and batteries.

13. A typical "servant of servants" always complains of not having money.

A "servant of servants" will always say he does not have resources! A "servant of servants" will say, "We have no money!" A typical "servant of servants" does not know how to do anything unless he gets a loan, a gift or a grant. Watch servants of servants when they are in leadership. Servants often beg for help and money because they cannot manage with their own resources. When a person is fully operating under this curse, he looks at you with dreamy eyes, expecting you to give him a handout. It never occurs to a "servant of servants" to roll up his sleeve to start digging or doing something productive. They immediately think of getting a loan or they start complaining about a lack of resources.

You must neutralize this curse by specifically not complaining about not having money. You must distance yourself from such statements. Isolate this particular point in your mind and determine that you can never be so described. Intentionally do the opposite of this point and declare that you have the money that you need for this project. Gradually, this particular feature of complaining about not having money will not be associated with you. God is giving you the wisdom to neutralize and diffuse a picture and a curse. Declare that we can do it and we will do it!

14. A typical "servant of servants" operates like a pompous chief.

Servants of servants are so amazed when they come into positions of power that they magnify themselves greatly and behave like pompous chieftains. They will never roll up their sleeves and do practical work. If a "servant of servants" is in charge of a construction site, he will never climb up or climb up to see things for himself. He stands aloof and sends people he esteems lower than himself to do the practical work.

He sits in his swivel chair in his air-conditioned office and receives inflated invoices which he never checks. He can approve a project that costs ten times as much as it should. He will build a house for ten million when he could have built it for one million. The "pompous chief" has no time to look into such details.

This "servant of servants" may not even be a thief but his "pompous chief" style of leadership puts him above practical things. Servants of servants will never check the state of the construction site, the toilets, the kitchens or the gardens. Such things are below him! He will sit in his air-conditioned office doing nothing much to lead or manage. As a result, things fall apart when they are under a "servant of servants".

The practical places like toilets, kitchens, and gardens all fall into disrepair when the "pompous chief" is the manager. He is too big for such matters. All he wants is his new Land Cruiser and his air-conditioned office so that he can sit there huffing and puffing all day long! No wonder things fall apart under this high and mighty manager.

You must neutralize this curse by specifically distancing yourself from the "pompous chief" leadership style. Isolate this particular point in your mind and determine that you can never be described as a "pompous chief" leader. Intentionally do the opposite of everything I described above. Gradually, this "pompous chief" feature will not be associated with you. God is giving you the wisdom to neutralize and diffuse the picture and the curse.

15.   A "servant of servants" is impractical.

When a leader is a "servant of servants", he cannot do practical work. He can only sit aloof from everything that is practical. Perhaps, such people are filled with lofty ideas and great imaginations of things they want to achieve. But they do not realise that they have to start small and with practical things. *As a result, when such people are in charge, they are unable to move forward because the first step in many great achievements involves doing small practical things.* Because they are not practical, they cannot understand how preventing waste can make everyone rich. When you show them how to work practically, they are reluctant to do it. They simply no longer accept practical things.

Indeed, servants of servants stand amazed, baffled and befuddled when you show them the practical steps they must take in order to build and achieve greatness. Many African nations do not need loans or gifts. They just need to be practical and to work with their hands. Unfortunately, the leaders are so high and mighty and have their heads in the clouds. If you were to suggest the practical things that should be done, they would look at you as if you just came from outer space. However, you did not just come from outer space. They, the bad leaders, are the ones who are completely out of their depth in the seat of leadership. Many African leaders are like class three children who have been given an airline to pilot in mid-air. They have no idea of what to do

219

next. Many African leaders are like school children who have just been given a massive ship loaded with containers and other goods to captain. They have no idea what to do. No wonder Africa is in the state that it is! All over Africa, the evidence of this stares at you! There are African countries that have come to an absolute and literal standstill since servants of servants took over the management and leadership of the nation.

16. A "servant of servants" does not communicate well.

When a person is a servant, he does not say much to his master. If you have ever been in countries where they have a lot of servants, you will notice how they work silently without lifting their eyes or talking much to the master. A typical "servant of servants" has very poor communication. You cannot get him to speak, relate or communicate appropriately. He communicates comfortably only when he is with low ranking members of the community. Such people can be disloyal. They stare at you blankly when you are speaking and have no reasonable contribution to make. A wise leader will take note of people who cannot rise out of poor communication.

17. Typical "servant of servants" have dirty toilets.

Wherever the curse of Noah is working itself out, the symptoms and signs of servanthood are seen. Typical "servant of servants" do not have beautiful toilets or bathrooms.

People who live under the curse of Noah usually have dirty eating-places and dirty toilets. Where this curse is working, you will find that toilets usually do not have running water. In many servant quarters, the water does not run and the toilets are not nice places.

Where the curse of Noah is working, people behave like servants of servants. A "servant of servants" is even worse than a servant. Decide that this curse will not work in your environment. Ensure that your kitchens and toilets have running water. Many real servants are simply not used to modern toilet facilities.

Where a "servant of servants' rules, public toilets are not nice places to visit. The water is likely not to be running and the toilets may be stuffed with layer after layer of faeces and rubbish.

Someone called the toilet in his university an "s.o.s" toilet. I asked what it meant and I was told it meant *"shit-on-shit"* toilets. (Please excuse the language). This is because person after person deposits a layer of faeces which cannot be flushed away because there is never enough water. Another person told me that when she was in secondary school she experienced the phenomenon of *"shot putt"* toilets. I asked what that was. She explained that the students defaecated into a polythene (plastic) bag and threw it over the wall (like a shot putt). She said, "This was the practice of all the students in the school because there was no running water."

Indeed, the management of a "servant of servants" toilet leaves much to be desired. Since there is no running water, servants of servants toilets creates a super "mountain" of unmoveable hardened stinking human excreta. Servants of servants create smelly unhygienic toilets and kitchens with lots of flies. Honestly, it is sad, pathetic and miserable to be under the leadership of servants of servants. This is why the embassies of western nations are full of people trying to migrate away from the places where servants of servants are ruling.

You must neutralize this curse by specifically not having dirty toilets. You must distance yourself from such horrible toilets. Ensure that water runs all the time. Fight the curse of not having running water with all your might. Do not have *"shit on shit"* toilets (again, please excuse my language) or *"shot putt"* toilets. Isolate this particular point of having dirty toilets in your mind and determine that you can never be described as having horrible toilets under your management. Intentionally do the opposite of having nasty toilets which have no running water. Gradually, this particular feature of nasty toilets will not be associated with you. God is giving you the wisdom to neutralize and diffuse the picture and the curse of being a "servant of servants".

18. A typical "servant of servants" has dirty kitchens and eating places.

Many "servant of servants" do not have the privilege of having beautiful state-of-the-art kitchens. A typical "servant of servants" will cook in the midst of filth and flies. You will be shocked to see kitchen floors flooded with cooking oil that has been left to stay for so long on the floor. You will be amazed to see mountains of unwashed plates, pans and bowls. You will be shocked to find flies everywhere. These flies, by the way, are coming from the dirty toilet next door. Almost every "servant of servant's" kitchen has this picture. Children who are in boarding school run by servants of servants, \ are forced to eat food that has been kissed by flies that came from the nearby toilet. Remember that these next-door toilets are full of diarrhoea and porridge-like faeces which cannot be flushed away because there is no running water. Please make sure that you fight the picture of being a "servant of servants" with such dirty kitchens.

19. A typical "servant of servants" is usually superstitious.

Servants of servants are not usually educated people and lean largely on superstitious beliefs. Because of a lack of education, servants of servants tend to believe more in superstition than in common sense. You could find a main street jammed with traffic because part of the road has been blocked up by the shrine of an idol. You would find a tree, a river, a stone that will be treated more importantly than a human being because it is believed to be a god.

A group of servants of servants were once building a dam that burst and killed over two hundred people. This dam was providing electricity for millions of people. After investigations, the servants of servants concluded that the river god was not happy with the project because he went from one end of the river to the other every year was being prevented from continuing to do so because the dam was blocking his passage. Instead of thinking of other technical reasons why the dam burst, superstitious beliefs prevailed.

20. A typical "servant of servants" is not analytical.

The opposite of being superstitious is being analytical.

Servants are not analytical. Many servants are not educated and do not read or analyse much. Therefore, typical servants of servants do not use maps. Typical servants of servants do not use data. Typical servants of servants do not analyse information and take decisions from them. Typical servants of servants do not use statistics. A typical "servant of servants" does not sit down to plan with maps, information, drawing boards and computers.

When it comes to nation building, the leaders do not know which roads are tarred but continue to develop the same old roads whilst leaving huge areas unattended to for a hundred years. It is not easy to be under the leadership of a "servant of servants". A "servant of servants" does not analyse nor discern the importance of certain people in their society. They frighten away the very people who are necessary and important for the development and improvement of the nation.

Few churches pastored by servants of servants use maps, information, statistics and data. Servants of servants are simply not into such things. They are more into prayer or even superstition.

21. A typical "servant of servants" does not read or study much.

Where the curse of Noah is in force, people do not read or buy books. A maidservant does not often buy books. A maidservant does not usually use libraries. You would not normally find domestic servants visiting libraries and spending money on books. Typical "servant of servants" are not studious. They do not read books nor quote from them. If you had a servant who did that you would consider him to be unusual. There are no chains of bookshops where servants of servants live. There are hardly any publishers nor publishing contracts where servants of servants reign.

Prove to yourself that the curse of Noah is broken in your life by becoming a reader of books. Decide to read all you can and to study all you can.

22. Typical "servant of servants" cannot maintain buildings.

A servant is a servant and a manager is a manager. Where this curse is working, beautiful structures are left for the servants to manage only for them to run them down until they are unusable. Servants of servants are most likely to run down a house and turn it into a decrepit and dilapidated structure. It is easy to see whether the real manager or the domestic servant is running affairs by just looking at the building.

If you visit a building that is being managed by a "servant of servants", you will notice unused building materials lying around. You will notice boxes, cartons, chairs, scaffolding, blocks, chippings scattered in different places. Where a "servant of servants" is in charge, some of the lights do not work. Many locks do not work! Toilets do not work! Water does not run! Electricity does not come on! Elevators do not work!

In places where this curse is working, you will see the poorest kind of management ever. You cannot expect very good management from the servant of another domestic servant. The management of resources, the management of people, the management of buildings is of the poorest kind. This is why large hotels, large companies and large institutions always avoid using servants of servants as their top management.

23. Typical "servant of servants" cannot make places beautiful.

You can almost tell who is in charge when you visit a large facility. If it is a "servant of servants" you will notice the shabbiness at the entrance. Which servants do you know who have homes with gardens? Typical servants of servants do not have lawns, gardens and beautiful mansions.

Where there are servants of servants you will notice hanging cables and wires everywhere. You will notice uncompleted structures. You will notice unfinished work and half-finished projects everywhere. Half-finished houses, half-finished roads, half-painted structures are the order of the day. Where there are servants of servants, the finishing is very poor. Tiles are not straight, windows are crooked, doors are slanted and there are dangerous hanging wires everywhere. Some years ago, my caddy was killed when he hang his work clothes on a wire outside his house. He did not know that it was a live electric wire.

When a "servant of servants" is put in charge of a place, there are no well-kept lawns, there are no well-kept gardens, no pavements, and no beautiful sights. If it is a run-down hotel, you will know that it is a "servant of servants" who is the manager. If it is a sharp expensive, clean, posh hotel you will know that another type of manager is at post.

Servants of servants cannot make a city beautiful. The city will be littered with kiosks, shacks, tables, sign boards, unplastered walls, half-painted buildings, different heights of walls and so on.

Where there are servants of servants, there is no order. Parts of the streets are used as markets to sell shoes, clothes, bags, jeans, cooked food, fish, phone chips, phone cards, dog chains, and videos. The other parts of the street are used for parking and loading passengers. Commotion, disorderliness, and chaos are the hallmarks of the places where servants of servants are in charge.

It is important to recognise such characteristics and peel them off your skin. You must distance yourself from such inabilities. It is a curse not to be able to make a place beautiful. When you visit the shanty towns and slums that exist in certain cities, you immediately know which group of people is living there.

You must neutralize this curse by specifically creating beautiful places. You must distance yourself from places which are disorderly. Isolate this particular point in your mind and determine that you can never be so described as I have done above. Let your leadership intentionally do the opposite of everything described above. Gradually, this particular feature will not be associated with you. God is giving you the wisdom to neutralize and diffuse a picture and a curse.

24. Typical servants of servants cannot manage complex things.

Woe to your company, business or nation, if it is given to a typical servant to manage. A "servant of servants" is simply not a good manager. Wherever things are poorly managed you can be sure the "servant of servants" is at post.

I was once in a hospital run by servants of servants. Patients were attended to in their cars, in the corridors and on the floor. Women would deliver their babies in out of service elevators and sometimes on the staircases. You would think that it is uneducated people who were in charge of the hospital. Indeed no! It was the most distinguished professors and medical experts who were running that hospital. Unfortunately, the picture of a "servant of servants" was clearly found in that hospital even though it had the most illustrious surgeons, eminent physicians and renowned professors. Why was such a reputable hospital being run like a village health post under a tree or in a war zone?

The poorest kind of management can be found in hospitals run by servants of servants. I was once in a hospital run by servants of servants and I saw patients sleeping under the bed on the floor and on top of the bed. You can imagine the mortuary run by servants of servants. You walk through floods of water and blood and the dead lie everywhere. A mortuary which is intended to hold seventy people has four hundred bodies, all because of the kind of people who are running the facility.

Typical servants of servants are simply unable to manage complex things like countries, currencies, airlines, companies or even banks. Anything that is out of visual contact receives no attention from these poor managers.

It is time to show that you are not operating under a curse. Rise up and become a good manager of your country, your church, your company and your business by specifically fighting against the scourge of "the inability to manage complex things".

You must neutralize this curse by specifically learning how to manage complex things. You must distance yourself from poor management. Isolate this particular point in your mind and determine that you can never be so described as I have done above. Let your leadership intentionally do the opposite of everything described above. Gradually, poor management will not be associated with you. God is giving you the wisdom to neutralize and diffuse a picture and a curse.

25. Typical servants of servants pile up rubbish and filth everywhere.

Many servants are surrounded by rubbish. Servants also keep a lot of unusable items that their masters have disposed of. When you drive through cities run by servants of servants, you will find the country is littered with rubbish. You will find entire rivers of filth, plastic waste, and human waste. You will find entire lagoons filled with the waste of an entire city. Sometimes the whole city has a terrible smell.

Where servants of servants are in charge, you will find massive piles of rubbish filling spaces all over the city. These massive piles of human waste are then burnt by educated people, polluting entire communities with poisonous gases that come from burning plastics, batteries and other dangerous items. People literally cannot breathe in their homes as the servants of servants do the unthinkable.

I once had a church by a rubbish dump. The rubbish dump became a mountain, as high as three floors. There was so much pollution and so many flies from this amazing rubbish dump that it was impossible to have communion in the church hall for several months. The flies from the rubbish dump would simply invade the church during communion time. There was nothing anyone could do since we were under the management and leadership of servants of servants. Servants are not used to having very clean environments.

It is time to prove that you are not under that curse. Clear up the rubbish in your world. Remove the tables, kiosks, signboards and rubbish that litter every space around you. Do not be angry with this message. Just prove that you are not a servant or a "servant of servants". Neutralize the curse by peeling off these characteristics now.

You must neutralize this curse by specifically ensuring that there is no rubbish and filth piling in your controlled area. You must distance yourself from the piling up of rubbish which is so typical of a "servant of servants". Isolate this particular point in your mind and determine that you can never be so described as I have done above. Let your leadership intentionally do the opposite of everything described above. Gradually, this particular feature will not be associated with you. God is giving you the wisdom to neutralize and diffuse a picture and a curse.

26. Typical servants of servants do not go out on adventures.

Typical servants of servants do not go mountain climbing, swimming or horse-riding. Most servants do not know how to swim unless they are fishermen. This lack of adventure leads to a certain dullness and placidity in the servant.

This is how come some people claimed to have discovered other types of human beings whom they then called "natives" and "savages". Do not let anyone call you a "native" or a "savage". Are they not savages who have nude beaches and behave like men from the stone age? It is time to shake off the characteristic of not being adventurous. It is time to become missionaries and go out where God is sending us to.

This characteristic of not being adventurous has affected Christians who should have become missionaries. Instead of stepping out, they stayed at home. When the season came, in which the gospel was entrusted into the hands of the black man, most of them did not go out. Today, the gospel is restricted to coastal mega cities whilst the hinterland is given over to other religions because of our inability to venture out with the gospel. Many white people went to Africa and died there for their beliefs. It is important to break and neutralize the curse of not being adventurous. Without being adventurous, man would not have climbed mountains, crossed rivers, discovered our earth and gone into outer space. You rarely hear of certain types of people climbing mountains.

27. A typical servants of servants does not appreciate nature.

Where the curse of Noah is in full bloom, nature is not appreciated much. Lowly servants are not used to enjoying nature for the pleasure of the moment. It is aristocrats, nobles, sophisticated, wealthy and enlightened individuals who enjoy the forests, beaches, swim in the sea, enjoy nature, preserve wildlife and create sanctuaries for endangered species.

Typical servants will kill all the wild animals and eat them up. They would also cut down the trees and use their beaches as toilets. In certain places, a tree can increase the value of a house by over ten thousand dollars. However, in other places a tree is a nuisance and is often cut down at the nearest opportunity.

It is important to break away from the curse of not appreciating nature.

Since you are not under that curse, show us that you appreciate nature and enjoy God's creation without destroying it. Don't destroy the beaches! Use them and benefit from what God has provided! Plant trees instead of cutting them down. Create and enjoy beaches and do not use them as toilets or rubbish dumps. Since you are not under that curse, preserve your wildlife and admire nature. A curse creates an unmistakeable and almost inexplicable picture.

28. A typical "servant of servants" does not document things.

Most servants do not keep a diary of their activities. They do not write down important things that are happening around them. Why would a servant sit down to write the history of his life? Do you know any maidservant who has written a biography?

A "servant of servants" is just happy to live for today, to enjoy the moment and to forget the past. You are not likely to find a servant wearing reading glasses and making notes about events that are happening around him so that he can leave a good record of events for his descendants. There is no written history and there are no biographies where the curse of Noah is dominant. Most of the history in the places where this curse is working is by oral tradition. They will tell you that a man came from another country and changed the lives of everyone in the town forever. It will be a story that is modified from generation to generation, until the story says that the man who changed their lives fell out of the clouds and landed in a lake which dried up instantly.

Where the curse of Noah is in manifestation, you will find that people struggle to record things. They struggle to record data, to fill forms, to record events, to write records and to keep notes about things. If you employ someone who is struggling under the curse of Noah, he will be happy to work but he will not be happy to keep records, write notes and enter information into a computer.

You are reading this book because this curse is ending in your life today! Begin to write down your life history. Write the history of your church! Write an autobiography! Write biographies of important people! Keep a diary. By specifically deciding to be a church and a ministry that has records, that has a written history and that has written biographies, you dismiss the picture of the curse from your life. It is very unusual for a servant to keep a written history, to write a biography or to make important records and archives. Fill forms, make notes and keep records as you work, so that the picture of the curse will be broken.

By doing these things you prove that you have dismantled the picture of the curse of Noah from your life forever. Set about to go against your very nature and do these things that completely dissociate you from the picture of the curse of Noah. You are free today from the curse of Noah!

29.   A typical "servant of servants" does not do research.

You are not likely to find the servant of your house doing research on anything. He is not likely to do research on the type of bulbs that save electricity. He is not likely to analyse the bacterial content of the water you are drinking in the house. He is not likely to analyse the bills in the home and understand why they go up or down. Servants did not carry out most of the great scientific researches of our world. Most of the great discoveries and research of our world were not carried out by servants. Inventions like electricity, nuclear science, cars, computers and phones were not developed by servants.

Where people are servants of servants, they are often unable to carry out research of any kind. Where there are servants of servants in charge, they are not interested to know why a church grows or why it does not. They are not interested in analysing the effect of the length of church services on the attendance. They are not interested in analysing the effect of taking the offering when people are standing or sitting. All they want to do is to pray and have nothing to do with research.

Today, your mind is being brightened with the ability to do research, to think and to analyse. The curse of Noah cannot and will not work in your life because you are declared a researcher and an analyst from today! No one will be able to say that you not interested in finding out things and analysing things.

Begin to invent and create new things by the power of God. God is giving you the ability to research, to think and to invent by the power of God. After today, no one will associate dullness and a lack of creativity with you! The curse is broken in your life in Jesus' name!

Do Not Believe the Lies and Insults of P. W. Botha and Lord Lugard

I was shocked to discover the speeches of some white men who ruled different sections of Africa at different times over the last one hundred years. It is important that you reject their speeches and their lies for what they are. Their speeches contain insults and derogatory statements about black people. Apart from being wrong, the Word of God does not support their statements. Read the Word of God for yourself. God does not look down on people! God respects every group of people! God's word shows that any human being who fears Him and works righteousness will be accepted and honoured.

Then Peter opened his mouth, and said, Of a truth I perceive that GOD IS NO RESPECTER OF PERSONS: But IN EVERY NATION HE THAT FEARETH HIM, AND WORKETH RIGHTEOUSNESS, IS ACCEPTED with him.

Acts 10: 34 - 35

The doctrine of the curse of Noah is not intended to be misused by anyone to humiliate, degrade, enslave and cheat other human beings. God is no respecter of persons but accepts everyone. *You must not, on any account believe the lies of P. W. Botha and Lord Lugard!* God did not make the white man superior to the black man. God made all men equal. It is up to you to behave equally and to fight curses with the wisdom of God.

Let us now notice a few points in a speech by P. W. Botha, a white man who ruled South Africa during the Apartheid era. His speech is full of insults, degrading remarks and some interesting observations. *It is important for every African leader to ensure that Botha's observations do not ever come true in their lives.* His words and negative predictions must be resisted fiercely by those he purported to describe. None of the negative words spoken by P. W. Botha should ever be fulfilled in any one of us!

However, if you take his words lightly, you will find out that you will fulfil his observations to the letter. Without fighting hard, curses have a way of descending and being fulfilled almost magically. That is why curses end up being described as "an astonishment and a wonder".

It is important for every one of us to ensure that none of P.W. Botha's predictions will ever be fulfilled under our leadership. Every leader must distance himself from fulfilling these terrible stereotypes.

I must warn you that if you do not unravel the curse of Noah in a step-by-step fashion, and set it aside, P. W. Botha will almost seem to be a prophet describing your future in detail. You must fight very hard to ensure that none of his words are fulfilled even in the slightest way. Every born again Christian leader can and must reject all negative characteristics described and live his life in the opposite of this prediction.

Excerpts From P.W. Botha's Speech - 1985

- *"Pretoria has been made by the White mind for the White man. We are not obliged even in the least to try to prove to anybody and to the Blacks that we are superior people. We have demonstrated that to the Blacks in a thousand and one ways.*

- *The Republic of South Africa that we know of today has not been created by wishful thinking. We have created it at the expense of intelligence, sweat and blood.*

- *We do not pretend like other Whites that we like Blacks. The fact that Blacks look like human beings and act like human beings, do not necessarily make them sensible human beings. Hedgehogs are not porcupines and lizards are not crocodiles simply because they look alike.*

- *If God wanted us to be equal to the Blacks, he would have created us all of a uniform colour and intellect. But he*

> *created us differently: Whites, Blacks, Yellow, rulers and the ruled.*
>
> • *Intellectually, we are superior to the Blacks; that has been proven beyond any reasonable doubt over the years. I believe that the Afrikaner is an honest, God-fearing person, who has demonstrated practically the right way of being. Nevertheless, it is comforting to know that behind the scenes, Europe, America, Canada, Australia - and all others are behind us in spite of what they say.*
>
> • *It is our strong conviction, therefore, that the Black is the raw material for the White man.*
>
> • *And here is a creature that lacks foresight. The average Black does not plan his life beyond a year.*
>
> • *By now every one of us has seen it practically that the Blacks cannot rule themselves.*
>
> • *Give them guns and they will kill each other.*
>
> • *They are good in nothing else but making noise, dancing, marrying many wives and indulging in sex.*
>
> • *Let us all accept that the Black man is the symbol of poverty, mental inferiority, laziness and emotional incompetence. Isn't it plausible, therefore that the White man is created to rule the Black man?"*

Notice also the speech of Lord Lugard, a British man who was the Governor of Hong Kong (from 1907-1912) and the Governor of Nigeria (from 1914 to 1919). One of the hostels in the secondary school I went to as a young man, Lugard House, was named after Lord Lugard.

His speech is full of observations, remarks and some insults. It is important for every one of us to ensure that his observations do not come through and are not repeated in our lives. None of the negative words spoken by Lord Lugard should ever be fulfilled in any one of us.

Then Peter opened his mouth, and said, Of a truth I perceive that GOD IS NO RESPECTER OF PERSONS: But IN EVERY NATION HE THAT FEARETH HIM, AND WORKETH RIGHTEOUSNESS, IS ACCEPTED with him.

Acts 10: 34 - 35

The doctrine of the curse of Noah is not intended to be misused by anyone to humiliate, degrade, enslave and cheat other human beings.   God is no respecter of persons but accepts everyone. *You must not, on any account believe the lies of P. W. Botha and Lord Lugard!*   God did not make the white man superior to the black man.   God made all men equal.   It is up to you to behave equally and to fight curses with the wisdom of God.   Curses can be overcome. That is why I am writing this book.

However, if you take Lord Lugard's words lightly, you will find out that you will fulfil his observations to the letter. Without fighting hard, curses have a way of descending and being fulfilled almost magically.   That is why curses end up being described as "an astonishment and a wonder".

The picture in certain regions of the world is the same; whether it is east, west, north or south. It is simply a wonder how the picture of non-development, non-building, poor organisation, mismanagement and confusion slaps itself inexorably on many places.

You must fight very hard to ensure that none of the negative observations made by Lord Lugard will be fulfilled even in the slightest way in your life.   Every leader must distance himself from fulfilling these terrible descriptions.

Excerpts from Lord Lugard's Speech - 1926

- *"In character and temperament"* wrote Lord Lugard, *"the typical African of this race-type is a happy, thriftless, excitable person, lacking in self control, discipline, and foresight, naturally courageous, and naturally courteous and polite, full of personal vanity, with little sense of veracity, fond of music and loving weapons as an oriental loves jewellery.*

- *His thoughts are concentrated on the events and feelings of the moment, and he suffers little from the apprehension for the future, or grief for the past.*

- *His mind is far nearer to the animal world than that of the European or Asiatic, and exhibits something of the animal's placidity and want of desire to rise beyond the state he has reached.*

- *Through the ages the African appears to have evolved no organized religious creed, and though some tribes appear to believe in a deity, the religious sense seldom rises above pantheistic animalism and seems more often to take the form of a vague dread of the supernatural.*

- *He lacks the power of organization, and is conspicuously deficient in the management and control of men or business.*

- *He loves the display of power, but fails to realize its responsibility... he will work hard with less incentive than most races. He has the courage of the fighting animal - an instinct rather than a moral virtue....*

- *In brief, the virtues and defects of this race-type are those of attractive children, whose confidence when it is won is given ungrudgingly as to an older and wiser superior and without envy....*

- *Perhaps the two traits which have impressed me as those most characteristic of the African native are his lack of apprehension and his lack of ability to visualize the future."*

Indeed, these speeches predict the picture of servants of servants - shabbiness, servants of servants - filth, servants of servants - inability to lead, servants of servants - inability to build, servants of servants - inability to prosper, servants of servants - inability to govern and servants of servants - inability to manage things.

It is clear that the people who wrote these speeches have no hope in the ability of the black people to ever rise up and manage their own affairs properly. I do not share those views. I do not believe in the words of P.W. Botha and Lord Lugard. I believe in the word of God. Black and white people are equal in the sight of God. Black people can arise and be excellent leaders and builders. There are many examples of this.

However, the curse can be neutralized only if it is not ignored or trivialized. The picture in Africa is sad and amazingly uniformly spread throughout the continent. It is easy to expect nothing good to come out of a place that is hundreds of years behind.

However, just as the curse of Adam on women has been neutralized, the curse of Noah can be diffused and neutralized. We can arise and neutralize, overcome and break out of the curse through the wisdom of God. Hear the wisdom of God for overcoming the curse of Noah! Always remember the curse of Adam and how it is being neutralized through wisdom. The same will happen to the curse of Noah. Wisdom will make all the effects of the curse of being "servant of servants" disappear from our horizon. As you believe this word, you will create an environment where that picture of shabbiness, poverty, disorganization, confusion, chaos, filth, difficulty, joblessness, hopelessness and a lack of development will be a thing of the past.

How to Overcome the Curse of Noah

1. **Have a proper respect for the curse of Noah which creates the picture of the "servant of servants".**

All those who do not have a proper respect for snakes can be bitten and die from them. Likewise all those who joke with these curses live to regret how serious and unfortunate their effects are.

The human race has taken the curse of Adam seriously, and has blocked the effects of the curse of Adam by developing schools and hospitals.

The human race has taken the curse of Eve seriously and developed the study of obstetrics and gynaecology. It is now very unlikely that a woman will die from childbirth according to the curse on Eve. The wisdom of medical science has made sure that that curse is greatly reduced in its effect.

The curse of Noah must also be taken seriously! Black people must not ignore the words of Noah. It is important to fight that curse with wisdom. Wisdom is the master key to overcoming impossible situation. When you understand the wisdom of God to unravel the curse, you will, in a step by step fashion, dismiss the picture of servant shabbiness, servant filth, servant inability to lead, servant inability to build, servant inability to prosper, servant inability to govern and servant inability to manage things.

If you joke with the curse of Noah, it will fasten itself to you and you will only be another confirmation that curses and blessings are real and powerful. You will confirm the existence of a curse through your shabbiness of the "servant of servants", the filth of the "servant of servants" the inability to lead of the "servant of servants", the inability to govern of the "servant of servants", the inability to prosper of the "servant of servants", the inability to build of the "servant of servants" and the inability to manage complex things which is typical of the "servant of servants".

2. Resist the picture and patterns of the "servant of servants".

The picture of a "servant of servants" must be resisted, fought against and overcome with wisdom, with honesty and with humility.

It is possible to escape, overturn and minimize the effects of the curse. Do not just sit down and let certain predictions, pictures and patterns be fulfilled in your life! Do not allow yourself to be another statistic in the well-known picture of: shabbiness of the "servant of servants", filth of the "servant of servants", disorganization of the "servant of servants", poor leadership of the "servant of servants", poverty of the "servant of servants", and confusion and backwardness of the "servant of servants". Do not allow yourself to have the picture of being two hundred years behind everybody else on the planet.

3.   Use the wisdom of this teaching to negate the pattern of the "servant of servants".

The curse of Adam was severe. Women were cursed to suffer through childbirth. Through the wisdom of medical science, fewer and fewer women are dying and suffering from the pain of childbirth. The wisdom of medical science has virtually wiped out the curse. In the same way, wisdom will neutralize the curse of Noah.

The curse of Noah is severe because it creates the picture of a "servant of servants". By taking each element of the picture of a "servant of servants," you can fight the curse. For instance, take the element of the servant's inability to build and decide to start building now. Take the element of the servant's inability to lead and start practicing good leadership now. Take the element of the servant's shabbiness and filth and clear your environment of all forms of shabbiness and filth.

People who respect this curse fight against the servant patterns of servant shabbiness, servant filth, servant inability to lead, servant inability to build, servant inability to prosper, servant inability to govern and servant inability to manage things. As black people dismiss the curse of Noah and ridicule this teaching, they will find themselves manifesting all the traits of a "servant of servants" such as shabbiness, filth, poverty, disorganization, lack of management, lack of order, and lack of leadership.

SECTION 3

THE END OF CURSES

CHAPTER 20

How You Can Use the Powers of the World to Come

And there came unto me one of the seven angels which had the seven vials full of the seven last plagues, and talked with me, saying, Come hither, I will shew thee the bride, the Lamb's wife.

And he carried me away in the spirit to a great and high mountain, and shewed me that great city, the holy Jerusalem, descending out of heaven from God, Having the glory of God: and her light was like unto a stone most precious, even like a jasper stone, clear as crystal.

And the city had no need of the sun, neither of the moon, to shine in it: for the glory of God did lighten it, and the Lamb is the light thereof.

And the nations of them which are saved shall walk in the light of it: and the kings of the earth do bring their glory and honour into it.

And the gates of it shall not be shut at all by day: for there shall be no night there.

And they shall bring the glory and honour of the nations into it.

And there shall in no wise enter into it any thing that defileth, neither whatsoever worketh abomination, or maketh a lie: but they which are written in the Lamb's book of life.

Revelation 21:9-11, 23-27

And he shewed me a pure river of water of life, clear as crystal, proceeding out of the throne of God and of the Lamb. In the midst of the street of it, and on either side of the river, was there the tree of life, which bare twelve manner of fruits, and yielded her fruit every month: and the leaves of the tree were for the healing of the nations.

And THERE SHALL BE NO MORE CURSE: but the throne of God and of the Lamb shall be in it; and his servants shall serve him:

Revelation 22:1-5

The passage above describes life in the world to come. There are several wonderful features about the world to come.

1. The world to come has a very beautiful city - the New Jerusalem.

2. All nations walk in the light of this city.

3. No evil thing enters the city.

4. Abominations cannot come to the city.

5. Anyone that tells a lie or makes a lie cannot come to the city.

6. There is a beautiful river of life in the city.

7. There is a tree of life in the city.

8. There will be no night in the city.

9. There will be no need of a candle or even the sun in the city.

10. There will be no curse there.

As you can see, there are many wonderful characteristics to be enjoyed in the world to come. We are going to have a great time in the world to come. Most of the evil things on earth will not be found in the world to come. Liars are a very common group to find on earth. But there will be no liars or makers of lies in the New Jerusalem. That is really significant! There is no tree of life or river of life on earth, but there will be a tree of life and a river of life in the world to come.

In the world to come, there are powers that will wipe out curses, sorrow, crying and death. The curses that affected Adam and Eve, Noah and Israel will no longer work. A great power would have wiped out these terrible judgments forever. Indeed, it will take a great power to end the sorrow and the pain that is in this world.

For it is impossible for those who were once enlightened, and have tasted of the heavenly gift, and were made partakers of the Holy Ghost, And have tasted the good word of God, and THE POWERS OF THE WORLD TO COME, If they shall fall away, to renew them again unto repentance; seeing they crucify to themselves the Son of God afresh, and put him to an open shame.

Hebrews 6:4-6

The wonderful scripture we read above, tells us that Christians on earth can actually experience the **powers of the world to come.** Hebrews 6:4 describes a Christian's experience of being enlightened, tasting the heavenly gift of salvation, being a partaker of the word of God and a partaker of the **powers of the world to come**. God will allow Christians on earth to taste of the **powers of the world to come.**

This scripture gives hope to all of us since we are operating under lingering global curses. This scripture is showing us that even whilst we are on earth, we can partake of the **powers of the world to come.** Indeed, in this life, you can invoke the **powers of the world to come** and thereby escape the tragedy of these global curses.

It is a fact that most of us have done things that arouse biblical curses. Most individuals, families and nations have some kind of lingering curse in effect somewhere. In order to deal with all curses in this life, you will have to invoke the **powers of the world to come.**

It is only by the **powers of the world to come** that ALL CURSES will be finally removed. It is time for you to operate in the **powers of the world to come**. According to the scripture, if you partake in the Word of God, and in the Holy Spirit, then you are qualified to operate in the **powers of the world to come**.

The **powers of the world to come** can deliver you from a legitimate curse. The **powers of the world to come** are the powers that will be used to create the beautiful world that is coming after this era. The world to come is not this world! This world is passing away! The glory of this world will soon be gone.

In the world to come everything is going to be different. If we trust the Lord, we will reign with Him in the world to come. There will be no more sorrow, pain or curse in the world to come because the **powers of the world to come** would have wiped out such things.

What the Powers of the World to Come Will Accomplish

1. The powers of the world to come will wipe away all TEARS.

    And GOD SHALL WIPE AWAY ALL TEARS FROM THEIR EYES; and there shall be no more death, neither sorrow, nor crying, neither shall there be any more pain: for the former things are passed away.

    Revelation 21:4

2. The powers of the world to come will wipe out all DEATH.

    And God shall wipe away all tears from their eyes; and THERE SHALL BE NO MORE DEATH, neither sorrow, nor crying, neither shall there be any more pain: for the former things are passed away.

    Revelation 21:4

3. The powers of the world to come will wipe out all SORROW.

    And God shall wipe away all tears from their eyes; and there shall be no more death, NEITHER SORROW, nor crying, neither shall there be any more pain: for the former things are passed away.

    Revelation 21:4

4.   The powers of the world to come will wipe out all
     CRYING.

     **And God shall wipe away all tears from their eyes;
     and there shall be no more death, neither sorrow, NOR
     CRYING, neither shall there be any more pain: for the
     former things are passed away.**

                                              Revelation 21:4

5.   The powers of the world to come will wipe out all
     PAIN.

     **And God shall wipe away all tears from their eyes;
     and there shall be no more death, neither sorrow, nor
     crying, NEITHER SHALL THERE BE ANY MORE
     PAIN: for the former things are passed away.**

                                              Revelation 21:4

6.   The powers of the world to come will wipe out all
     CURSES.

     **AND THERE SHALL BE NO MORE CURSE: but the
     throne of God and of the Lamb shall be in it; and his
     servants shall serve him:**

                                              Revelation 22:3

7.   The powers of the world to come will wipe out all
     DARKNESS.

     **And THERE SHALL BE NO NIGHT there; and they
     need no candle, neither light of the sun; for the Lord
     God giveth them light: and they shall reign for ever
     and ever.**

                                              Revelation 22:5

Through the **powers of the world to come**, all these terrible
things, which characterize life on earth, will be removed.   Pain,
sorrow, crying, death and darkness will be permanently removed.
Curses will also be no more.

If you, as a Christian, according to Hebrews 6:5 are able to exercise powers of the world to come, you will live a curse-free life.

I release the **powers of the world to come** to set you free as you read this book.

Whatever curse followed you before you started reading this book drops off by the **powers of the world to come!**

Whatever curse you have brought upon yourself before you started reading this book is finally driven away by the powers of the world to come!

Whatever curse your father or mother have contracted for you and your children, you are set free from its implications from this moment!

Through the **powers of the world to come**, you are walking away and enjoying an absolutely curse-free life. Read on, and you will discover more secrets about the powers of the world to come!

CHAPTER 21

How You Can Cancel a Curse by Sacrifice

Christ hath REDEEMED US from the curse of the law...

                                        Galatians 3:13

One of the ways to deploy the powers of the world to come is to deploy the mysterious power of sacrifice. The mysterious power that is released through sacrifice, has been known to stop a ravaging curse from continuing to destroy the people in its way. Indeed, the power of a sacrifice can stop a curse from continuing. Let us see several examples in which a great sacrifice was made and a curse stopped.

1.   The sacrifice of Jesus saved us from the curse.

Christ hath redeemed us from the curse of the law, being made a curse for us: for it is written, Cursed is every one that hangeth on a tree:

Galatians 3:13

We know that Christ has redeemed us from the curse. But exactly how did he redeem us from the curse? What method or power was used? The power that was used to redeem us was not the power of corruptible things. It was the power of the sacrifice of His Life and Blood. "Forasmuch as ye know that ye were not redeemed with corruptible things, as silver and gold, from your vain conversation received by tradition from your fathers; But with the precious blood of Christ, as of a lamb without blemish and without spot" (1 Peter 1:18-19). The curse was stopped by Jesus' sacrifice of hanging on the cross.

...Cursed is every one that hangeth on a tree:

Galatians 3:13

The sacrifice of Jesus Christ on the cross stopped the curse of death. By Jesus' sacrifice on the cross, we are redeemed from the curse. Through the mystery of the cross, great power is released into the world to deliver us from the curse. "For the preaching of the cross is to them that perish, foolishness; but to us which are saved it is the power of God" (1 Corinthians 1:18). The cross of Jesus Christ releases the powers of the world to come and blocks the curse. Today, we are set free from the curse of eternal death. This is through the Blood of Jesus. One day, we will see thousands and thousands of people in heaven. These were accursed people who were once doomed and damned. They will walk the streets of heaven and praise the Saviour. What was able to stop the curse in their lives? What is the secret that broke the power of the curse in their lives? How were they able to make it to heaven? It is the Blood of Jesus that enables the multitudes to escape the curse of death and eternal separation from God.

> After this I beheld, and, lo, a great multitude, which no man could number, of all nations, and kindreds, and people, and tongues, stood before the throne, and before the Lamb, clothed with white robes, and palms in their hands; And cried with a loud voice, saying, Salvation to our God which sitteth upon the throne, and unto the Lamb.
>
> And all the angels stood round about the throne, and about the elders and the four beasts, and fell before the throne on their faces, and worshipped God, Saying, Amen: Blessing, and glory, and wisdom, and thanksgiving, and honour, and power, and might, be unto our God for ever and ever. Amen.
>
> And one of the elders answered, saying unto me, What are these which are arrayed in white robes? and whence came they?
>
> And I said unto him, Sir, thou knowest. And he said to me, THESE ARE THEY WHICH CAME OUT OF GREAT TRIBULATION, AND HAVE WASHED THEIR ROBES, AND MADE THEM WHITE IN THE BLOOD OF THE LAMB. Therefore are they before the throne of God, and serve him day and night in his temple: and he that sitteth on the throne shall dwell among them. They shall hunger no more, neither thirst any more; neither shall the sun light on them, nor any heat.
>
> Revelation 7:9-16

2.   The sacrifice of Noah stopped the curse.

And Noah builded an altar unto the Lord; and took of every clean beast, and of every clean fowl, and OFFERED BURNT OFFERINGS on the altar.

And THE LORD SMELLED A SWEET SAVOUR; and the Lord said in his heart, I WILL NOT AGAIN CURSE the ground any more for man's sake; for the imagination of man's heart is evil from his youth; neither will I again smite any more every thing living, as I have done.

While the earth remaineth, seedtime and harvest, and cold and heat, and summer and winter, and day and night shall not cease.

Genesis 8:20-22

Sacrifices are well known to stop curses. This is why giving is an important spiritual activity. Giving sacrificially stops the curse of poverty and supernaturally opens the doors of prosperity. People who have not learnt to give have not learnt to stop the curse. The curse on Adam was basically a curse to struggle, to sweat and to be poor. Do you want to be poor? Do you want to struggle? Do you want to sweat all your life and have little to show for it all?

The sacrifice of Noah was a great and wise effort to stop the curse. Through this wonderful sacrifice that Noah made, the curse of death and destruction, which wiped out the whole human race was stopped.

When God smelled the sweet sacrifice of Noah, God said in His heart, "I will not again curse the ground." This means that God could have continued cursing the earth for the wickedness that was still there. The flood did not end the wickedness of mankind. Ham, the son of Noah, was a wicked and ungrateful child. Even more wickedness was released into the earth after the flood. From the behaviour of Ham and the wickedness that continued after the flood, we see that God would have had to flood the earth on several more occasions.

The sacrifice of Noah changed the mind of God and that is why there has been no more worldwide flood to wipe out the human race.

3. The sacrifice of the king of Moab stopped a curse.

And when the king of Moab saw that the battle was too sore for him, he took with him seven hundred men that drew swords, to break through even unto the king of Edom: but they could not.

Then he took his eldest son that should have reigned in his stead, and offered him for a burnt offering upon the wall. And there was great indignation against Israel: and they departed from him, and returned to their own land.

2 Kings 3:26-27

The Bible records a famous battle between the king of Judah, the king of Israel, the king of Edom and the king of Moab. It was a battle of one against three. All the three kings were out to eliminate Moab. This battle was inspired when Elisha the prophet prophesied the defeat of the Moabites to Jehoshaphat. So great was the defeat of the Moabites, according to the prophecy of Elisha, that they faced total annihilation.

When the king of Moab realised that he had lost the war, he attempted to break through to kill the king of Edom whom he thought he could get to. Unable to break through, he knew that his end had come and decided to make a sacrifice of his own son. When Israel saw the wicked king of Moab burning his own son who was to reign in his stead in front of them, a great indignation fell on them.

The power to drive away the surrounding armies of Israel, Judah and Edom was somehow released. From that point onwards, the armies of Israel, Judah and Edom were forced to return and go back home. The Bible says furious anger, wrath and indignation were released against Israel. The armies of Israel turned back and went home. The sacrifice of a king's son released so much power that an entire army was halted in its tracks.

Once again a sacrifice had stopped the curse of defeat and death that was descending on Moab. Why do you think witches, wizards and diviners make sacrifices? Sacrifice is a well-known key for the release of spiritual power.

Paul said, the preaching of the cross is the power of God. The preaching of the cross is the preaching of sacrifice.

It may sound incredible, but there is spiritual power in a sacrifice. The spiritual power produced through a sacrifice will stop every curse in your life in the name of Jesus. Whatever was molesting you before you started reading this book is finally broken today!

4. **God saved His people from the curse through the prophet.**

    And by a prophet the LORD brought Israel out of Egypt, and by a prophet was he preserved.

    Hosea 12: 13

Indeed, through a prophet, God saved His people from the curse of bondage, slavery, cruelty and death. Through a prophet God saved Israel out of Egypt! And through a prophet He preserved them! The prophet Zechariah also prophesied about how the people of Israel would be saved from the curse of the east country and the curse of the west country.

> Thus saith the Lord of hosts; Behold, I WILL SAVE MY PEOPLE FROM THE EAST COUNTRY, AND FROM THE WEST COUNTRY;
>
> And I will bring them, and they shall dwell in the midst of Jerusalem: and they shall be my people, and I will be their God, in truth and in righteousness.
>
> Thus saith the Lord of hosts; Let your hands be strong, ye that hear in these days these words by the mouth of the prophets, which were in the day that the foundation of the house of the Lord of hosts was laid, that the temple might be built.

For before these days there was no hire for man, nor any hire for beast; neither was there any peace to him that went out or came in because of the affliction: for I set all men every one against his neighbour. But now I will not be unto the residue of this people as in the former days, saith the Lord of hosts. For the seed shall be prosperous; the vine shall give her fruit, and the ground shall give her increase, and the heavens shall give their dew; and I will cause the remnant of this people to possess all these things.

And it shall come to pass, that AS YE WERE A CURSE AMONG THE HEATHEN, O HOUSE OF JUDAH, AND HOUSE OF ISRAEL; SO WILL I SAVE YOU, AND YE SHALL BE A BLESSING: fear not, but let your hands be strong.

Zechariah 8:7-13

You must know when the time has come for you to be saved from the curse. For seventy years, Israel was in captivity as determined by the Lord. There was no way to break from this captivity until the seventy years came to pass. It was after the seventy years that Zechariah began to prophesy. Zechariah prophesied the release and the prosperity of God's people because the time was right. When the time is right, your deliverance from the curse will be instant. Instead of the curse, a blessing will begin to follow you. This is why the same prophet said, "Ask ye of the Lord rain, in the time of the latter rain." It is important to ask for things in the season that God is giving those things. If He is not giving those things there is no point in asking.

A key to being saved from a curse has to do with the mind that God has towards you. You can be saved from a curse when God decides to change His mind towards you and conveys it through His prophet. Pray to the Lord so that His mind towards you will be good. Do not be stubborn-hearted, lest God be angry with you! Receive the prophesying of the prophet and be delivered from the curse!

It is possible to be saved from great evil by the blessing of the Lord. In this wonderful passage, God tells His people that He has changed His mind about them. He says, "I will not be unto the residue of this people as in the former days." Notice that God had a change of mind and heart towards these people. The curse exists because of God's anger. God is able to save you from your curse. His mind about you has to change. His mind towards you must be good and not evil.

You will notice the blessings that come when you are saved from the curse. There will be hire for man (Zechariah 8:10). This means that there will be jobs. There will be peace and every one will not be against his neighbour (Zechariah 8:10). There will also be prosperity when you are saved from the curse (Zechariah 8:12). The vine shall give her increase and the ground shall give her increase (Zechariah 8:12).

Another significant change will be that you will possess all things. All these will happen when God saves you from a curse. By this scripture you must believe that you too can be saved from a curse.

CHAPTER 22

How You Can be Saved from a Curse by Redemption

As the bird by wandering, as the swallow by flying, so the curse causeless shall not come.

Proverbs 26:2

A curse is a legally binding declaration that is difficult to revoke, remove or cancel. If a judge declares that you are sentenced to prison for twenty years, it would take a great miracle to change it. Those words spoken by the judge are very powerful and are backed by the entire government of your nation. When a judge declares that a person is sentenced to death, it is very difficult for that person to ever go free.

I know of an African head of state who was once very powerful, living in luxury and in great affluence. He was sentenced to life imprisonment by powerful judges in Holland. Today, those words spoken by the judge are being implemented by the army, the police and the security forces of all European nations. He is locked behind bars and is most likely to die in the midst of his fellow prisoners.

The words spoken by the judge are legally binding. There are good reasons why this man is forced to live the rest of his life as a prisoner. He caused the deaths and mutilation of thousands of ordinary people and is receiving human judgment for his crimes. When the judge declared that he would be in prison, it was as though a powerful curse was declared over the rest of his days on the earth.

I also know a pastor who has visited this head of state in his prison. The reality is that none of the prayers and declarations of the pastor have been able to set this man free. There are good reasons for this man's current bondage. The declaration of the judge has released the army, the police, the immigration forces, the prison service, the secret service, Interpol and other special forces against him. These powers have secured him in the prison.

This is how a curse works. It causes and allows demons to have access to you when they would otherwise not have had such access.

Indeed, it is very difficult to undo such declarations spoken by the judge against your life. The judge did not speak without a cause. The curse causeless does not come. The authority figure does not speak without a good reason.

A curse can be legally challenged, removed and revoked. The way by which a curse can be cancelled in your life is by being *"redeemed from the curse"*. To be redeemed is for someone to pay for the crime so that you no longer have to pay for your sins. If you have to pay for your crimes by being executed, someone would have to be executed in your place. Once the person is executed in your place, you can demand freedom using the evidence that one person has died already as a payment for that crime.

How You Can be Redeemed From a Curse

Christ hath REDEEMED US FROM THE CURSE of the law, being made a curse for us: for it is written, Cursed is every one that hangeth on a tree:

Galatians 3:13

Redemption is a payment or atonement for a sin, fault or mistake because *there is a legal reason for the curse*. It is all well and good for people to say that a curse cannot come into their lives. The revelation of positive faith confessions is a genuine truth that God has given to us. But it does not negate or cancel other realities that are equally in the Word of God.

One day I went to a prison with the love of God and with my Bible. I preached the Word of God and many people gave their lives to God. I fell in love with the people, especially the leader of the Bible study group. I wanted to set him free. Actually, I wanted to set many of them free because they looked so harmless and pitiful. I desperately wanted them to be free.

No matter how strong my desire and faith was, I was forced to come to terms with the reality that there were legal reasons why every one of them was in prison. Indeed, the leader of the fellowship who appeared the most spiritual explained to me that he had actually murdered his own son and that was why he was in prison.

I was stunned when I discovered that this Bible-wielding, tongue-talking prisoner was actually a murderer. There was a solid legal reason why this gentleman and all the other prisoners were in prison. Making declarations of sudden miraculous freedom will not set such murderers free from the prison where they are legally bound to be. There must be some kind of legal settlement to enable someone like that to go free.

This is one of the reasons why Jesus Christ died on the cross. He died to shed His Blood for us and to wash our sins away. But He also died to redeem us from the curse of the law. The curse of the law is so strong, that some legal payments needed to be made in order to set us free from those declarations.

Christ hath REDEEMED US FROM THE CURSE OF THE LAW, being made a curse for us: for it is written, Cursed is every one that hangeth on a tree:

Galatians 3:13

To redeem means to buy. The word "redeem" is an old English word which means to pay for something. Once your debt is paid, you do not have to pay for it any more. If your debt is twenty years in prison and someone serves those twenty years for you, then you do not have to serve those twenty years. God paid for your legal deliverance from the curse of the law. A curse is not something you can just walk away from, because it did not come without a reason.

How Rebekah redeemed her son Jacob from the curse.

Rebekah redeemed her son from his curse! Rebekah paid for her son's curse with her own life. She said, "I will take the punishment and the death so that you can live and have a good life."

Rebekah advised her son Jacob to deceive his father, Isaac, and pretend that he was Esau. Jacob knew that he could easily be cursed instead of being blessed. A curse could come on him because he was deceiving his own father.

And Rebekah spake unto Jacob her son, saying, Behold, I heard thy father speak unto Esau thy brother, saying, Bring me venison, and make me savoury meat, that I may eat, and bless thee before the Lord before my death. Now therefore, my son, obey my voice according to that which I command thee. Go now to the flock, and fetch me from thence two good kids of the goats; and I will make them savoury meat for thy father, such as he loveth: And thou shalt bring it to thy father, that he may eat, and that he may bless thee before his death.

And Jacob said to Rebekah his mother, Behold, Esau my brother is a hairy man, and I am a smooth man: My father peradventure will feel me, and I shall seem to him as a deceiver; and I SHALL BRING A CURSE UPON ME, and not a blessing.

And his mother said unto him, UPON ME BE THY CURSE, my son: only obey my voice, and go fetch me them.

Genesis 27:6-13

Jacob knew he would be placing himself in great danger by deceiving and dishonouring his father. He only agreed to go ahead with the plan when his mother decided to take his place and receive his curse for him. She said clearly, "Upon me be thy curse." She took the curse of Jacob so that he could experience only the blessing. This is the legal implication of a curse. It has a right to be there and it needs to be paid for if it is to be set aside. After this act, Rebekah was heard of only once; the next and final time she is mentioned is when she said she was weary of her life. No mention is made of her again. Even the event of her death was not mentioned. She fully absorbed the curse that Jacob should have received.

And Rebekah said to Isaac, I am weary of my life because of the daughters of Heth: if Jacob take a wife of the daughters of Heth, such as these which are of the daughters of the land, what good shall my life do me?

Genesis 27:46

Which Curses Are We Redeemed from?

What does the Bible mean when it says that in Heaven there will be no more curse? Why does the Bible say there will be no more curse if all curses have been redeemed by Jesus? Obviously, not all curses have been redeemed and removed by Jesus Christ. It is when we get to Heaven that there will be no more curse. Here on earth, there are curses everywhere. Most things are working out on the basis of a curse. The wickedness of man has brought about many intractable curses. Heaven is the sure place where there will be no more curse. Let us have a look at the specific curses that you can be redeemed from through the sacrifice of Jesus.

Jesus has redeemed us from the curse of the law that came under Moses.

The curses that are found in the Law of Moses have been paid for and we are set free from them. Therefore, if you go against the things written in the Law of Moses you will not experience a curse. You are redeemed from that curse. For instance, if you eat pork, you should not expect the curse for disobeying the law to fall on you. The Law of Moses is very strong against eating pork. Just have a look at what the Law of Moses says about eating pork. In spite of this law, many Christians eat pork and are blessed as they eat it because they have been redeemed from the curse of the law.

> And the Lord spake unto Moses and to Aaron, saying unto them, Speak unto the children of Israel, saying, these are the beasts which ye shall eat among all the beasts that are on the earth. Whatsoever parteth the hoof, and is clovenfooted, and cheweth the cud, among the beasts, that shall ye eat.
>
> And the swine, though he divide the hoof, and be clovenfooted, yet he cheweth not the cud; he is unclean to you.

They shall be even an abomination unto you; ye shall not eat of their flesh, but ye shall have their carcases in abomination.

Leviticus 11:1-3, 7, 11

Another law which millions of Christians apparently break is the law on the type of fabric to wear. You are not under a curse because you wear clothes that are a mixture of fabrics. Most clothes today are made up of a mixture of fabrics. There are many dresses, suits and shirts that are a mixture of fabrics. Christ has redeemed us from the curse of disobeying that law.

Thou shalt not wear a garment of divers sorts, as of woollen and linen together.

Deuteronomy 22:11

Yet another law which people disobey, is women wearing clothes that pertain to men and men wearing clothes that pertain to women. Most women wear trousers that are originally designed for men whilst many men in some cultures wear long shirts that look like dresses. Under the Law, you would be an abomination to God and most definitely experience a curse. Christ has redeemed us and paid the price for disobeying that Law.

The woman shall not wear that which pertaineth unto a man, neither shall a man put on a woman's garment: for all that do so are abomination unto the Lord thy God.

Deuteronomy 22:5

At the beginning of this book, I shared about three categories of curses. Many of these curses are not in the category of the curse of the law. It is important to understand that there are still many curses that are on going and are still operational. They are powerful and effective because they have causes that are real.

1.   Jesus has not redeemed us from the curse of Adam.

This is why we still eat bread in the sweat of our faces according to the curse of Adam even though we are Christians.

2.   Jesus has not redeemed us from the curse of Eve.

This is why women still struggle under the curse of Eve to desire husbands and to suffer in childbirth.

3.   Jesus has not redeemed us from the curse of Noah.

This is why descendants of Ham all over the world labour under the difficulty of being servants of servants according to the curse of Noah.

4.   Jesus has not redeemed us from the curse of Jacob.

This is also why enemies of Israel labour under various difficulties when they fight against Israel.

Also, Jesus has not redeemed you from the curse of the boy who cursed you last week. Jesus has not redeemed you from the curse of the girl who cursed you four years ago. If those curses have a legal right and basis, they may come flying at you. That is why it is important to conduct your life in such a way that you do not cause curses to come to you.

When a man removes his mother's wig from her head and slaps her with it, he creates for himself a custom-made curse. When a young man dishonours his father and sneers at his father's wisdom, he creates for himself a custom-made curse that he will have to contend with in his life. When a man goes out stealing, he opens the door to curses and punishments that have a cause to come.

Your salvation does not redeem you from all these things. It would have been nice if it were the case that salvation took away all these awful punishments.

It is important to stop saying you are redeemed from the curse and expect to be redeemed from every kind of curse in the world. That only gives the impression that the Word of God is not true.

CHAPTER 23

How You Can Escape from a Curse through Wisdom

There was a little city, and few men within it; and there came a great king against it, and BESIEGED IT, and built great bulwarks against it: Now there was found in it a poor wise man, and he BY HIS WISDOM DELIVERED THE CITY; yet no man remembered that same poor man.

Ecclesiastes 9:14-15

It is possible to be released from a curse. To be cursed is to be surrounded! What is it like when you are surrounded? When you are surrounded, you cannot escape; if you try to escape to the north you meet the enemy. If you try to escape to the south, you meet the same enemy! If you try to escape to the south-west, you meet the enemy! If you try to escape to the east, you still meet the enemy! That is what it means to be surrounded. There is a kind of wisdom however, that will enable you to escape when you are besieged and surrounded. You can be released from the curse!

For INNUMERABLE EVILS HAVE COMPASSED ME ABOUT: mine iniquities have taken hold upon me, so that I am not able to look up; they are more than the hairs of mine head: therefore my heart faileth me.

Be pleased, O Lord, to deliver me: O Lord, make haste to help me.

Let them be ashamed and confounded together that seek after my soul to destroy it;

let them be driven backward and put to shame that wish me evil.

Psalm 40:12-14

When a curse is in place you have the same result no matter what you do. If you are cursed to poverty, whether you live in America, Amsterdam, Lagos, Johannesburg, Toronto or Paris, you will still be poor. Whichever direction you take, poverty is the end result!

Whichever way you turn, it will lead to the same outcome. The enemy awaits you in every direction because you are cursed.

To be released from the curse, you must use the wisdom of the old man who delivered the city when it was surrounded.

There was a little city, and few men within it; and there came a great king against it, and BESIEGED

IT, and built great bulwarks against it: Now there was found in it a poor wise man, and he BY HIS WISDOM DELIVERED THE CITY; yet no man remembered that same poor man.

Ecclesiastes 9:14-15

God has a wisdom key that can help you escape from any apparent curse. When you discover that a curse is in operation, your mind must quickly go to the solution that God has provided to come out of the curse. The master key to overcoming curses is wisdom. The wisdom of God is the only way to circumvent, overcome, override and defeat a curse. The wisdom of God is the light that will make you shine in the midst of darkness. You will shine when you receive the light of God's wisdom in your life. There will be darkness all over the world and in everybody's life. But there will be light in your life because you have received the wisdom of God.

Arise, shine; for thy light is come, and the glory of the Lord is risen upon thee.

For, behold, the darkness shall cover the earth, and gross darkness the people: but the Lord shall arise upon thee, and his glory shall be seen upon thee.

And the Gentiles shall come to thy light, and kings to the brightness of thy rising.

Isaiah 60:1-3

Some curses are such that you cannot escape from them completely. However, there is no curse that is not alleviated somehow by applying a little wisdom from God. Anyone who applies the light of wisdom to a curse will be able to escape most of its terrible effects.

Daniel the prophet had been unfortunately subjected to castration and his life had been turned into the cursed existence of a eunuch. Yet, through the light of God's wisdom, he enjoyed some level of deliverance and escaped from that accursed state.

The light and the wisdom that was found in him was a master key to rising above the unfortunate state he found himself in. He was elected to become the prime minister under three different governments because of the great light and wisdom that was found in him.

> **There is a man in thy kingdom, in whom is the spirit of the holy gods; and in the days of thy father LIGHT AND UNDERSTANDING AND WISDOM, like the wisdom of the gods, was found in him; whom the king Nebuchadnezzar thy father, the king, I say, thy father, made master of the magicians, astrologers, Chaldeans, and soothsayers; Forasmuch as an excellent spirit, and knowledge, and understanding, interpreting of dreams, and shewing of hard sentences, and dissolving of doubts, were found in the same Daniel, whom the king named Belteshazzar: now let Daniel be called ...**
>
> **Daniel 5:11-12**

All mankind has been cursed to die. Death can be delayed and greatly postponed by applying the wisdom of medical science in your life. Death can be delayed in human beings for so long that they actually begin to wish to die. Wisdom, somehow, alleviates the curse and grants a limited escape from it. Women, for instance, have been cursed to suffer in childbirth. The wisdom of God has greatly alleviated women's suffering in childbearing. Accepting the wisdom of medical science greatly changes the outcome of women's suffering in childbirth. Wisdom is a master key for escaping from the full effects of curses.

The curse of futility on man's life can be overcome by applying the wisdom of God. The wisdom of God is not the wisdom of this world. If you apply the wisdom of God, you will escape the futility of life of this earth. Life on this earth is doomed to end in dust, futility and emptiness.

> **Howbeit we speak wisdom among them that are perfect: yet NOT THE WISDOM OF THIS WORLD, nor of the princes of this world, that come to nought:**

267

But we speak the wisdom of God in a mystery, even the hidden wisdom, which God ordained before the world unto our glory.

1 Corinthians 2:6-7

God's wisdom from above is the master key to overcoming the curse on this earth. Anything in the Word of God is the wisdom from above. Following any aspect of the Word of God will lift you above the curse.

For instance, the wisdom of God says, " Seek ye first the kingdom of God and His righteousness and all these things will be added" (Matthew 6:33). When you seek the kingdom of God, you set aside frustrating earthly ambitions. When you set your heart on seeking God's kingdom, the supernatural power of God is released to make you prosper. Do not ask me how it happens because I do not know.

When you work for God, the curse that is in the ground is avoided because your work is not just to get bread. You must remember that the ground is cursed. "In the sweat of thy face shall thou eat bread..." (Genesis 3:19). In serving the Lord, you are not serving your own interest. You are not tilling the ground for bread. You are working in His supernatural vineyard! You will receive a supernatural harvest! When you seek the kingdom of God, you invoke many promises that are reserved for servants of God. For instance, those who serve Him are promised to spend their days in prosperity. Serving God is different from working for yourself.

If they obey and serve him, they shall spend their days in prosperity, and their years in pleasures.

Job 36:11

Following God's word and doing His work will cause you to spend your life on earth in such a way that it is not futile any more. You are lifted above the earthly limitations and frustrations that exist in the world.

As many as are led by the Spirit of God, they are the sons of God (Romans 8:14). As soon as you give yourself to the Holy Spirit and allow yourself to be led by Him, you enter the supernatural state of being a son of God. Instead of being a son of man who lives in a cursed existence, you are lifted into a supernatural existence. This is why following the Holy Spirit is one of the wisest things to do.

Many Christians have forsaken the wisdom of being led by the Spirit. This is the reason for the poverty! This is the reason for the sweating! This is the reason for the struggle! The curse is everywhere. You need the wisdom of God to circumnavigate it and escape the molestation of the curse! You need the wisdom of God to circumnavigate the road of sweating, struggles and stagnation.

CHAPTER 24

How You Can Break a Curse by the Anointing

And it shall come to pass in that day, that his BURDEN shall be taken away from off THY SHOULDER, and his YOKE from off THY NECK, and the YOKE shall be destroyed because of the anointing.

Isaiah 10:27

The curse is the greatest burden on mankind. The curse is a yoke on your neck. A curse follows you everywhere and colours everything you do. It is only by the power of the Holy Spirit that you can break away from the curse. In Isaiah, you learn that the yoke can be removed from your shoulders and your neck by the anointing of the Holy Spirit.

The curse is found all over the earth. The coming of our Lord Jesus and the coming of the new Heaven and earth will usher in an era in which there is no curse. For now, there are curses everywhere and almost everyone walks into a curse somewhere.

It is virtually impossible to live on this earth without having some kind of a curse working in your life. Many of the steps that human beings take activate existing curses and multiply frustration in their lives. Most people do things that tend to poverty and difficulty. Stubbornness in children leads to many curses. Men naturally walk into the futility of working life with little to show for their lives at the end of it all.

Women are inexorably drawn to men and live their lives in a way that fulfils the curse on women. Haters of Jews instinctively fight against Israel, thereby multiplying the curse. Black people all over the world continue to take steps that make them the last and the least in most things.

It is time to break curses. It is time to break the curse that is following you. It is time to break away from the path of molestation! You can break with a curse by exiting the cursed path! That is how to break a curse! Break away from the cursed path!

The master key to breaking away from the curse, the burden and the yoke, is the anointing. The anointing is the Holy Spirit. The master key to exiting the cursed path is to follow the direction of the Holy Spirit! How is the anointing going to break the curse?

The master key to rising above the cursed existence on this earth, is to be led by the Holy Spirit!

The master key to exiting a cursed path is to listen to the voice of God!

The master key to rising above the cursed existence of your fellow human beings, is to be totally influenced by the light that comes from God's Word!

Let me prove this to you by the Word of God.

1. **Israel exits the cursed path of other nations by following the voice of God.**

   And it shall come to pass, IF THOU SHALT HEARKEN DILIGENTLY UNTO THE VOICE OF THE LORD THY GOD, to observe and to do all his commandments which I command thee this day, that the Lord thy God will set thee on HIGH ABOVE ALL NATIONS of the earth:

   Deuteronomy 28:1

   Notice how Israel was to be different from other nations by doing this one thing. Following God's voice would change their destiny and make them rise above all other nations. The cursed existence on all human beings would be alleviated if they followed the voice of God. Following the voice of God will cause you to be far above all your colleagues.

2. **Christians exit the cursed path of ordinary people by being led by the Holy Spirit.**

   For as many as are LED BY THE SPIRIT of God, they are the SONS OF GOD.

   Romans 8:14

   When you are led by the Holy Spirit, you will not live your life as an ordinary person. You will live your life as a son of God. Living like a son of God depends on your ability to be led by the Spirit of God.

Kenneth Hagin taught that the difference between ministers is their ability to be led by the Holy Spirit. Your ability to be led by the Holy Spirit is probably the most important skill that you must develop as a Christian. If you can learn how to be led by the Spirit, you will constantly be led away from an ordinary human existence to a higher and better life.

On many occasions, being led by the Spirit of God caused me to exit the cursed path. Whenever God leads you, do not struggle with Him. He is leading you to the exit that takes you away from the curses in this world.

When I finished medical school, the Holy Spirit directed me to give myself wholly to the ministry. This meant that I was to pursue ministry and forget about all other possible ways of making money and prospering in this life. That direction which came from the Holy Spirit and the Word of God caused me to rise above most of my colleagues and fellow strugglers. The life I now live could never have been given to me by being a medical doctor.

On another occasion, I found the Lord leading me away from debt. By leading me into a life without debt, I entered into a realm of unusual prosperity. Today, most of the struggles of businessmen, ministries and nations are the struggles of paying back debts owed. Little did I know, when I was being directed away from debt, that I was being made to exit the cursed path of indebtedness, frustration and poverty. I was being made to rise above the curse of frustration that is everywhere.

On many occasions, I found the Lord leading me to build something. Little did I know that simply getting involved in building was enabling my exit from the cursed existence that is everywhere. The curse of Noah was a curse to be a servant of servants. Servants do not build. The day you start building is the day you start rising above the curse of inferiority.

Each time I have a meeting and share with other Christians certain key things that lead us away from the curse of Noah, they look at me in disbelief. I have experienced such struggles with my own leaders when I encouraged them to build. Perhaps I would not have had such struggles if I had been organising an anniversary celebration in which we make T-shirts, spend money and celebrate endlessly. People operating under the curse of Noah love to celebrate endless anniversaries even though they have accomplished little and built nothing.

As I look back, I realise that the Holy Spirit has been leading me to take decisions and turns that seem peculiar to many. It is those very Holy Spirit influenced decisions that were the exit from the accursed path. Many leaders who were supposed to assist me were so opposed to my ideas that I had to bypass them and use people who would simply implement my instructions.

Those who could not assist me were often people who could not rise above the curse nor understand the direction of the Holy Spirit. Listen to me my friend! Black people generally struggle to rise above being the last or lowest in anything that they do. It is a mysterious and amazing reality! Only the direction of the Holy Spirit can supernaturally lead you out of this curse and into a glorious existence. The Word of God and the direction of the Holy Spirit is ordained for your glory. The combination of the Word of God and the Holy Spirit is the wisdom of God for your life. Notice this wonderful scripture that is one of the most important scriptures in the whole of the New Testament.

> **But we speak the wisdom of God in a mystery, even the hidden wisdom, which God ordained before the world unto our glory:**
>
> **1 Corinthians 2:7**

3. **God's people exit the cursed path of darkness through the light of God.**

    Arise, SHINE; for thy light is come, and the glory of the Lord is risen upon thee.

    For, behold, THE DARKNESS SHALL COVER THE EARTH, AND GROSS DARKNESS THE PEOPLE:

but the Lord shall arise upon thee, and his glory shall be seen upon thee.

Isaiah 60:1-2

You will notice that you begin to shine when the light of God and the glory of God rise upon you. Most human beings do not shine in this life. The vast majority of people live in frustration and difficulty. That cannot be called shining. Notice in this beautiful prophecy, that darkness covers the entire earth and gross darkness covers all people. The gross darkness that covers all people is the condition that the whole world is struggling under.

Darkness represents the curse, difficulty and evil. The light represents God's word, God's wisdom and God's direction for your life. You begin to shine when the light of God comes into your life. The light of God is the Word of God. The light of God is the direction that comes from the Holy Spirit. The light of God is the wisdom that comes to you from the wisdom of God. The Word of God is always light and it is always delivering you from the darkness and the gross darkness that is upon the world today.

Thy word is a lamp unto my feet, and a light unto my path.

Psalm 119:105

Through the Word of God and the direction that comes to you from the voice of God, the Gentiles shall come to thy light, and kings to the brightness of thy rising. Through the wonderful direction that comes to you from the Word of God, many will come to you to study and understand what you are doing.

Through the Word of God and the direction that comes to you from the voice of God, thy sons shall come from far, and thy daughters shall be nursed at thy side. Many people will come to you and call you their father. You will enjoy the blessing of daughters being nursed at your side.

Through the Word of God and the direction that comes to you from the voice of God, your sons will be brought from far, their silver and their gold with them, unto the name of the Lord thy God, and to the Holy One of Israel, because He hath glorified thee.

Through the Word of God and the direction that comes to you from the voice of God, the sons also of them that afflicted thee shall come bending unto thee; and all they that despised thee shall bow themselves down at the soles of thy feet; and they shall call thee, the city of the Lord, the Zion of the Holy One of Israel.

As you can see, the curse of darkness is blocked, totally stopped and overcome by the light that comes from God. You begin to shine because the light of God has risen up upon your life. Frustration, struggles, molestation and difficulty become a thing of the past as you allow the light of God to shine in your life.

CHAPTER 25

How You Can Avert a Curse by Restoring Father-Son Relationships

Behold, I will send you Elijah the prophet before the coming of the great and dreadful day of the Lord:

And he shall turn the heart of the fathers to the children, and the heart of the children to their fathers, LEST I COME AND SMITE THE EARTH WITH A CURSE.

Malachi 4:5-6

One of the main reasons for the curse in the world is the continual disconnection between children and their fathers. Establishing the link between the hearts and the lives of sons and fathers is a master key to averting the curse.

Re-establishing the broken link between fathers and children is a vital key to averting a curse. You will notice in the scripture that there is a threat to unleash fresh curses in the world.

The Word of God says, honour your father and you mother that it may be well with you. But if you do not even know your father, how can you honour him? If you have nothing to do with your father, how can you honour him? If you have been told bad things about your father and have nothing to do with him, how can you honour him?

Malachi 4:6 above talks about the hearts of the fathers and the hearts of the children. When you have been told negative things about your father, your heart and your mind are far from him. You have nothing to do with him and you do not want to know about him. We learn from Malachi that the disconnection at the level of the heart is dangerous and brings about a curse.

You can avert the curse by establishing or re-establishing the link between yourself and your father in your heart.

You can also avert the curse by re-establishing the link between yourself and your son.

It is an important process for you to turn yourself towards your father or towards your children in your heart.

In the ministry, people's hearts are turned away from the one who brought them up, trained them and ordained them. They may never openly insult their spiritual fathers, but their hearts are turned away. It is important to establish a link at the heart level between yourself and your spiritual father in the ministry.

It is important to re-establish every important relationship that God ordained for you in life and ministry. This is how to avert a curse. Analyse your life very carefully. See if you are disconnected at the heart level from any important father-son relationship. God is seeking to shield you from the smiting of a curse! You are delivered from all forms of wickedness and punishment in the Name of Jesus, as you turn your heart in the right direction.

CHAPTER 26

How You Can Neutralize a Curse with Blessings

Thus saith the Lord, As the new wine is found in the cluster, and one saith, DESTROY IT NOT; FOR A BLESSING IS IN IT: so will I do for my servants' sakes, that I may not destroy them all.

Isaiah 65:8

This scripture teaches that you cannot be destroyed because a blessing is found in you. "Destroy it not, because there is a blessing in it." Even though you may have brought upon yourself a curse, the presence of a blessing can prevent you from being destroyed.

Most of the problems in our lives arise from curses. Most of the things we do not want for ourselves have been spoken to people as curses. Most of the good things we desire in lives have already been spoken over people as blessings.

Somehow, we believe that these things we desire came upon people because they had the right attitudes. We are brought up to believe that everything we will ever have must be as a result of hard work and sacrifice. Reading the Bible will show you that many of the things you desire actually happen to people as a result of blessings being spoken over their lives, rather than them working very hard.

Indeed, many things come to us because of our hard work. But many things also come to people because a specific blessing has been spoken over their lives.

There are many people who work very hard and still do not have the good things we all desire. If you work very hard but do not have the blessing of the Lord over your life, your hard work amounts to nothing.

It is important to desire blessings that have already been declared and that are already governing our world. Look carefully and you will see that it is blessings that lift people up and determine the outcome of their destiny. Desire each one of these blessings and speak them over your life and over the lives of those you love.

You must desire powerful blessings and work towards them, because they can absolutely neutralize the power of any curse in your life. You may never know if you have done anything to incur a curse in your life. It is very likely that you may have. You must work towards triggering off blessings in your life. These blessings are very important to you because they neutralize all lingering curses.

Curses can be neutralized by blessings. A blessing often results in the exact opposite of a curse. Therefore, if you receive a blessing to go up, it neutralizes the curse that makes you go down. A curse to go down is neutralized by a blessing that makes you go up!

Let's have a look at how curses and blessings neutralize each other in the scripture.

Seven Neutralizing Blessings

1. **I want you to notice how the curse of *demotion* in Deuteronomy 28:43 is completely neutralized by the blessing of *promotion* in Deuteronomy 28:13.**

But it shall come to pass, if thou wilt not hearken unto the voice of the Lord thy God, to observe to do all his commandments and his statutes which I command thee this day; that ALL THESE CURSES shall come upon thee, and overtake thee:

The stranger that is within thee shall get up above thee very high; and THOU SHALT COME DOWN VERY LOW.

Deuteronomy 28:15, 43

And ALL THESE BLESSINGS shall come on thee, and overtake thee, if thou shalt hearken unto the voice of the Lord thy God. Blessed shalt thou be in the city, and blessed shalt thou be in the field.

And the lord shall make thee the head, and not the tail; AND THOU SHALT BE ABOVE ONLY, AND THOU SHALT NOT BE BENEATH; if that thou hearken unto the commandments of the Lord thy God, which I command thee this day, to observe and to do them:

Deuteronomy 28:2-3, 13

2. **I want you to notice how the curse of *financial difficulty* in Malachi 3:9 is completely neutralized by the blessing of *super abundance* Malachi 3:10-12.**

Invoking the blessing by paying tithes rebukes the agents of the curse. Who are the agents of the curse? The agents of the curse are the devourers who have been sent to swallow up your increase. The blessings of paying tithes totally wipe out the agents that bring the curse. This is one of the clearest examples of how a blessing neutralizes curse.

YE ARE CURSED WITH A CURSE: for ye have robbed me, even this whole nation.

Malachi 3:9

Bring ye all the tithes into the storehouse, that there may be meat in mine house, and prove me now herewith, saith the Lord of hosts, if I will not open you the windows of heaven, and POUR YOU OUT A BLESSING, that there shall not be room enough to receive it.

And I will rebuke the devourer for your sakes, and he shall not destroy the fruits of your ground; neither shall your vine cast her fruit before the time in the field, saith the Lord of hosts.

And all nations shall call you blessed: for ye shall be a delightsome land, saith the Lord of hosts.

Malachi 3:10-12

3. **I want you to notice how the curse *in all that you set your hand to do* in Deuteronomy 28:20 is completely neutralized by the blessing *on all that you set your hand to do* in Deuteronomy 28:8.**

The curse is declared on everything you do with your hands. But the blessing is equally declared on everything you do with your hands. The curse is targeted at what you set your hands on and the blessing is targeted at the same hands. If you have made a mistake and brought upon yourself a curse on the work of your hands, you can take a step that will bring a blessing on the work of your hands.

The Lord shall send upon thee CURSING, vexation, and rebuke, IN ALL THAT THOU SETTEST THINE HAND UNTO FOR TO DO, until thou be destroyed, and until thou perish quickly; because of the wickedness of thy doings, whereby thou hast forsaken me.

Deuteronomy 28:20

The Lord shall command the BLESSING upon thee in thy storehouses, and IN ALL THAT THOU SETTEST THINE HAND UNTO; and he shall bless thee in the land which the Lord thy God giveth thee.

Deuteronomy 28:8

4. **I want you to notice how the curse of *sickness* in Deuteronomy 28:21-22 is completely neutralized by the blessings of *health* in Exodus 23:25.**

    The opposite of sickness is health. The curse brings sickness and the blessing brings health. Every curse of sickness in your body is completely neutralized by the blessing of health!

The Lord SHALL MAKE THE PESTILENCE CLEAVE UNTO THEE, until he have consumed thee from off the land, whither thou goest to possess it. The Lord shall SMITE THEE WITH A CONSUMPTION, AND WITH A FEVER, AND WITH AN INFLAMMATION, AND WITH AN EXTREME BURNING, and with the sword, and with blasting, and with mildew; and they shall pursue thee until thou perish.

Deuteronomy 28:21-22

And ye shall serve the Lord your God, and he shall bless thy bread, and thy water; and I WILL TAKE SICKNESS AWAY from the midst of thee.

Exodus 23:25

5. **I want you to notice how the curse of *drought* in Deuteronomy 28:24 is completely neutralized by the blessings of *rain* in Deuteronomy 28:12.**

   The blessing of rain brings the much needed water. The curse of drought takes away the much needed water. As you can see, the blessing is the direct opposite of the curse.

   The Lord SHALL MAKE THE RAIN OF THY LAND POWDER AND DUST: from heaven shall it come down upon thee, until thou be destroyed.

   Deuteronomy 28:24

   The Lord shall open unto thee his good treasure, THE HEAVEN TO GIVE THE RAIN UNTO THY LAND IN HIS SEASON, and to bless all the work of thine hand: and thou shalt lend unto many nations, and thou shalt not borrow.

   Deuteronomy 28:12

6. **I want you to notice how the curse of *being an astonishment and a byword* in Deuteronomy 28:37 is completely neutralized by the blessings of *being an awesome wonder* in Deuteronomy 28:10.**

   If somebody has cursed you to become an astonishment and a byword, the blessing of God to become a wonder will neutralize that curse. You must do things that will bring about blessings in your life. The more blessings that are spoken over your life, the further you are from having terrible curses being fulfilled in your life.

   And thou shalt become an astonishment, a proverb, and a byword, among all nations whither the Lord shall lead thee.

   Deuteronomy 28:37

Then all the nations of the world will see that you are a people claimed by the Lord, and they will stand in AWE of you.

Deuteronomy 28:10 (NLT)

7. **I want you to notice how the curse of a *failed harvest* in Deuteronomy 28:38-42 is completely neutralized by the blessing of an *abundant harvest* in Deuteronomy 28:11.**

Thou shalt carry much seed out into the field, and SHALT GATHER BUT LITTLE IN; for THE LOCUST SHALL CONSUME IT. Thou shalt plant vineyards, and dress them, but shalt neither drink of the wine, nor gather the grapes; for THE WORMS SHALL EAT THEM. Thou shalt have olive trees throughout all thy coasts, but thou shalt not anoint thyself with the oil; for thine olive shall cast his fruit. Thou shalt beget sons and daughters, but THOU SHALT NOT ENJOY THEM; for they shall go into captivity. All thy trees and fruit of thy land shall THE LOCUST CONSUME.

Deuteronomy 28:38-42

And the Lord shall make thee PLENTEOUS IN GOODS, in the FRUIT OF THY BODY, and in the FRUIT OF THY CATTLE, and in the FRUIT OF THY GROUND, in the land which the Lord sware unto thy fathers to give thee.

Deuteronomy 28:11

May the blessings that make you go up far outweigh the curses that make you go down!

CHAPTER 27

How You Can Stop a Curse with a Multitude of Blessings

Joseph is a fruitful bough, even a fruitful bough by a well; whose branches run over the wall: The archers have sorely GRIEVED HIM, and SHOT AT HIM, and HATED HIM: But his bow abode in strength, and the arms of his hands were made strong by the hands of the mighty God of Jacob; (from thence is the shepherd, the stone of Israel:)

Even BY THE GOD OF THY FATHER, WHO SHALL HELP THEE; and by the Almighty, who shall bless thee WITH BLESSINGS of heaven above, blessings of the deep that lieth under, blessings of the breasts, and of the womb:

The BLESSINGS OF THY FATHER HAVE PREVAILED above the blessings of my progenitors unto the utmost bound of the everlasting hills: they shall be on the head of Joseph, and on the crown of the head of him that was separate from his brethren.

Genesis 49:22-26

Joseph began to feel the presence of the curse quite early in life. He experienced hatred, rejection, slavery, poverty and imprisonment. These are definitely curses of frustration. Yet, Joseph overcame and annulled these terrible curses.

You can stop a curse in your life through the variety of blessings you receive. If your father gives you a variety of gifts, you would have been helped more than someone who received one little gift from his father. The many gifts you receive will help you prevail in life. Why have one blessing when you can have many different blessings? Joseph was fortunate because he received many unusual and unrelated blessings. The extraordinary blessings of the womb, the unusual blessings of the breast, the rich blessings of the deep and the amazing blessings of the heavens above. This cocktail of blessings lifted Joseph from the curse of prison and slavery. Through the many blessings that his father spoke over his life, Joseph became the famous prime minister we read about.

Blessings are a great source of help in this life. The life of Joseph is an illustration of how blessings can help an ordinary person rise above his difficulty.

Joseph had three main problems in this life.

The first problem that Joseph had was the problem of being hated and rejected by his brethren. Hatred is a very painful thing to sense, especially from those who are supposed to be close to you. Hatred is a difficult thing to rise above. Rejection is an equally painful experience.

The second problem that Joseph had was that he was hurt, grieved and sorely wounded by his brethren.

The third problem that Joseph had was that he was shot at, attacked and vilified by his own brethren (Genesis 49:23). Indeed, many of us have experienced these three problems in one way or another.

Perhaps people who should have loved you have hated you. Perhaps you have been hurt so much in this life. Perhaps you have been rejected. Sadness, sorrow and weeping may be common in your life. Today, God has a solution for the hatred, the rejection and the many attacks and hurts of your life.

Joseph Annuls the Curse

1.   **Joseph overcame because he had a variety of blessings from his father.**

Some people only receive one blessing in their lives. But Joseph received many blessings from his father. All the different blessings you receive will help you in this life.

How did God help Joseph? God helped Joseph by blessing him with a variety of blessings. Notice the scripture below. Joseph remained strong because God made his hands strong. God the Father helped him by blessing him with the blessings of heaven, the blessings of the deep, the blessings of the breasts and the blessings of the womb.

But his bow abode in strength, and the arms of his hands were made strong

by the hands of the mighty God of Jacob; (from thence is the shepherd, the stone of Israel:)

Even BY THE GOD OF THY FATHER, WHO SHALL HELP THEE; and by the Almighty, who shall bless thee WITH BLESSINGS of heaven above, blessings of the deep that lieth under, blessings of the breasts, and of the womb:

Genesis 49:24-25

Whenever God blesses you, you are helped! You must do whatever you can to induce the blessing of God in your life. God has a plan to release His blessing as you obey His Word and walk in His light. The blessings of the womb, the blessings of the breasts, the blessings of heaven above and the blessings of the deep, are the mystical blessings that were given to Joseph by Almighty God. May you encounter all these four dimensions of mysterious blessings.

i) *The blessings of heaven* above speak of being blessed
    with spiritual things. Joseph was blessed with visions and
    dreams from above. He was also blessed with the power
    of interpreting dreams. Those are surely the blessings of
    heaven above. Joseph was a gifted man. He had spiritual
    insight. He had spiritual wisdom. He had the gift of
    leadership. He had the gift of management. He had the
    blessings of heaven above.

ii) *The blessings of the deep* speak of the blessings of wealth.
    All the wealth of our world is down below, hidden deep
    in the earth. The gold, the silver, the diamonds and the
    oil are buried below the earth's surface and in the deepest
    parts of the earth. Joseph became one of the most powerful
    and richest men in the whole world. These are surely the
    blessings of the deep.

iii) *The blessings of the breast* speak of the blessings of comfort
    and the blessings of provision. The breast is a source of
    comfort. The breast is a source of provision for a child. A
    baby does not need rice, meat, orange juice or even water,
    when it has breast milk. The breast milk is everything
    that the child needs. This is why the breast is a symbol of
    provision. The softness of the breast symbolises the comfort
    and the consolation that it ministers.

Joseph was comforted by the Lord from all his sufferings.
God gave him a beloved and a wife called Asenath. He enjoyed
the practical comfort of Asenath's wonderful breasts. He enjoyed
the practical comfort of the Lord through the restoration of his
life back to him. Those were the blessings of the breast.

Joseph enjoyed the practical comfort of the Lord because
God took care of him and provided for him everywhere he
went. Throughout his experiences of being a slave and then to
Potiphar's house and then to prison, he was taken care of. God
gave him favour everywhere he went. All he needed was God's
favour and he had it. Surely, these are the blessings of the breast.
The blessing of the breast is the blessing of abundant supply of

your needs. Through the blessings of the breast, Joseph was mightily helped by God to overcome the hatred and the hurts of his youth.

iv) *The blessings of the womb* are the blessings of having children and the blessings of fruitfulness. Joseph was blessed with two wonderful children, Ephraim and Manasseh. These two boys became tribes of Israel. God blessed him with the blessing of a large heritage. His children multiplied and grew into millions. These definitely are the blessings of the womb. Receive the blessing of fruitfulness in your life today!

2. Joseph overcame because his father's blessings prevailed against hatred and rejection.

The BLESSINGS OF THY FATHER HAVE PREVAILED above the blessings of my progenitors unto the utmost bound of the everlasting hills:

they shall be on the head of Joseph, and on the crown of the head of him that was separate from his brethren.

Genesis 49:26

The blessings of Joseph's father prevailed against the hatred that was unleashed against Joseph by his brothers. The blessings of your father will prevail against any hatred that is unleashed against you from now on. This is why you need to receive the blessing of a father. Receive the prevailing blessing of a father. The blessings of Joseph also prevailed against the rejection that he experienced in life.

The blessings of Jacob prevailed against the hurts that his son experienced in life. A person who is wounded cannot walk straight. A person who is wounded cannot accomplish the same things that a person without injuries accomplishes. This is why wounded soldiers are removed from battle. In spite of the fact that Joseph was sorely grieved and greatly hurt, he overcame and became the greatest person in Egypt, second only to Pharaoh. The blessings of his father had prevailed in his life. The blessings of your father will prevail in your life. You are finally coming into the place of prosperity because of the blessings of your father.

The blessings of Jacob prevailed against the attacks that were unleashed against Joseph by his brothers. The archers shot at Joseph, intending to wipe him out. But Joseph overcame because the blessing of his father prevailed in his life.

The blessings of his father were even more than the blessings of Jacob's progenitors, which are Abraham and Isaac. Joseph had indeed received a very strong blessing from his father. May the Father's blessings come upon you and prevail against all those who hate you! May your father find you worthy to bless you with such abundant blessings.

CHAPTER 28

How You Can Be Delivered From a Curse through a Prophet

And by a prophet the Lord brought Israel out of Egypt, and by a prophet was he preserved.

Hosea 12:13

The ministry of the prophet is an amazing agency through which you can be delivered from many curses. Israel was locked up in Egypt, suffering under the curse of slavery. God's power appeared to them through the ministry of the prophet, Moses. Through the ministry of the prophet, the political power of Egypt was unravelled. The military might of Egypt was neutralized. The curse of bondage, struggling and molestation by the Egyptians was broken through the ministry of Moses the prophet.

Israel was stuck in the mud! Israel was stuck in Egypt! Israel was bound in Egypt! Israel had no freedom!

Therefore they did set over them TASKMASTERS to AFFLICT them with their burdens. And they built for Pharaoh treasure cities, Pithom and Raamses. But the more they AFFLICTED them, the more they multiplied and grew. And they were GRIEVED because of the children of Israel. And the Egyptians made the children of Israel to serve with rigour: And they made their lives BITTER WITH HARD BONDAGE, in morter, and in brick, and in all manner of service in the field: all their service, wherein they made them serve, was with RIGOUR.

Exodus 1:11-14

The future of Israel was dark and gloomy until the prophet came on the scene. Bitterness, hard bondage, affliction and slavery, was the portion of all Israelites. Perhaps, this is how you could describe your life. It is a cursed existence and God wants to set you free from every curse. A prophet is a senior minister and agent of God. Through the ministry of a prophet you can be miraculously liberated from a curse just as Israel was miraculously liberated from Egypt. "And by a prophet the Lord brought Israel out of Egypt, and by a prophet was he preserved." Let us now look at several more examples of how a prophet's ministry delivered people from the curse.

Twelve Curses that You Can Be Delivered from Through a Prophet

1. **The curse of poisonous water, the curse of barren lands, the curse of unfruitfulness and the curse of poverty are broken by the ministry of the prophet.**

A prophet is a powerful agent for the deliverance of all kinds of curses. Read your Bible and believe in the powerful ministry of a prophet. You can be delivered from curses by the ministry of a prophet.

> And the men of the city said unto Elisha, Behold, I pray thee, the situation of this city is pleasant, as my lord seeth: but the water is naught, and the ground barren. And he said, Bring me a new cruse, and put salt therein. And they brought it to him.
>
> And he went forth unto the spring of the waters, and cast the salt in there, and said, Thus saith the Lord, I have healed these waters; there shall not be from thence any more death or barren land.
>
> So the waters were healed unto this day, according to the saying of Elisha which he spake.
>
> 2 Kings 2:19-22

2. **By a prophet you are delivered from the curse of ridicule, insults, mockery and scorn.**

All those who laugh at you will receive a shock as God overturns the situation. Anyone who mocks God's servant is due for a curse. You must be careful when you lift up your horn to make fun of God's servant. May all mockers receive a shock that they will not like! Your house, your life and your ministry can burn down because you mocked at God's servant. Anyone who tries to inflict the curse of ridicule, insults, accusations and mockery on God's servant is due for a curse himself.

> And he went up from thence unto Bethel: and as he was going up by the way, there came forth little children out of

the city, and mocked him, and said unto him, Go up, thou bald head; go up, thou bald head.

And he turned back, and looked on them, and cursed them in the name of the Lord. And there came forth two she bears out of the wood, and tare forty and two children of them.

                                                    2 Kings 2:23-24

3.   By the ministry of the prophet you are delivered from the curse of indebtedness.

The curse of being dispossessed of your home and possessions is broken in your life! You will not live your life any more in bondage. Many people in this world are in debt. They live their lives drowning in debts they have incurred. The world system is full of deception, always encouraging innocent victims to go into debt. The banks reach out to unsuspecting victims and draw them into debts which they do not need. Through the curse of indebtedness, many people live in fear and bondage and are unable to serve God. Today, by the ministry of a prophet, you are coming out of every kind of debt. Mortgages, loans, and all forms of debts are finally wiped out of your life, by the ministry of the prophet. Have faith in God! Your day of freedom has come!

Now there cried a certain woman of the wives of the sons of the prophets unto Elisha, saying, Thy servant my husband is dead; and thou knowest that thy servant did fear the Lord: and the creditor is come to take unto him my two sons to be bondmen.

And Elisha said unto her, What shall I do for thee? tell me, what hast thou in the house? And she said, Thine handmaid hath not any thing in the house, save a pot of oil.

Then he said, Go, borrow thee vessels abroad of all thy neighbours, even empty vessels; borrow not a few.

And when thou art come in, thou shalt shut the door upon thee and upon thy sons, and shalt pour out into all those vessels, and thou shalt set aside that which is full.

So she went from him, and shut the door upon her and upon her sons, who brought the vessels to her; and she poured out.

And it came to pass, when the vessels were full, that she said unto her son, Bring me yet a vessel. And he said unto her, There is not a vessel more. And the oil stayed.

Then she came and told the man of God. And he said, Go, sell the oil, and pay thy debt, and live thou and thy children of the rest.

2 Kings 4:1-7

4. By the ministry of a prophet you are delivered from the curse of barrenness.

God's power comes to your life through the prophet. Every curse in your family is broken by the power of God.

And he said, what then is to be done for her? And Gehazi answered, Verily she hath no child, and her husband is old.

And he said, call her. And when he had called her, she stood in the door. And he said, About this season, according to the time of life, thou shalt embrace a son. And she said, Nay, my lord, thou man of God, do not lie unto thine handmaid.

And the woman conceived, and bare a son at that season that Elisha had said unto her, according to the time of life.

2 Kings 4:14-17

5. By a prophet you are delivered from the curse of sudden death, demonic surprises, poisoning, wicked traps and snares of the devil.

It was through the ministry of a prophet that the curse of death in the pot was overcome. The sons of the prophets had already eaten poisonous food. The curse of death was about to envelope the entire family of prophets. This curse was averted because of the ministry of the prophet, Elisha. Whatever curse and whatever surprise satan has for you is foiled today by the ministry of the prophet.

And Elisha came again to Gilgal: and there was a dearth in the land; and the sons of the prophets were sitting before him: and he said unto his servant, Set on the great pot, and seethe pottage for the sons of the prophets. And one went out into the field to gather herbs, and found a wild vine, and gathered thereof wild gourds his lap full, and came and shred them into the pot of pottage: for they knew them not.

So they poured out for the men to eat. And it came to pass, as they were eating of the pottage, that they cried out, and said, O thou man of God, THERE IS DEATH IN THE POT. And they could not eat thereof.

But he said, Then bring meal. And he cast it into the pot; and he said, Pour out for the people, that they may eat. And THERE WAS NO HARM IN THE POT.

2 Kings 4:38-41

6. By a prophet you are delivered from the curse of sickness and incurable diseases.

It was through the ministry of a prophet that healing came to Naaman the Syrian. There was no way that Naaman would have been healed from leprosy without the intervention of the prophet. Today, through the ministry of the prophet, you will experience the miracle of healing. The curse of sickness and disease is finally broken in your life today.

Now Naaman, captain of the host of the king of Syria, was a great man with his master, and honourable, because by him the Lord had given deliverance unto Syria: he was also a mighty man in valour, but he was a leper.

So Naaman came with his horses and with his chariot, and stood at the door of the house of Elisha. And Elisha sent a messenger unto him, saying, Go and wash in Jordan seven times, and thy flesh shall come again to thee, and thou shalt be clean. But Naaman was wroth, and went away, and said, Behold, I thought, He will surely come out to me, and stand, and call on the name of the Lord his God, and strike his hand over the place, and recover the leper. Are not Abana and Pharpar, rivers of Damascus, better than all the waters of Israel? May I not wash in them, and be clean? So he turned and went away in a rage.

And his servants came near, and spake unto him, and said, My father, if the prophet had bid thee do some great thing, wouldest thou not have done it? How much rather then, when he saith to thee, Wash, and be clean?

Then went he down, and dipped himself seven times in Jordan, according to the saying of the man of God: and his flesh came again like unto the flesh of a little child, and he was clean.

2 Kings 5:1, 9-14

7. By a prophet you are delivered from the curse of indebtedness and financial loss.

Today, many people have borrowed money and their businesses are turning into accursed pools of debt and bondage. For many people it will take the ministry of a prophet for them to come out of that cursed financial state.

And the sons of the prophets said unto Elisha, Behold now, the place where we dwell with thee is too strait for us. Let us go, we pray thee, unto Jordan, and take thence every man a beam, and let us make us a place there, where we may dwell. And he answered, Go ye.

And one said, Be content, I pray thee, and go with thy servants. And he answered, I will go. So he went with them. And when they came to Jordan, they cut down wood. But as one was felling a beam, the axe head fell into the water: and he cried, and said, Alas, master! for it was borrowed.

And the man of God said, Where fell it? And he shewed him the place. And he cut down a stick, and cast it in thither; and the iron did swim. Therefore said he, Take it up to thee. And he put out his hand, and took it.

2 Kings 6:1-7

Through the ministry of the prophet, the young men were saved from financial crisis.

8.   By a prophet you are delivered from the curse of defeat, humiliation and destruction.

Through the prophet there was foreknowledge about the enemy's plans. The armies of satan were defeated and destroyed through the ministry of the prophet.

Then the king of Syria warred against Israel, and took counsel with his servants, saying, In such and such a place shall be my camp.

And the man of God sent unto the king of Israel, saying, Beware that thou pass not such a place; for thither the Syrians are come down.

And the king of Israel sent to the place which the man of God told him and warned him of, and saved himself there, not once nor twice.

Therefore the heart of the king of Syria was sore troubled for this thing; and he called his servants, and said unto them, Will ye not shew me which of us is for the king of Israel? And one of his servants said, None, my lord, O king: but Elisha, the prophet that is in Israel, telleth the king of Israel the words that thou speakest in thy bedchamber.

2 Kings 6:8-12

9.   By a prophet you are delivered from the curse of the siege.

By a prophet you are delivered from the curse of an impossible situation. By a prophet, you are delivered from the curse of a crisis.

And there was a great famine in Samaria: and, behold, they besieged it, until an ass's head was sold for fourscore pieces of silver, and the fourth part of a cab of dove's dung for five pieces of silver.

2 Kings 6:25

Then Elisha said, Hear ye the word of the Lord; Thus saith the Lord, To morrow about this time shall a measure of fine flour be sold for a shekel, and two measures of barley for a shekel, in the gate of Samaria.

2 Kings 7:1

10. By a prophet you are delivered from the curse of famine, starvation and hunger.

By a prophet, a twenty-four hour miracle of provision is coming to your life.

And there was a great famine in Samaria: and, behold, they besieged it, until an ass's head was sold for fourscore pieces of silver, and the fourth part of a cab of dove's dung for five pieces of silver.

2 Kings 6:25

Then Elisha said, Hear ye the word of the Lord; Thus saith the Lord, To morrow about this time shall a measure of fine flour be sold for a shekel, and two measures of barley for a shekel, in the gate of Samaria.

2 Kings 7:1

11. By a prophet you are delivered from the curse of famine.

Then spake Elisha unto the woman, whose son he had restored to life, saying, Arise, and go thou and thine household, and sojourn wheresoever thou canst sojourn: for the Lord hath called for a famine; and it shall also come upon the land seven years.

And the woman arose, and did after the saying of the man of God: and she went with her household, and sojourned in the land of the Philistines seven years.

And it came to pass at the seven years' end, that the woman returned out of the land of the Philistines: and she went forth to cry unto the king for her house and for her land.

2 Kings 8:1-3

12. By a prophet you are delivered from the curse of injustice.

Through a prophet, receive the miracle of political favour, justice and fair treatment.

...And Gehazi said, My lord, O king, this is the woman, and this is her son, whom Elisha restored to life. And when the king asked the woman, she told him. So the king appointed unto her a certain officer, saying, Restore all that was hers, and all the fruits of the field since the day that she left the land, even until now.

2 Kings 8:5-6

CHAPTER 29

How You Can Overturn a Curse by Valuing Blessings

That there be no immoral or godless person like Esau, who sold his own birthright for a single meal. For you know that even afterwards, when **HE DESIRED TO INHERIT THE BLESSING, he was rejected, for he found no place for repentance, though he sought for it with tears.**

Hebrews 12:16-17 (NASB)

The curses in your life are overturned by the release of blessings. As you receive more and more blessings, they will overturn and overpower the curses that seek to destroy you. As you induce blessings in your life, they completely overpower and overcome the curses that exist everywhere.

For this reason, it is important to desire blessings and to seek them. You must actually fight to be blessed! You must seek to induce all kinds of blessings into your life.

The best example of someone who valued blessings and sought after them was Jacob. The fight between Jacob and Esau was a fight over blessings. I have never heard of Christians fighting over blessings pronounced by their father. I have heard of people fighting over inheritance and property, but not over the pronouncement of blessings. Unfortunately, Esau like many unspiritual people did not value his birthright or his spiritual blessings.

The Bible describes him as a profane person. The word "profane" is translated from the Greek word "bebelos". "Bebelos" means an irreligious person who despises sacred things. Anyone who despises sacred things will despise blessings! Esau despised the blessings that were rightfully his.

> And Jacob sod pottage: and Esau came from the field, and he was faint: And Esau said to Jacob, Feed me, I pray thee, with that same red pottage; for I am faint: therefore was his name called Edom. And Jacob said, Sell me this day thy birthright. And Esau said, Behold, I am at the point to die: and what profit shall this birthright do to me? And Jacob said, Swear to me this day; and he sware unto him: and he sold his birthright unto Jacob. Then Jacob gave Esau bread and pottage of lentiles; and he did eat and drink, and rose up, and went his way: thus Esau despised his birthright.
>
> Genesis 25: 29-34

If you are not spiritual, you will despise the concept of receiving blessings. Esau despised blessings and ended up as a struggler. I want you to desire each and every single blessing that is listed here because each one of them will have a powerful effect on your life.

The blessing that Esau despised was received happily by Jacob. This blessing gave him three advantages in this world and drowned out the effect of the curse on his life. The blessings that Jacob received overwhelmed the curses on the earth that affected everyone. This is going to be the effect of powerful blessings on your life. These blessings will completely overpower, overcome and overturn whatever curse is working in your life.

1. The blessings that Esau despised were given to Jacob and made him into a great and famous nation!

   ...Behold, I HAVE MADE HIM thy lord...

   Genesis 27:37

2. The blessings that Esau despised were given to Jacob and made him the master of his brethren.

   ...ALL HIS BRETHREN HAVE I GIVEN TO HIM for servants...

   Genesis 27:37

3. The blessings that Esau despised were given to Jacob and sustained him throughout his life!

   ...with corn and wine have I SUSTAINED HIM...

   Genesis 27:37

CHAPTER 30

How to Overcome Curses by Inducing Blessings

And YE SHALL SERVE the Lord your God, and
HE SHALL BLESS thy bread, and thy water; and I
will take sickness away from the midst of thee.

Exodus 23:25

FIFTEEN BLESSINGS YOU MUST INDUCE

1. **You can induce and produce a blessing on your life by serving God.**

    And YE SHALL SERVE the Lord your God, and HE SHALL BLESS thy bread, and thy water; and I will take sickness away from the midst of thee. There shall nothing cast their young, nor be barren, in thy land: the number of thy days I will fulfil.

    Exodus 23:25-26

    It is a great thing to serve the Lord because to serve God is to be blessed. God is actually looking for someone to bless and not really someone to work. There is nothing we can do to add to the height or the stature of God, nor to His work or His will.

2. **You can induce and produce a blessing on your life by accepting the call of God to be close to Him.**

    BLESSED IS THE MAN WHOM THOU CHOOSEST, and causest to approach unto thee, that he may dwell in thy courts: we shall be satisfied with the goodness of thy house, even of thy holy temple.

    Psalm 65:4

    God is a God who blesses those whom He has chosen to serve Him. To be called to work for God is a blessing. You cannot improve God in any way. You cannot make God look good or bad. You and I are nothing. We need God! God does not need us! The scripture above says, "Blessed is the man whom God chooses..." When you are chosen by God you are blessed. It is you who is blessed when you are chosen. "For, behold, those who are far from You will perish; You have destroyed all those who are unfaithful to You. But as for me, the nearness of God is my good; I have made the Lord GOD my refuge, that I may tell of all Your works" Psalms 73:27-28 (NASB).

3. You can induce and produce a blessing on your life by following the voice of God.

And it shall come to pass, if thou shalt hearken diligently unto the voice of the Lord thy God, to observe and to do all his commandments which I command thee this day, that the Lord thy God will set thee on high above all nations of the earth:

And ALL THESE BLESSINGS SHALL COME ON THEE, AND OVERTAKE THEE, IF THOU SHALT HEARKEN UNTO THE VOICE OF THE LORD THY GOD.

Deuteronomy 28:1-2

BLESSED IS THE MAN THAT HEARETH ME, watching daily at my gates, waiting at the posts of my doors.

Proverbs 8:34

... Blessed are all they that put their trust in him.

Psalm 2:12

The most important skill for a Christian to develop is the art of hearing God's voice. God's voice is what keeps you in the supernatural plain. The great promise of Deuteronomy 28 is that "Hearing the voice of God and obeying it will change your levels". You will be higher than any colleague anywhere. God said He will lift you above all the nations in the earth. Trust in the Lord with all your heart and lean not on your own understanding. People who trust in God have a special blessing on their lives.

Some people complain about how difficult it is to follow the will of God and to obey His voice. Instead of complaining about how difficult it is to obey the will of God, you should rather be talking about the blessing that comes from obeying the voice of God. I cannot say that I have experienced blessings because I became a medical doctor. Any blessing that I can count in my life today comes from following the voice of God. It is as simple as that! The voice of God led me to the ministry and led me to preach what I preach. That voice has brought me glory and honour.

For HE RECEIVED FROM GOD THE FATHER HONOUR AND GLORY, when there came such A VOICE to him from the excellent glory, This is my beloved Son, in whom I am well pleased.

2 Peter 1:17

4.   **You can induce and produce a blessing on your life by making great sacrifices for the Lord.**

And said, By myself have I sworn, saith the Lord, for BECAUSE THOU HAST DONE THIS THING, and hast not withheld thy son, thine only son: THAT IN BLESSING I WILL BLESS thee, and in multiplying I will multiply thy seed as the stars of the heaven, and as the sand which is upon the sea shore; and thy seed shall possess the gate of his enemies; and in thy seed shall all the nations of the earth be blessed; because thou hast obeyed my voice.

Genesis 22:16-18

The greatest blessings came on Abraham when he offered Isaac up as a sacrifice to God. God's declaration to Abraham came on the heels of his great sacrifice. You may not agree but God does notice the extent of our sacrifices. It is important for you to understand that there is no kind of service to God without sacrifice. Abel, Noah, Abraham, Isaac, Jacob, Moses, Joshua, David, Solomon and Gideon are just a few of the people who served God with many sacrifices. If you want to serve God, you will have to make sacrifices. Amazingly, a sacrifice induces blessings onto those who make the sacrifice. Notice the scripture below, which speaks about Jesus Christ the Lamb. The Lamb was declared worthy to receive power, riches, wisdom, strength, honour and glory!

Why was the Lamb declared worthy to receive power, riches, wisdom, strength, honour and glory? Because the Lamb gave Himself up as a sacrifice and was slain for all mankind. When you give up yourself in great sacrifice, you become worthy to receive many things that others can only read about.

Saying with a loud voice, worthy is the Lamb that was slain to receive power, and riches, and wisdom, and strength, and honour, and glory, and blessing.

Revelation 5:12

Do you want God to bless you with power, riches, wisdom, strength, honour and glory? Then give yourself up for His will and allow yourself to be slain like the Lamb.

5. **You can induce and produce a blessing in your life by having compassion on the helpless.**

Then the King will say to those on His right, 'Come, YOU WHO ARE BLESSED OF MY FATHER, inherit the kingdom prepared for you from the foundation of the world.

FOR I WAS HUNGRY, AND YOU GAVE ME SOMETHING TO EAT; I was thirsty, and you gave Me something to drink; I was a stranger, and you invited Me in; naked, and you clothed Me; I was sick, and you visited Me; I was in prison, and you came to Me.

Matthew 25:34-36 (NASB)

To care for helpless people is to set aside your selfish and myopic nature of wickedness and think like God does. God cares for everyone who is in need and who is afflicted by the devil. Few people in this world care for the helpless and the handicapped. Mighty blessings await those who care for the helpless, the weak and the handicapped.

6. **You can induce and produce a blessing in your life by having a love for the poor.**

    Blessed is he that considereth the poor: the Lord will deliver him in time of trouble.

    Psalm 41:1

    The poor are similar to the handicapped and the helpless. When you consider the poor, you bring God and His blessings into your life in an amazing way. God loves the poor. There are many scriptures that shower blessings on those who remember the poor. The poor must have the gospel preached to them. The poor have nothing to give you in return. The poor are the special objects of God's love and mercy. Reach out to them and God will reach out to you!

7. **You can induce and produce a blessing by honouring fathers and mothers.**

    Honour thy father and mother; (which is the first commandment with promise;) that it may be well with thee, and thou mayest live long on the earth.

    Ephesians 6:2-3

    God will bless those who honour fathers and mothers. To honour a father, you must be inspired by God. Carnally minded children do not honour their parents very much. Demonized children do not love and honour their parents. Many children have devils in them and do not honour their parents. Whenever a child grows to honour his father, he induces, invokes and stirs up blessings for himself. He is completely departed from a curse and demonic influence found in many children. Jesus Himself said I don't have a devil! And I know I don't have a devil because I honour my father!

    Jesus answered, I have not a devil; but I honour my Father, and ye do dishonour me.

    John 8:49

8.   You can induce and produce a blessing by ministering to the man of God.

And it fell on a day, that Elisha passed to Shunem, where was a great woman; and she constrained him to eat bread.

And so it was, that as oft as he passed by, he turned in thither to eat bread. And she said unto her husband, Behold now, I perceive that this is an holy man of God, which passeth by us continually.

Let us make a little chamber, I pray thee, on the wall; and let us set for him there a bed, and a table, and a stool, and a candlestick: and it shall be, when he cometh to us, that he shall turn in thither.

And it fell on a day, that he came thither, and he turned into the chamber, and lay there. And he said to Gehazi his servant, call this Shunammite. And when he had called her, she stood before him.

And he said unto him, say now unto her, Behold, thou hast been careful for us with all this care; what is to be done for thee? wouldest thou be spoken for to the king, or to the captain of the host? And she answered, I dwell among mine own people. And he said, what then is to be done for her?

And Gehazi answered, Verily she hath no child, and her husband is old. And he said, call her. And when he had called her, she stood in the door. And he said, about this season, according to the time of life, thou shalt embrace a son. And she said, Nay, my lord, thou man of God, do not lie unto thine handmaid.

2 Kings 4:8-16

Indeed, when the Shunammite woman ministered to Elisha, she stirred up the gift of God and provoked the miracle anointing that was on the man of God. By constantly ministering to him, providing a room for him, a table, food and shelter, the anointing was stirred up and she received a great miracle of childbirth. Her old husband was completely revived and enabled to impregnate her. A great miracle happened to her. This great historic miracle happened to her simply because she ministered to the man of God. The blessings of Galatians 6:7 comes to those who fulfil Galatians 6:6.

Let him that is taught in the word COMMUNICATE UNTO HIM THAT TEACHETH IN ALL GOOD THINGS. Be not deceived; God is not mocked: for whatsoever a man soweth, that shall he also reap.

Galatians 6:6-7

9. **You can induce and produce a blessing by being humble.**

Blessed are the meek: for they shall inherit the earth.

Matthew 5:5

Humble people are attractive. They attract blessings constantly. Little children who are orphaned and pitiful attract help from all over the world. As soon as the children are a little older, they become less attractive and fewer people want to help. The attractive thing about little children is their humility and purity. If you want to attract the blessings of your boss, learn to be genuinely humble. A proud look, a defiant attitude, aloofness and standoffishness, are the most unattractive characteristics you could ever carry with you. Arguments, denials, heated rebuffs are the most unattractive characteristics you could ever allow to be associated with you.

10. **You can induce and produce a blessing by hungering and thirsting after righteousness.**

Blessed are they which do hunger and thirst after righteousness: for they shall be filled.

Matthew 5:6

What a blessing it is to receive the anointing! My life changed when the Lord anointed me. It is because of the anointing that you are reading this book. The anointing comes to those who are hungry and thirsty for the things of God. The power of God comes to those who are thirsty. "O God, thou art my God; early will I seek thee: my soul thirsteth for thee, my flesh longeth for thee in a dry and thirsty land, where no water is; to see thy power and thy glory, so as I have seen thee in the sanctuary" (Psalm 63:1-2). It is very difficult to make someone drink water when he is not thirsty.

This is why people do not receive the anointing. They are simply not hungering and thirsting after the anointing. When you develop a strong desire for God and His power, you will be ninety percent nearer to receiving the anointing. It is a strong desire to see His power and glory that drives you to do all the things you must do to experience the anointing.

11. You can induce and produce a blessing by being merciful.

Blessed are the merciful: for they shall obtain mercy.

Matthew 5:7

The blessing of having your mistakes overlooked is the blessing that you induce by being merciful. Do you want the blessing of having your sins, mistakes and errors overlooked? You can induce that blessing by being merciful. Being merciful produces great blessings!

The world is like a soccer match and we are like the footballers chasing after the ball. There are match rules that are broken so many times. A referee who blows his whistle at every mistake will spoil the match and take away the blessing of the game. When you are in a relationship or in a marriage and you blow the whistle at every mistake, you take away the blessing of life itself.

This is why it is difficult to stay around super-melancholic people who only see your faults and point them out constantly. Blessed are the merciful because they will have the blessing of their mistakes being overlooked.

314

12. **You can induce and produce a blessing by being a peacemaker.**

Blessed are the peacemakers: for they shall be called the children of God.

Matthew 5:9

If the world had more peacemakers, there would be much more blessing in the world. The world is full of "case-makers" and quarrelsome people. Wars continue to be fought in our world because people do not forgive and do not make peace. When the devil is released from the pit of hell, he comes to gather the nations to battle against each other. Satan is the direct inspirer of all family quarrels, feuds, inter-tribal wars, terrorism and unending wickedness in our world. A great blessing will come into your life when you learn to step back and allow yourself to be "cheated" so that there can be peace.

13. **You can induce and produce a blessing by being pure in heart.**

Blessed are the pure in heart: for they shall see God.

Matthew 5:8

Being pure in heart induces one of the greatest blessings. Youthfulness, being clear, humble confessions and openness remove all shadows, glitches, spots and impurities from our lives. When these impurities of wickedness are not present, God will not only see through us but He will also reveal Himself to us.

There are few people who really see visions, trances and have significant dreams. The master key to seeing God is purity in the heart. Daniel was told by the angel, "You are greatly loved by the Lord."

Daniel was one of the people blessed with significant dreams, trances and visions. John, the beloved, called himself "the disciple whom Jesus loved." His great love for God was the amazing key that opened him up to the fantastic visions recorded in the book of Revelation. Do you want to see God? Do you

315

want the blessing of seeing God? You can induce it and produce it by becoming pure in heart.

How do you know when you are not pure in heart? You are not pure in heart when you are not open, clear or full of humility. Pride covers up terrible impurities and creates a world of hypocrisy with many attendant evils. Openness and humility will drive all forms of wicked impurities from our hearts.

Watch out for people who pretend and who cover up most of their lives. They are not pure in heart!

14. You can produce a blessing by believing without seeing.

Jesus saith unto him, Thomas, because thou hast seen me, thou hast believed: BLESSED ARE THEY THAT HAVE NOT SEEN, AND YET HAVE BELIEVED.

John 20:29

Those who have not seen and yet believe, bring upon themselves a great blessing. There are many people who claim to have received visions of Jesus calling them into the ministry. There are those who have heard voices and receive commands from Heaven. Such people are really fortunate to have had such experiences.

However, there is a large group of people who have never experienced such things and yet believe greatly in the call of God and the will of God. People who accomplish great things for God without seeing such visions are even more blessed than those who have seen the visions. John Wesley accomplished great things for God. His fruits are all over the world today. In his writings, I never read of him having any visions of Jesus. Without any visions, apparitions or trances, this man has borne fruits that are still in the earth today. Blessed are those who have not seen and yet believe! It is sad to say that there are many who have received fantastic visions from the Lord and yet have accomplished little.

15. You can induce and produce a blessing by being a reader.

BLESSED IS HE THAT READETH, and they that hear the words of this prophecy, and keep those things which are written therein: for the time is at hand.

Revelation 1:3

A great blessing can come into your life by reading books. If you want to induce a blessing on your life, you have to open yourself to reading special books that God brings to you. Martin Luther received the greatest blessing of his entire life by reading the Bible. Even though he was an ordained priest, he had not read much of the Bible. His great shock and transformation came when he read the books of Romans, Ephesians and the book of Psalms. He discovered to his amazement that salvation comes to man by faith and not by works.

I had been an ordinary Christian for years till I encountered books written by Kenneth Hagin. The great blessing of being anointed with the Holy Spirit and power came to me as I encountered Kenneth Hagin through books.

When I read the biography of John Wesley, I received one of the greatest boosts to my spiritual life. I was super-encouraged by his life, his trials and his wisdom. It was one of the turning points of my life. Reading about God's Generals through Roberts Liardon has been to me like watching a movie in which God speaks to me. I can hardly read any of those stories without being charged and without a fire being kindled in me.

O, how I wish ministers of the gospel would recognize the blessing that can come to them through reading!

CHAPTER 31

How You Can Counteract the Curse by Seeking Out Major Blessings

I call heaven and earth to record this day against you, that I have set before you life and death, blessing and cursing: therefore choose life, that both thou and thy seed may live:

Deuteronomy 30:19

Being a blessed person is more important than working hard or going to school. A curse is very effective in neutralizing your hard work and turning everything into nothing. A curse is very good at turning your efforts at education into nought. There is no explanation for the survival of the people of Israel, unless you accept the reality of blessings and curses. You must completely overturn the curses in your life and in your world by properly seeking the major blessings that are recorded in the Bible. Many people do not even know what a blessing is. Through this chapter, I want you to discover what a blessing is. When you know that something is a blessing, you must seek it.

It is time for you to seek the right thing. Seek for a blessing! Seek for these blessings to be pronounced and declared over your life. Learn about blessings! Discover what a blessing is! Study about blessed people! Read this book again! Target blessings! Choose blessings! Ask for blessings! Ask for a prayer! Honour your father! Let your heart turn towards your father! Serve God! Ask for hands to be laid on you! Do things that induce blessings!

A blessing in your life is more important than your hard work, your efforts and your family background. You would think that everyone would choose a blessing when it is set before them. Sadly, many people do not! They either despise blessings or they do not understand what blessings are.

Through a blessing you can counteract a curse, no matter how strong it is. It is the blessing that *makes you, sustains you* and *gives you* what you need! Pronounced blessings are mysterious because they lead to a series of apparently unrelated developments. Your life goes forward when a blessing is working in your life. I want you to study each of these blessings and seek them with all your heart. The presence of these blessings on your life will change everything for you.

Anyone who thought you were cursed will have to think again. Every curse in your life is overturned by the presence of a blessing! The following are blessings you must seek all the days of your life. Believe in them! Seek them! Pray for them! Ask for them! Your life will change and the curse will be overturned! God is giving you powerful blessings that will counteract every curse in your life. Through the reality of these blessings, you will counteract any curses that are operational in your life.

1. THE BLESSING OF FRUITFULNESS.

And GOD BLESSED THEM, and God said unto them, BE FRUITFUL, and multiply, and replenish the earth, and subdue it: and have dominion over the fish of the sea, and over the fowl of the air, and over every living thing that moveth upon the earth.

Genesis 1:28

And GOD BLESSED NOAH and his sons, and said unto them, BE FRUITFUL, and multiply, and replenish the earth.

Genesis 9:1

There is a blessing in being fruitful. It is worth stepping into the blessing of fruitfulness. God blessed Adam with the blessing of fruitfulness. This is a blessing. It is a blessing to be fruitful and it is a blessing that God wants you to have. Recognize that it is a blessing to bear fruit. You are walking in blessings when you walk in fruitfulness. Anyone who bears good fruit has a blessing working in his life. Do not be satisfied with little fruit! Remember that the more fruit you bear, the more blessed you are. The more souls you win, the more blessed you are.

2. THE BLESSING OF THE SABBATH.

And GOD BLESSED THE SEVENTH DAY, and sanctified it: because that in it he had rested from all his work which God created and made.

Genesis 2:3

There is a blessing on the seventh day, the day that God rested. There is a blessing for all those who respect the concept of rest on the Sabbath day. Step into the blessing of the Sabbath by allowing yourself to rest. Step into the blessing by resting from the money-making activities you are engaged in.

Today, people have discovered the health benefits of resting. Lions that live in zoos live up to twenty years because they rest much more than lions in the wild, which only live up to eight years. The lions in the zoo are enjoying the blessing of the Sabbath and the blessing of rest!

3.   THE BLESSING OF LAND OWNERSHIP.

And give thee THE BLESSING OF ABRAHAM, to thee, and to thy seed with thee; THAT THOU MAYEST INHERIT THE LAND wherein thou art a stranger, which God gave unto Abraham.

Genesis 28:4

Abraham had many blessings. The blessings of Abraham are ours for the taking. "That the blessing of Abraham might come on the Gentiles through Jesus Christ; that we might receive the promise of the Spirit through faith" (Galatians 3:14). One of the blessings of that Abraham received was the blessing of owning land.

You must see the ownership of land as a blessing. You are also receiving the blessing of owning land. Step into the blessing of acquiring land and owning land on the earth. Owning land is a greater blessing than owning lots of clothes, shoes, bags or even cars. That is why property is called *real* estate.

God gave Abraham a real blessing when He blessed him with land. It is important for you to recognize what blessings are and how you can walk into those blessings yourself. Don't be deceived into just having clothes, shoes, bags, parties, celebrations, mortgages and other debts. Believe and accept that owning land and property is a blessing. Aim for that blessing and become a landowner and a property owner.

4.   THE BLESSING OF VICTORY OVER ENEMIES.

And Melchizedek king of Salem brought forth bread and wine: and he was the priest of the most high God.

And HE BLESSED HIM, and said, Blessed be Abram of the most high God, possessor of heaven and earth:

And blessed be the most high God, which HATH DELIVERED THINE ENEMIES INTO THY HAND. And he gave him tithes of all.

Genesis 14:18-20

Melchizedek blessed Abraham and called him someone whose enemies had been delivered into his hand. It is a blessing when your enemies are under your control and when they do not have power over you. Receive the blessing of having your enemies in subjection to you! Some people do not even know who their enemies are. How can you have the blessing of your enemies being under your control if you do not even know who they are?

I once preached a message called "Know your enemies". God was about to deliver the enemies of the people I spoke to, into their hands. I was teaching them about the enemy of disloyalty. But they looked bewildered when I spoke about "Know your enemies". "Who are the enemies?" they asked, "We don't have enemies!" God was about to deliver unto them the blessing that Melchizedek blessed Abraham with and yet they did not value it.

When I began to preach about "Loyalty and Disloyalty," many despised this teaching that would cause their enemies to be delivered into their hands. Today, many of these churches that despised my teachings, have allowed their enemies to grow stronger and torment them grievously.

Dan was blessed to overcome a superior and overpowering enemy. He was described as being small like an adder but able to bring down a mighty horse.

Dan shall be a serpent by the way, an adder in the path, that biteth the horse heels, so that his rider shall fall backward.

Genesis 49:17

The blessing of Dan is the blessing of overcoming superior enemies and bringing an end to oppression and all forms of stalemates.

Step into the blessing of Dan that makes you overcome powerful enemies. Begin to overcome the bigger, stronger and more powerful enemies of your life.

5. THE BLESSING OF BEING A MOTHER OF MANY.

And THEY BLESSED REBEKAH, and said unto her, Thou art our sister, BE THOU THE MOTHER OF THOUSANDS OF MILLIONS, and let thy seed possess the gate of those which hate them.

Genesis 24:60

There is a blessing in being the mother of many children. Rebekah was blessed to become the mother of thousands of millions. This is a powerful blessing upon any woman. May you be a woman with such a blessing in your life! You must strive to have many children in your life. It is time to have many people that call you mother. Do not only focus on a few biological children. Like an elephant, you can only have one child at a time. You can also only bring forth very few biological children. God wants to lead you to great blessings. Become a mother to many people. Care for many children and you will discover that it is a truly blessed thing to be the mother of millions.

6. THE BLESSING OF MULTIPLICATION.

Sojourn in this land, and I will be with thee, and WILL BLESS THEE; for unto thee, and unto thy seed, I will give all these countries, and I will perform the oath which I sware unto Abraham thy father;

323

And I will MAKE THY SEED TO MULTIPLY as the stars
of heaven, and will give unto thy seed all these countries;
and in thy seed shall all the nations of the earth be blessed;

Genesis 26:3-4

The blessing of multiplication is the blessing that causes
everything to increase and multiply supernaturally. Money
multiplies! Members multiply! Customers multiply! Fruits
multiply! Cars multiply! Houses multiply! Projects multiply!
Contracts multiply! Friends multiply! Bank accounts multiply!
Everything multiplies.

Receive the blessing of multiplication! Multiplication is a
specific blessing that God spoke over Isaac! I will multiply thy
seed! May all the good things that you do begin to multiply! May
you walk in the blessings of multiplication! May everything you
touch receive the blessing of multiplication! May you no longer
be limited to a few things! You have the blessing of multiplication
on your life from today! In all that you set your hand to do from
today, you will experience the blessing of multiplication.

7. THE BLESSING OF GREATNESS.

Then Isaac sowed in that land, and received in the same
year an hundredfold: AND THE LORD BLESSED HIM.

AND THE MAN WAXED GREAT, AND WENT
FORWARD, AND GREW UNTIL HE BECAME VERY
GREAT:

For he had possession of flocks, and possession of herds,
and great store of servants: and the Philistines envied him.

For all the wells which his father's servants had digged in
the days of Abraham his father, the Philistines had stopped
them, and filled them with earth.

And Abimelech said unto Isaac, Go from us; for thou art
much mightier than we.

And Isaac departed thence, and pitched his tent in the
valley of Gerar, and dwelt there.

Genesis 26:12-17

Notice the blessing of being a great person. It is a blessing to be great because greatness is a gift from God. Isaac grew until he became very great. May you experience the great blessing that Isaac did!

May you have a good testimony and a good story to tell! Receive the blessings of greatness in every area that you operate in! Seek the blessings that Isaac received.

It is your prophetic destiny to be great like Isaac. Read this amazing scripture in the book of Galatians. It is telling us that we are just like Isaac was. We are destined to be great.

Now we, brethren, as Isaac was, are the children of promise.

Galatians 4:28

Be great in your church! Be great in your business! Be great in your ministry! Be great in your work place! Be great in your field! Be great in your nation! Be the great one among your classmates and your colleagues! Be great in the eyes of God! Be great wherever you go!

8. THE BLESSING OF MASTERY AND DOMINION.

And he came near, and kissed him: and he smelled the smell of his raiment, and blessed him, and said, See, the smell of my son is as the smell of a field which the LORD hath blessed:

Therefore God give thee of the dew of heaven, and the fatness of the earth, and plenty of corn and wine:

LET PEOPLE SERVE THEE, AND NATIONS BOW DOWN TO THEE: be lord over thy brethren, and let thy mother's sons bow down to thee: cursed be every one that curseth thee, and blessed be he that blesseth thee.

Genesis 27:27-29

Except God makes you a master you will never become the leader. Jacob received the blessing of people and nations bowing down to him. God is making you a leader to whom people will submit.

Unless God lifts you up, your mother's children will have no reason to bow down to you.

Look into every family. You will notice that some are lifted up and some are not. You will notice that sometimes one of the children is particularly lifted up and blessed. This is the blessing that Jacob received from the Lord. He became the master and had dominion over people and even over his own family. Notice what scripture says: Let people serve thee! Let nations bow down to thee! Be lord over thy brethren! Let thy mother's sons bow down to thee!

Receive dominion and mastery in your sphere of operation! Receive God's help to be the lord over your brethren.

9.   THE BLESSING OF THE BROKEN YOKE.

And Isaac his father answered and said unto him, Behold, thy dwelling shall be the fatness of the earth, and of the dew of heaven from above;

And by thy sword shalt thou live, and shalt serve thy brother; and it shall come to pass when thou shalt have the dominion, that THOU SHALT BREAK HIS YOKE FROM OFF THY NECK.

Genesis 27:39-40

The blessing of the broken yoke is the blessing of being set free from what limits you and binds you. Most of us are limited in one way or another. Most of us are subject to forces we would rather not be under, but when God blesses you with the blessing of a broken yoke, you will escape from your limitation, your bondages and restrictions. You will soar out into a higher level and begin to shine.

Sometimes, it is your relatives who prevent you from rising and shining. Sometimes, it is your country that restricts you and keeps you down.

Receive the breaking of the chain that holds you down and keeps you at a low level. You are delivered from all your inferiority complexes. You are free to be yourself and to express yourself away from those who have despised you!

10. THE BLESSING OF BECOMING A PRINCE.

And God appeared unto Jacob again, when he came out of Padanaram, AND BLESSED HIM.

And God said unto him, thy name is Jacob: thy name shall not be called any more Jacob, BUT ISRAEL SHALL BE THY NAME: AND HE CALLED HIS NAME ISRAEL.

And God said unto him, I am God Almighty: be fruitful and multiply; a nation and a company of nations shall be of thee, and kings shall come out of thy loins;

And the land which I gave Abraham and Isaac, to thee I will give it, and to thy seed after thee will I give the land.

Genesis 35:9-12

The name "Israel" means "prince". It is a blessing to be called a prince. Jacob received this blessing when his name was changed to Israel. To be a prince is to be a special man with a special status. It is to come into this world, needing nothing and never having to struggle.

The Prince of Wales and the Saudi Princes come into this world and never really have to work. You are blessed when you are turned into a prince by a spoken blessing. When you are declared to be a prince, you are no longer an ordinary person, you are royalty! Pray for the blessing of becoming a prince. Pray for your children to be princes. Call your child a prince. He will be outstanding! He will shine! He will stand out! He will be the leader!

Receive the blessing of becoming a prince as God changes your status from being a commoner into royalty!

11.   THE BLESSING FOR CHILDREN.

**BLESSED SHALL BE THE FRUIT OF THY BODY,
and the fruit of thy ground, and the fruit of thy cattle,
the increase of thy kine, and the flocks of thy sheep.**

Deuteronomy 28:4

It is a blessing to have good children. When the fruit of your body is blessed you experience the blessing of having wonderful children. Be blessed with the blessing of having good children.

Continually speak the blessings of the Lord over your children. It is important that your children are blessed by God. If your children are not blessed by God, they will turn out to be monsters you cannot control.

When your children are not blessed, you will send them to school and they will bring back a pregnancy instead of a degree. When your children are not blessed, you will send them to school but they will not attend the classes. When your children are not blessed, you will send them to school and they will return as homosexuals. When the blessing of the Lord is not upon your children, you will send them to school and they will return as atheists. You can give birth to blessed children or to cursed children. Your children can grow up and bring you curses, sorrow and pain. Every evil person has a mother and a father.

Today, anyone who was ever called Hitler has probably changed their name. Even some families of Hitler's henchmen have changed their names. It is a sad thing to bring cursed children into this world. It is a sad thing to bring forth children who multiply sorrows, curses and evil in this world. No one plans to give birth to a prostitute! No one plans to bring up a murderer, a serial killer or a terrorist. And yet people's children turn into these things all the time.

I declare today that none of these things will happen to you or your children!

Your children are declared to be blessed children! Your children will bring you happiness! Your children will bring you joy! Your children will bring sunshine into your life and your children will make you smile! Receive grace and power for your children's salvation unto the ways of the Lord and the love of Christ.

And he blessed Joseph, and said, God, before whom my fathers Abraham and Isaac did walk, the God which fed me all my life long unto this day, the angel which redeemed me from all evil, BLESS THE LADS; and let my name be named on them, and the name of my fathers Abraham and Isaac; and let them grow into a multitude in the midst of the earth.

Genesis 48:15-16

Jacob spoke blessings over Joseph's children.

Joseph's children were blessed to have the name of Jacob named on them. Jacob adopted Joseph's children as his own children. They were forever to be associated with Israel. Today, instead of the tribe of Joseph we have the tribe of Manasseh and the tribe of Ephraim. These are Joseph's children. Joseph's children are forever linked to the prince of Israel, Jacob.

God is the creator of associations. He is the one who links, who joins, creates, shuffles and re-creates families. One of the blessings you can receive for your life is the blessing of being associated with a far greater person with whom you may have had little to do.

May a great person adopt you! May you receive the greatest association and the greatest linkage in your life! May you be associated with good and great people! May your association bring you many benefits! May your association bring you more benefits than your salary and your job can!

12.   THE BLESSING OF TRANSPOSITION.

And HE BLESSED THEM THAT DAY, saying, in thee shall Israel bless, saying, God make thee as Ephraim and as Manasseh: and HE SET EPHRAIM BEFORE MANASSEH.

Genesis 48:20

The blessing of transposition is the blessing of being lifted from your junior position and being made into the senior. It is a blessing to be divinely lifted above those greater than you.

Manasseh was born before Ephraim but Ephraim became senior to Manasseh. This was a blessing that Ephraim received from his grandfather, Jacob. Through spoken blessings, you will be lifted up and made to be above those who were born before you.

Through the blessing of transposition, you will be more important than those who came before you! May you receive the blessing of transposition! May you be transposed from your inferior position and lifted into a level you could never create for yourself.

13.   THE BLESSING OF BEING MADE THE LEADER.

The sceptre shall not depart from Judah, nor a lawgiver from between his feet, until Shiloh come; and unto him shall the gathering of the people be.

Genesis 49:10

It is a blessing to be a leader. A leader is a blessed person! A leader is also a blessing to many people! Judah received the blessing of leadership. Judah received the blessing of being supernaturally made a leader.

Many books are written about leadership. Although leadership is often a natural gift that people possess, leadership is also a blessing that God bestows on certain people.

The gift of being a leader is so natural that leaders are not aware when they are taking charge. Judah was promised the blessing that the sceptre would not depart from him until the arrival of Shiloh.

Leadership was given to Judah and it was a blessing for him. When a nation has a good leader, it is obvious that a blessing has fallen on that nation. What blessedness comes upon a people when they have a good leader over them! What a curse is bestowed on a people when they are led by incompetent and incapable people! There will be no roads, no water, no light, no order, no security, no hospitals, no schools, no good universities and no airports because there is no good leader.

Even in nations that characteristically do not have good leaders, when one person stands out as a good leader, he creates an island of blessings that many benefit from. May you become one of the good leaders of this world!

14.   THE BLESSING OF THE HEAVENS, THE DEEP, THE BREASTS AND THE WOMB.

Joseph is a fruitful bough, even a fruitful bough by a well; whose branches run over the wall:

The archers have sorely grieved him, and shot at him, and hated him:

But his bow abode in strength, and the arms of his hands were made strong by the hands of the mighty God of Jacob; (from thence is the shepherd, the stone of Israel:) even by the God of thy father, who shall help thee; and by the Almighty, who shall bless thee with BLESSINGS OF HEAVEN ABOVE, BLESSINGS OF THE DEEP THAT LIETH UNDER, BLESSINGS OF THE BREASTS, AND OF THE WOMB:

Genesis 49:22-25

The blessings of Joseph were in four parts!

The blessings of the heavens above are the blessing of having spiritual gifts. Joseph was blessed with visions and dreams and the power to interpret dreams. It was this power that got him out of prison and into the Prime Minister's office.

Joseph was also blessed with the blessings of the deep. The blessings of the deep are the blessings of long-lasting wealth. Within the deep lie the reserves of gold, oil, diamond, iron ore, cobalt, bauxite and uranium. Joseph received the blessings of the deep and became the wealthiest and most powerful man in Egypt, second only to Pharaoh. He bought all the land of Egypt and bought the people in the country for Pharaoh (Genesis 47:23). He was second to Pharaoh, so the land and the people virtually belonged to him. God gave him unimaginable wealth and power!

Joseph also received the blessings of the breast. The blessings of the breast are the blessings of comfort, softness and delight. He was comforted after his trials in Potiphar's house and being in prison. God gave him a wife and a family and made him forget the painfulness of his youth. The ministry of the Holy Spirit is the ministry of the comforter. Comfort is one of the greatest things you can ever receive. Most pastors are unable to change the unfortunate things that happen to people, but they are able to minister the comfort of the Lord. This is why the blessings of the breast are so powerful. If Joseph had received all the power and money but had not been comforted, he may have had a psychological breakdown and suffered from the effects of his rejection and traumatic childhood.

Joseph was also blessed with the blessings of the womb. God blessed Joseph with children and offspring who would look up to him and carry his seed. Children are a blessing and many people are sad when they have no one to work for and give their inheritance to. Why do I labour and bereave my soul of good? What is the point of all my hard work when there is no one to come after me and benefit from it all? (Ecclesiastes 4:8).

Seek for these four powerful blessings. Seek for the blessings of the deep and the blessings of the heavens above. Seek for the blessings of the breast and the blessings of the womb. When these blessings are on your life, curses will have no effect on you. The multiplied blessings on your life will surely render the curses powerless.

15. THE BLESSING OF PROSPERITY EVERYWHERE, NO MATTER WHERE.

BLESSED shalt thou be in the CITY, and blessed shalt thou be in the FIELD.

Deuteronomy 28:3

Some people are only blessed in small towns but cannot thrive in a big city. It is a blessing to experience prosperity everywhere. Step into the blessings of being blessed in the city! Receive the blessing of being blessed in a large metropolitan city. You are delivered from being limited to "village prosperity".

Not only can some people survive in the city, but they can also be blessed in the village! You can also experience the blessing of being blessed in the field or a city. With this kind of blessing you can live anywhere, whether it is a village or a city. You can have "city prosperity" and you can have "village prosperity"!

Years ago, Europeans came to Africa and established mission posts there. They thrived in the villages and in the fields of Africa. In Ghana, they built churches, botanical gardens, golf courses, schools and cemeteries. They lived there because they had the blessing of being blessed in the field. You are declared capable of experiencing blessings in the cities and blessings in the field! You are declared capable of experiencing city prosperity as well as village prosperity!

16.   THE BLESSING ON YOUR BUSINESS.

Blessed shall be the fruit of thy body, and THE FRUIT OF THY GROUND, and the fruit of thy cattle, the increase of thy kine, and the flocks of thy sheep.

Deuteronomy 28:4

Your fruits and your profits can be blessed. The fruit of your ground is the profit of your business. I am sorry to say that most businesses do not make profit. God is raising you up so that whatever you do will be truly profitable.

There was a lady who was selling milk, sardines, mackerel, sugar and soap by the roadside. One day, she was asked, "Do you make any profit from your business?" She answered, "No, I do not make profit. My husband gives me money all the time. I just sit by the roadside to while away the time. My business is absolutely unprofitable."

Unfortunately, this is the story of many people. They have an activity they call a "business" but there is no real profit from this business.

Another lady frying doughnuts for sale in an African country worked for twelve hours a day and made two dollars profit every month for all her efforts. Such is the story of many people whose businesses are not yet blessed. Begin to pray for a blessing on the fruit of your ground and on the fruit of your cattle.

When your cattle and goats and sheep are blessed, there will be a true and genuine profit for all your labour. Your labour will not be in vain any more. You will not say, "I do not make profit. I just work for the sake of working." You will not work for nothing any more. The fruit of your ground and your cattle are declared blessed from now on!

17.   THE BLESSING ON YOUR BASKET.

Blessed shall be thy basket and thy store.

Deuteronomy 28:5

There are different types of baskets. There are blessed baskets and there are baskets that have no blessings on them. Pray that your basket will be blessed! Your basket and your store speak of your bank account and any other storage place you may have.

Moses declared a blessing on the storerooms of the Israelites. There are many people who have bank accounts with nothing in them. Sometimes, these bank accounts are more of a burden to the banks than anything else. It is for this reason that Moses declared a blessing for the basket and store.

Speak a blessing over your account and watch it grow by leaps and bounds. God is able to fill your bank account so that you can write cheques that will never bounce. Some of you have stopped writing cheques because you are never sure if it will bounce or not. Pray for a blessed basket! Seek for blessings on your basket! Your basket is declared blessed! Your cheque will never bounce again after you read this paragraph. A blessing has finally come upon your basket and your store!

18.   THE BLESSING OF SUCCESSFUL AND SAFE JOURNEYS.

Blessed shalt thou be when thou comest in, and blessed shalt thou be when thou goest out.

Deuteronomy 28:6

It is a blessing to experience safe journeys. Step into the blessing of successful, safe and fruitful journeys. Many journeys that started out with laughter, excitement and hope have ended in tragedy, sadness and despair. Today, God's Word is showing you the need for a blessing to be upon your travels. When your journeys are blessed, you will go rejoicing and come back with even more joy.

One day, I thought of the numerous journeys that some evangelists had made in their lifetime. They travelled up and down many times. God took them and brought them back safely! They were blessed going and blessed coming! This will be your story and your testimony!

You will not go and return with a broken leg. You will not go in a seat and return in a coffin! You will not go full of joy and return empty-handed! Receive the blessing of blessed and fruitful journeys!

Respect the blessing of the blessed journeys. You may not have thought about having a blessing for your journey but it is one of the important blessings you need. Every time you travel, you are very vulnerable. Your journeys will be blessed journeys from today. Your journeys are declared safe, successful and fruitful from now onwards!

19.   THE BLESSING OF BEING BLESSED IN YOUR COUNTRY.

The Lord shall command THE BLESSING upon thee in thy storehouses, and in all that thou settest thine hand unto; and HE SHALL BLESS THEE IN THE LAND which the Lord thy God giveth thee.

Deuteronomy 28:8

In every nation, there is a group that has the best kind of life. Perhaps you have not met that group yet. But they exist in every country. The people who enjoy the nation are the people who are blessed in the land.

Dear friend, every country has a group of people who are completely and totally enjoying their country. They are happy to live there and they are prosperous in the land. You may not know them but they exist. There is a blessing that can come upon you so that you will be blessed in the nation wherein you dwell. When you are blessed in a land, you begin to enjoy it. You will not feel the need to travel or to migrate. It is because people are not blessed in their land that they seek to relocate to other nations.

May you rise in your nation and be called "blessed" in your own country. May you enjoy the good of the land. I see you rising to take your place among those who enjoy the good of the land. Your story has changed from today. Experience a blessing of being blessed in the land, which the Lord God giveth thee!

20. THE BLESSING OF GOOD COMPANY.

Blessed is the man that walketh not in the counsel of the ungodly, nor standeth in the way of sinners, nor sitteth in the seat of the scornful.

Psalm 1:1

Blessed are those who have good friends and who stay in the company of righteous men. A blessing has been pronounced on those who can stay away from bad company. Your life changes from the day you are delivered from bad company. When sinners, the ungodly and mockers of God are far away from your life you are experiencing true blessings.

God has desired to bless you by delivering you from mockers. That is a great blessing.

Many evil spirits come to you because you are in bad company. Sometimes the lot of evil men falls to you because you are standing near them in the day of their judgment.

A blessing is on your life just because these people are not in your life. Separate yourself from all those who fall into these categories. Do not have a sinner as a friend. Do not have an ungodly person as a close friend! Do not sit down to eat with people who mock the anointing and mock the anointed. Earnestly seek to be far away from evil men so that you can enjoy the blessings of God!

CHAPTER 32

How You Can Quench a Curse by Saying "Amen" to Blessings

Else WHEN THOU SHALT BLESS with the spirit,
HOW SHALL HE that occupieth the room of the
unlearned SAY AMEN at thy giving of thanks ...

1 Corinthians 14:16

Y
ou can overcome a curse by learning to say "Amen" when blessings are spoken over your life. "Amen" is the biblical response to the Word of God. "Amen" is the biblical response to prophecies. "Amen" is the biblical response to the ministry of the prophet! By learning to say "Amen", shout "Amen", and scream "Amen" at the blessings and prophecies, you will discover a master key that overturns and overcomes curses.

When someone speaks out a blessing in the spirit, you are expected to say "Amen". Say "Amen" to the blessings! Amen is the Bible response to the word of God. Amen is the proper response to spoken blessings. Amen is the single word that confirms and establishes a supernatural prophecy that is spoken.

Let the blessings of God come onto His people as they shout "Amen".

Saying "Amen" establishes a thing.

This is an appropriate response to the Word of God that you must develop as a Christian.

Some people respond to the Word of God by saying nothing! Others respond by shouting, "Yeah! Aah! Ooh!"

Some say, "Yes"! Some say "Mercy"! Some say "Forgive"!

Some go further and say, "Preach on! Say it! You are the best! Sharp shooter!"

Others scream when they hear the Word and say, "I love that man! I love you Bishop! What a word! What a preacher! Fine teaching!"

Yet still, some people stand up, when they hear the Word of God. Some clap, some jump and some even come forward and place an offering on the altar. I have experienced every one of these responses.

However, "Amen" is the right response that we must have to the Word of God. The proper and appropriate response to the Word of God is simply "Amen". Learn the art of saying "Amen". You will be surprised how your life will change when you learn to say "Amen" to the Word of God. Amen means "Let it happen"! Amen means "Let it be so!" Amen means "Let the words that came out of your mouth come to pass in my life."

Amen is a Bible word. It is better to shout "Amen" than to shout, "I love you Bishop." It is better to shout "Amen" than to get up and shout, "You are a sharp shooter, Bishop."

All through the Bible the proper response to God's word was "Amen". Perhaps, you should study the entire Bible and you will discover how the Old Testament saints responded to blessings and curses with the word "Amen". You will also discover that almost every book in the New Testament ended with the word, "Amen."

In my personal experience, I have found that people who say faith filled "Amens" experience greater breakthroughs, greater empowerment, greater blessing, greater shining and greater rising! You will now experience the greatness of God's blessing as you learn to say "Amen". Learn to say short "Amens", long "Amens", sustained "Amens", and quiet "Amens". But make sure you say "Amen"!

Agree with God! Be on God's side! Join your faith with what will certainly happen. Make it come to pass by saying "Amen." Say "Amen" to the blessings that come from God.

You must also say "Amen" to the curses! Let the enemies of God be judged by the curses that fall on them. You can never be kinder than God. Our God is a God of vengeance. In the day that He redeems you, He executes judgment on your enemies. "For the day of vengeance is in mine heart, and the year of my redeemed is come" (Isaiah 63:4). The anointing that was on Jesus is also an anointing that executes vengeance on the enemies of God.

The Spirit of the Lord God is upon me; because the Lord hath anointed me to preach good tidings unto the meek; he hath sent me to bind up the brokenhearted, to proclaim liberty to the captives, and the opening of the prison to them that are bound;

To proclaim the acceptable year of the Lord, and THE DAY OF VENGEANCE OF OUR GOD; to comfort all that mourn;

Isaiah 61:1-2

Say "Amen" to the curses on God's enemies. Through the power of curses God will send judgment into the camp of the enemy.

Seeing it is a righteous thing with God to recompense tribulation to them that trouble you;

2 Thessalonians 1:6

Overcome Curses by Saying "Amen" to Blessings Declared Over Your Life

1. Say "Amen" when someone blesses the Lord.

And EZRA BLESSED THE LORD, the great God. And all the people answered, AMEN, AMEN, with lifting up their hands: and they bowed their heads, and worshipped the Lord with their faces to the ground.

Nehemiah 8:6

2. Say "Amen" when God is praised.

BLESSED BE THE LORD GOD of Israel from everlasting, and to everlasting. AMEN, and AMEN.

Psalm 41:13

3. Say "Amen" when a blessing is spoken over your life.

THE GRACE of our Lord Jesus Christ BE WITH YOU ALL. AMEN.

Romans 16:24

4. Say "Amen" when God promotes you with an amazing blessing.

AND HATH MADE US KINGS AND PRIESTS unto God and his Father; to him be glory and dominion for ever and ever. AMEN.

Revelation 1:6

5. Say "Amen" when powerful prayers are spoken.

And LEAD US NOT INTO TEMPTATION, but deliver us from evil: For thine is the kingdom, and the power, and the glory, for ever. AMEN.

Matthew 6:13

6. Say "Amen" when you receive instructions from the Lord.

Go ye therefore, and teach all nations, baptizing them in the name of the Father, and of the Son, and of the Holy Ghost:
Teaching them to observe all things whatsoever I have commanded you: and, lo, I am with you alway, even unto the end of the world. AMEN.

Matthew 28:19-20

7. Say "Amen" to powerful declarations and ministrations of God's love.

My love be with you all in Christ Jesus. AMEN.

1 Corinthians 16:24

Overcome Curses by Saying "Amen" to Prophecies Declared Over Your Life

Let the remaining days of your life be days of goodness and mercy! Amen!

Whatever curse is in operation against your financial prosperity is declared cancelled today in Jesus' name! Amen!

Every horn that seeks to prevent you from rising is cut off! Amen!

Judgment day has finally come for the enemies of your progress! Amen!

Every evil calculated against your future crashes today in the name of Jesus! Amen!

Let wonderful blessings go forth and descend on all those who are part of this spiritual family! Amen!

Every one appointed to premature death: that appointment is cancelled in Jesus' name! Amen!

No one reading this book is permitted to bury his children! Amen!

Let the grace of God finally lift you out of the mud and the clay where you are stranded! Amen!

Let the Lord thy God in the midst of thee rise up and save you! Amen!

Your day of shining has come. Arise and shine! Your light has come! Amen!

Whatever gate has been shut against you is finally declared open from today! Amen!

Overcome Curses by Saying "Amen" to Prophecies Declared Over Your Children

None of your parents will ever weep over your life again! Amen!

Your parents will see you take root downwards and bear fruit upwards! Amen!

Your parents will see you graduate from universities! Amen!

Your parents will see you take great positions in life! Amen!

Your parents will see you having children! They will see your children having children. Amen!

You will never be a source of concern to your parents! Amen!

You shall never be a disappointment to your parents! Amen!

You will never be a problem to this world! Amen!

You will be a blessing to this world and a blessing to your parents! Amen!

You are an asset to this world and a blessing to many people! Amen!

You shall never be molested or cheated or raped ever in your life! Amen!

Every wicked and jealous eye that is set against you goes blind today! Amen!

The enemies that hoped to see your downfall are finally destroyed forever! Amen!

Every step of your life will be marked with dignity from now onwards! Amen!

You will become a source of pride and joy to your parents and guardians! Amen!

Overcome Curses by Saying "Amen" to Prophecies Declared Over Your Ministry

Your ears are declared open to the voice of God! Amen!

Your paths are directed by the Holy Spirit! Amen!

Whatever mistake you have made in the past, you will recover from it! Amen!

You will run this race successfully to the end in the name of Jesus! Amen!

Whatever invisible enemy is fighting you is declared destroyed from now on! Amen!

All invisible barriers in your way are removed by the Blood of Jesus! Amen!

All invisible frustrations that slow down your ministry are declared cursed. Judgment comes on them today! Amen!

You are blessed of the Lord who has made heaven and earth! Amen!

Your ministry is preserved and protected by the Blood of the Lamb! Amen!

The arrows of the wicked will no longer be able to strike at you! Amen!

You are declared to be a fruitful tree! Amen!

You are protected by the Blood of the Lamb! Amen!

You will make full proof of your ministry! Amen!

You will fulfil your calling! Amen!

[77]The number of your days you will fulfil! Amen!

References

Chapter 2

Excerpts from:

"Curse | Definition, meaning & more | Collins Dictionary" *Collinsdictionary.com*. Web. 24 Jan 2017. Retrieved from https://www.collinsdictionary.com/dictionary/english/curse

"Curse" *En.wikipedia.org*. Web. 24 Jan 2017. Retrieved from https://en.wikipedia.org/wiki/Curse

"Imprecation – Free definitions by Babylon" *Babylon-software.com* Web. 24 Jan 2017. Retrieved from www.babylon-software.com/definition/imprecation/English

Chapter 3

Excerpts from:

Crowley, Cathleen F. "How are you likely to die? Here are the odds of dying" *The Pulse* Web. 24 Jan 2017. Retrieved from http://blog.timesunion.com/healthcare/how-are-you-likely-to-die-here-are-the-odds-of-dying/2515/

"According to the National Safety Council, the odds of an "American" dying from various causes are as follows:" *Imgur*. Web. 24 Jan 2017. Retrieved from http://imgur.com/gallery/at97PQn

"Causes of death in the world 1990 2005 2010" *healthintelligence. drupalgardens*. Web. 24 Jan 2017. Retrieved from http://healthintelligence.drupalgardens.com/content/causes-death-world-1990-2005-2010

Chapter 13

Excerpts from:

"Women | Anxiety and Depression Association of America ADAA" *Adaa.org*. Web. 24 Jan 2017. Retrieved from https://www.adaa.org/category/help/women?page=12

"British Women's Emancipation since the Renaissance" *Historyofwomen.org.* Web.. 24 Jan 2017. Retrieved from http://www. historyofwomen.org/oppression.html

Chapter 14

Excerpts from:

Brooks, David (January 11, 2010). "The Tel Aviv Cluster: The New York Times."

"Titus' Siege of Jerusalem – Livius" *Livius.org.* Web. 24 Jan 2017. Retrieved from http://www.livius.org/articles/concept/roman-jewish-wars/roman-jewish-wars-4/?

"The Diaspora | Jewish Virtual Library" *Jewishvirtuallibrary.org.* Web. 24 Jan 2017. Retrieved from http://www.jewishvirtuallibrary.org/jsource/History/Diaspora.html

"Learn more about Russian Empire with micro-learning cards" *Snappico App.* Web. 24 Jan 2017. Retrieved from https://www.snappico.com/sets/history/russian-empire

"Notable Russian Jews genealogy project" *Geni_family_tree.* Web. 24 Jan 2017. Retrieved from https://www.geni.com/projects/Notable-Russian-Jews/17049

"History of the Jews in Russia" *En.wikipedia.org.* Web. 24 Jan 2017. Retrieved from https://en.wikipedia.org/wiki/History_of_the_Jews_in_Russia

"Persecution of Jews" *En.wikipedia.org.* Web. 24 Jan 2017. Retrieved from https://en.wikipedia.org/wiki/Persecution_of_Jews

"Spanish Empire" *Infogalatic.com.* Web. 24 Jan 2017. Retrieved from https://infogalactic.com/info/Spanish_Empire

"History of the Jews in Spain" *En.Wikipedia.org.* Web. 24 Jan 2017. Retrieved from https://en.wikipedia.org/wiki/History_of_the_Jews_in_Spain

"The Spanish Expulsion (1492) | Jewish Virtual Library" *Jewishvirtuallibrary.org.* Web. 24 Jan 2017. Retrieved from http://www.jewishvirtuallibrary.org/jsource/Judaism/expulsion.html

"Jews in Germany" *Newworldencyclopedia.org*. Web. 24 Jan 2017 . Retrieved from http://www.newworldencyclopedia.org/entry/Jews_in_Germany

"History of the Jews in Germany" *En.wikipedia.org*. Web. 24 Jan 2017. Retrieved from https://en.wikipedia.org/wiki/History_of_the_Jews_in_Germany

"The British White Papers | Jewish Virtual Library" *Jewishvirtuallibrary.org*. Web. 24 Jan 2017. Retrieved from http://www.jewishvirtuallibrary.org/jsource/History/whitetoc.html

"Jews are the Richest Religious Group in the USA" *AARP*. Web. 24 Jan 2017. Retrieved from https://community.aarp.org/t5/Politics-Current-Events/Jews-are-Richest-Religious-Group-in-the-USA/td-p/1643658/page/6

"How did American Jews get so rich?" *Ynetnews*. Web. 24 Jan 2017. Retrieved from http://www.ynetnews.com/articles/0,7340,L-4099803,00.html

"European church attendance" *Via Integra*. Web. 24 Jan 2017. Retrieved from https://viaintegra.wordpress.com/european-church-attendance/

"History of religion in the Netherlands" *En.wikipedia.org*. Web. 24 Jan 2017. Retrieved from https://en.wikipedia.org/wiki/History_of_religion_in_the_Netherlands

"Christianity in Qatar" *En.wikipedia.org*. Web. 24 Jan 2017. Retrieved from https://en.wikipedia.org/wiki/Christianity_in_Qatar

"Catholic Church in Saudi Arabia" *En.wikipedia.org*. Web. 24 Jan 2017. Retrieved from https://en.wikipedia.org/wiki/Catholic_Church_in_Saudi_Arabia

"Religion in Iran" *En.wikipedia.org* Web. 24 Jan 2017. Retrieved from https://en.wikipedia.org/wiki/Religion_in_Iran

"Christianity in Iraq" *En. wikipedia.com*. Web. 24 Jan 2017. Retrieved from https://en.wikipedia.org/wiki/Christianity_in_Iraq#cite_note-3

"Christianity in the United Arab Emirates" *En.wikipedia.com*. Web. 24 Jan 2017. Retrieved from https://en.wikipedia.org/wiki/Christianity_in_the_United_Arab_Emirates#cite_note-3

"Encyclopedia Coptica: The Christian Coptic Orthodox Church" *Coptic.net*. Web. 24 Jan 2017. Retrieved from http://www.coptic.net/EncyclopediaCoptica/

"Persian Jews" *En. wikipedia.com*. Web. 24 Jan 2017. Retrieved from https://en.wikipedia.org/wiki/persian_jews

"Yarsanism" *En.wikipedia.org*. Web. 24 Jan 2017. Retrieved from https://en.wikipedia.org/wiki/yarsan

"Bahá'í Faith" *En.wikipedia.org*. Web. 24 Jan 2017. Retrieved from https://en.wikipedia.org/wiki/baha%27i_faith

"Mandaeism" *En.wikipedia.org*. Web. 24 Jan 2017. Retrieved from https://en.wikipedia.org/wiki/mandaeism

"Religious Minorities in Iran" *En.wikipedia.org*. Web. 24 Jan 2017. Retrieved from https://en.wikipedia.org/wiki/religious_minorities_in_iran

"Iran" *En.wikipedia.org*. Web. 24 Jan 2017. Retrieved from https://en.wikipedia.org/wiki/iran

"Crucifix" *En.wikipedia.org*. Web. 24 Jan 2017. Retrieved from https://en.wikipedia.org/wiki/crucifix

"Bible" *En.wikipedia.org*. Web. 24 Jan 2017. Retrieved from https://en.wikipedia.org/wiki/bible

"Islam" *En.wikipedia.org*. Web. 24 Jan 2017. Retrieved from https://en.wikipedia.org/wiki/islam

"Christian Denomination" *En.wikipedia.org*. Web. 24 Jan 2017. Retrieved from https://en.wikipedia.org/wiki/christian_denomination

"Irreligion" *En.wikipedia.org*. Web. 24 Jan 2017. Retrieved from https://en.wikipedia.org/wiki/irreligion

Chapter 15

Excerpts from:

"The Romans Destroy the Temple at Jerusalem 70 AD" *Eyewitnesstohistory.com*. Web. 24 Jan 2017. Retrieved from http://www.eyewitnesstohistory.com/jewishtemple.htm

"The War of the Jews and the Fall of Jerusalem" *Angelfire.com.* Web. 24 Jan 2017. Retrieved from http://www.angelfire.com/nt/theology/18-ad70.html

World Congress | "A third of Nazi's war effort funded with money stolen from Jews, study finds: World Jewish Congress" *Worldjewishcongress.org.* Web. 24 Jan 2017. Retrieved from https://www.worldjewishcongress.org/en/news/a-third-of-nazis-war-effort-funded-with-money-stolen-from-jews-study-finds?printable=true

"Children in the Holocaust" *En.wikipedia.org.* Web. 24 Jan 2017. Retrieved from https://en.wikipedia.org/wiki/Children_in_the_Holocaust

"God's Truth" *The christadelphianns.org.* Web. 24 Jan 2017 Retrieved from http://www.thechristadelphians.org/htm/books/Gods_Truth/Gods_Truth_03.htm

"Reasons to believe – Reason 5" *Bridgetothebible.com.* Web. 24 Jan 2017. Retrieved from http://www.bridgetothebible.com/12%20 reasons/Reason%205.htm

"BBC – Religions – Judaism: Children and the Holocaust" *Bbc.co.uk.* Web. 24 Jan 2017. Retrieved from http://www.bbc.co.uk/religion/religions/judaism/holocaust/children_1.shtml

"The Siege of Jerusalem, AD 70, by Falvius Josephus" *Rjgeib.com* Web.. 24 Jan 2017. Retrieved from http://www.rjgeib.com/thoughts/desolation/josephus.html

"The Spanish Expulsion (1492)" *Jewishvirtuallibrary.org.* Web.. 24 Jan 2017. Retrieved from http://www.jewishvirtuallibrary.org/jsource/Judaism/expulsion.html

Chapter 16

Excerpts from:

"History & Overview of the Maccabees" *Jewishvirtuallibrary.org.* Web. 24 Jan 2017. Retrieved from http://www.jewishvirtuallibrary.org/jsource/History/Maccabees.html

"First Jewish-Roman War" *En.wikipedia.org.* Web. 24 Jan 2017. Retrieved from https://en.wikipedia.org/wiki/First_Jewish–Roman_War

"Flavian Dynasty" *En.wikipedia.org* . Web. 24 Jan 2017. Retrieved from https://en.wikipedia.org/wiki/First_Jewish–Roman_War

"Jewish Deicide" *En.wikipedia.org.* . Web. 24 Jan 2017. Retrieved from https://en.wikipedia.org/wiki/Jewish_deicide

"Timeline of Anti-Semitism" *En.wikipedia.org.* Web. 24 Jan 2017. Retrieved from https://en.wikipedia.org/wiki/Timeline_of_antisemitism

"Adversus Judaeos" *En.wikipedia.org.* Web. 24 Jan 2017. Retrieved from https://en.wikipedia.org/wiki/Adversus_Judaeos

"Jewish History 410 – 419" *Jewishhistory.org.il.* Web. 24 Jan 2017. Retrieved from http://www.jewishhistory.org.il/history.php?startyear=410&endyear=419

"Bryn Mawr Classical Review 1998.12.15" *Bmcr.brynmawr.edu..* Web. 24 Jan 2017. Retrieved from http://bmcr.brynmawr.edu/1998/1998-12-15.html

"Yazdegerd II" *En.wikipedia.org.* Web. 24 Jan 2017. Retrieved from https://en.wikipedia.org/wiki/Yazdegerd_II

"France Virtual Jewish History Tour" *Jewishvirtuallibrary.org.* Web. 24 Jan 2017. Retrieved from http://www.jewishvirtuallibrary.org/jsource/vjw/France.html

"The 1990 Massacre: History of York" *Historyofyork.org.uk.* Web. 24 Jan 2017. Retrieved from http://www.historyofyork.org.uk/themes/norman/the-1190-massacre

"Louis VIII of France" *En.wikipedia.org.* Web. 24 Jan 2017. Retrieved from https://en.wikipedia.org/wiki/Louis_VIII_of_France

"ANJOU – JewishEncyclopedia.com" *Jewishencyclopedia.com.* Web. 24 Jan 2017. Retrieved from http://www.jewishencyclopedia.com/articles/1543-anjou

"Saint Dominic Del Val" *Holy Redeemer Altar Servers* . Web. 24 Jan 2017. Retrieved from http://altarserversgroup.weebly.com/saint-dominic-del-val.html

"Disputation of Barcelona" *En.wikipedia.org.* Web. 24 Jan 2017. Retrieved from https://en.wikipedia.org/wiki/Disputation_of_Barcelona

"Jewish History 1260 – 1269" *Jewishhistory.org.il*. Web. 24 Jan 2017. Retrieved from http://www.jewishhistory.org.il/history.php?startyear=1260&endyear=1269

"Jewish History 1270 – 1279" *Jewishhistory.org.il*. Web. 24 Jan 2017. Retrieved from http://www.jewishhistory.org.il/history.php?startyear=1270&endyear=1279

"Yellow Badge" *En.wikipedia.org* . Web. 24 Jan 2017. Retrieved from https://en.wikipedia.org/wiki/Yellow_badge

"Leper Scare" *En.wikipedia.org*. Web. 24 Jan 2017. Retrieved from https://en.wikipedia.org/wiki/Yellow_badge

"Arnold von Ulssigheim" *En.wikipedia.org*. Web. 24 Jan 2017. Retrieved from https://en.wikipedia.org/wiki/Arnold_von_Uissigheim

"Black Death Jewish Persecutions" *En.wikipedia.org*. Web. 24 Jan 2017. Retrieved from https://en.wikipedia.org/wiki/Black_Death_Jewish_persecutions

"Jewish History 1340 – 1349" *Jewishhistory.org.il*. Web. 24 Jan 2017. Retrieved from http://www.jewishhistory.org.il/history.php?startyear=1340&endyear=1349

"Erfurt massacre (1349)" *En.wikipedia.org*. Web. 24 Jan 2017 Retrieved from https://en.wikipedia.org/wiki/Erfurt_massacre_(1349)

"Brussels massacre" *WikipediaTLDR*. Web. 24 Jan 2017. Retrieved from http://www.wikipediatldr.com/wiki/Brussels_massacre/

"History of Christianity" *Historyofchristianity.info*. Web. 24 Jan 2017. Retrieved from http://historyofchristianity.info/christian-history-1360-to-1391.html

"The History of The Jewish People 600-1850 Part 1" *Jewishandisraeltimeline.blogspot.com*. Web. 24 Jan 2017. Retrieved from http://jewishandisraeltimeline.blogspot.com/2015/11/the-history-of-jewish-people.html

"Majorca | Jewish Currents" *Jewish Currents*. Web. 24 Jan 2017. Retrieved from http://jewishcurrents.org/old-site/tag/majorca/

"Mellah" *En.wikipedia.org*. Web. 24 Jan 2017. Retrieved from https://en.wikipedia.org/wiki/Mellah

"Anti-semitism" *En.wikipedia.org.* Web. 24 Jan 2017. Retrieved from https://en.wikipedia.org/wiki/Antisemitism

"100-1850" *Defendheritage.blogspot.com.* Web. 24 Jan 2017 Retrieved from http://defendheritage.blogspot.com/2011/06/1776-1820.html

"Hep – Hep riots" *En.wikipedia.org.* Web. 24 Jan 2017. Retrieved from https://en.wikipedia.org/wiki/Hep-Hep_riots

"Pogroms" *Jewishvirtuallibrary.org.* Web. 24 Jan 2017. Retrieved from http://www.jewishvirtuallibrary.org/jsource/History/pogroms.html

"Kishinev Pogrom" *En.wikipedia.org.* Web. 24 Jan 2017. Retrieved from https://en.wikipedia.org/wiki/Kishinev_pogrom

Yadvashem.org. Web. 24 Jan 2017. Retrieved from http://www.yadvashem.org/untoldstories/database/index.asp?cid=283

"Hebron Massacre" *En.wikipedia.org.* Web. 24 Jan 2017. Retrieved from https://en.wikipedia.org/wiki/1929_Hebron_massacre

"Bill Wagner –Rogers" *En.wikipedia.org.* Web. 24 Jan 2017. Retrieved from https://en.wikipedia.org/wiki/Wagner–Rogers_Bill

"Claudius" *En.wikiipedia.org.* Web. 24 Jan 2017. Retrieved from https://en.wikipedia.org/wiki/claudius

"Tax resistance" *En.wikipedia.org.* Web. 24 Jan 2017. Retrieved from https://en.wikipedia.org/wiki/tax_resistance

"Cestius Gallus" *En.wikipedia.org.* Web. 24 Jan 2017. Retrieved from https://en.wikipedia.org/wiki/cestius_gallus

"Legatus" *En.wikipedia.org.* Web. 24 Jan 2017. Retrieved from https://en.wikipedia.org/wiki/legatus

"Syria Roman Province" *En.wikipedia.org.* Web. 24 Jan 2017. Retrieved from https://en.wikipedia.org/wiki/syria_roman_province

"Shabbat Explained" *Everything.explained.today.* Web. 24 Jan 2017. Retrieved from http://everything.explained.today/shabbat/

"Jews Explained" *Everything.explained.today.* Web. 24 Jan 2017. Retrieved from http://everything.explained.today/jews/

"Isfahan Explained" *Everything.explained.today.* Web. 24 Jan 2017. Retrieved from http://everything.explained.today/isfahan/

"Ostrogoths" *En.wikipedia.org.* Web. 24 Jan 2017. Retrieved from http://en.wikipedia.org/wiki/ostrogoths

"Hebrew Language" *En.wikipedia.org.* Web. 24 Jan 2017. Retrieved from http://en.wikipedia.org/wiki/hebrew_language

"Shema Yisrael" *En.wikipedia.org.* Web. 24 Jan 2017. Retrieved from https://en.wikipedia.org/wiki/shema_yisrael

"Trinity" *En.wikipedia.org.* Web. 24 Jan 2017. Retrieved from https://en.wikipedia.org/wiki/trinity

"Chalcedonian Christianity" *En.wikipedia.org.* Web. 24 Jan 2017. Retrieved from https://en.wikipedia.org/wiki/chalcedonian_Christianity

"Sisebar" *En.wikipedia.org.* Web. 24 Jan 2017. Retrieved from https://en.wikipedia.org/wiki/sisebur

"Heraclius" *En.wikipedia.org.* Web. 24 Jan 2017. Retrieved from https://en.wikipedia.org/wiki/heraclius

"Quinisext Council" *En.wikipedia.org.* Web. 24 Jan 2017. Retrieved from https://en.wikipedia.org/wiki/quinisext_council

"Leo III The Isaurian" *En.wikipedia.org* Web. 24 Jan 2017. Retrieved from https://en.wikipedia.org/wiki/leo_iii_the_isaurian

"Domus Conversorom" *En.wikipedia.org.* Web. 24 Jan 2017 Retrieved from https://en.wikipedia.org/wiki/domus_conversorom

"Blood Libel" *En.wikipedia.org.* Web. 24 Jan 2017. Retrieved from https://en.wikipedia.org/wiki/blood_libel

"Nahmanides" *En.wikipedia.org.* Web. 24 Jan 2017. Retrieved from https://en.wikipedia.org/wiki/nahmanides

"Judenhut" *En.wikipedia.org.* Web. 24 Jan 2017. Retrieved from https://en.wikipedia.org/wiki/judenhut

"Statute of the Jewry" *En.wikipedia.org.* Web. 24 Jan 2017. Retrieved from https://en.wikipedia.org/wiki/statute_of_the_jewry

"Edward I of England" *En.wikipedia.org.* Web. 24 Jan 2017. Retrieved from https://en.wikipedia.org/wiki/edward_i_of_england

"Dominican Order" *En.wikipedia.org.* Web. 24 Jan 2017. Retrieved from https://en.wikipedia.org/wiki/dominican_order

"Albert I of Germany" En.wikipedia.org Web. 24 Jan 2017. Retrieved from https://en.wikipedia.org/wiki/albert_i_of_germany

"Rintfleish Pogrom" Web. 24 Jan 2017. Retrieved from En.wikipedia. org https://en.wikipedia.org/wiki/rintfleisch_pogrom

"Louis of France" *En.wikipedia.org*. Web. 24 Jan 2017. Retrieved from https://en.wikipedia.org/wiki/louis_of_france

"Henry II of Castile" *En.wikipedia.org*. Web. 24 Jan 2017. Retrieved from https://en.wikipedia.org/wiki/henry_ii_of_castile

"Badge of Shame" *En.wikipedia.org*. Web. 24 Jan 2017. Retrieved from https://en.wikipedia.org/wiki/badge_of_shame

"Philip V of France" *En.wikipedia.org*. Web. 24 Jan 2017. Retrieved from https://en.wikipedia.org/wiki/philip_v_of_france

"1321 Leper Scare" *En.wikipedia.org*. Web. 24 Jan 2017. Retrieved from https://en.wikipedia.org/wiki/1321_leper_scare

"Lepers" *En.wikipedia.org*. Web. 24 Jan 2017. Retrieved from https://en.wikipedia.org/wiki/lepers

"Solomon Grayzel" *En.wikipedia.org*. Web. 24 Jan 2017. Retrieved from https://en.wikipedia.org/wiki/solomon_grayzel

"Franconia" *En.wikipedia.org*. Web. 24 Jan 2017. Retrieved from https://en.wikipedia.org/wiki/franconia

"Alsace" *En.wikipedia.org*. Web. 24 Jan 2017. Retrieved from https://en.wikipedia.org/wiki/alsace

"Arnold Von Uissigheim" *En.wikipedia.org* Web. 24 Jan 2017. Retrieved from https://en.wikipedia.org/wiki/arnold_von_uissigheim

"Uissigheim Family" *En.wikipedia.org* Web. 24 Jan 2017. Retrieved from https://en.wikipedia.org/wiki/uissigheim_family

"Toulon France" *En.wikipedia.org*. Web. 24 Jan 2017. Retrieved from https://en.wikipedia.org/wiki/toulon_france

"Strasbourg Pogrom" *En.wikipedia.org*. Web. 24 Jan 2017. Retrieved from https://en.wikipedia.org/wiki/strasbourg_pogrom

"Isabella I of Carlile" *En.wikipedia.org*. Web. 24 Jan 2017. Retrieved from https://en.wikipedia.org/wiki/isabella_i_of_carlile

"Ferdinand II of Aragon" *En.wikipedia.org* Web. 24 Jan 2017. Retrieved from https://en.wikipedia.org/wiki/ferdinand_ii_of_aragon

"Alhambra Decree" *En.wikipedia.org* Web. 24 Jan 2017. Retrieved from https://en.wikipedia.org/wiki/alhambra_decree

"Land of Israel" *En.wikipedia.org.* Web. 24 Jan 2017. Retrieved from https://en.wikipedia.org/wiki/land_of_israel

"Marrano" *En.wikipedia.org.* Web. 24 Jan 2017. Retrieved from https://en.wikipedia.org/wiki/marrano

"Bradenburg Germany" *En.wikipedia.org.* Web. 24 Jan 2017. Retrieved from https://en.wikipedia.org/wiki/bradenburg_germany

"Ghetto" *En.wikipedia.org.* Web. 24 Jan 2017. Retrieved from https://en.wikipedia.org/wiki/ghetto

"Venice" *En.wikipedia.org.* Web. 24 Jan 2017. Retrieved from https://en.wikipedia.org/wiki/venice

"Protestant Reformation" *En.wikipedia.org.* Web. 24 Jan 2017. Retrieved from https://en.wikipedia.org/wiki/protestant_reformation

"Martin Luther" *En.wikipedia.org.* Web. 24 Jan 2017. Retrieved from https://en.wikipedia.org/wiki/martin_luther

"Corpus Jurius Cirllus" *En.wikipedia.org.* Web. 24 Jan 2017 Retrieved from https://en.wikipedia.org/wiki/corpus_jurius_cirllus#servitus_judaeorum

"Tunis" *En.wikipedia.org.* Web. 24 Jan 2017. Retrieved from https://en.wikipedia.org/wiki/tunis

"On the Jews and their Lies" *En.wikipedia.org.* Web. 24 Jan 2017. Retrieved from https://en.wikipedia.org/wiki/on_the_jews_and_their_lies

"Religious Conversion" *En.wikipedia.org.* Web. 24 Jan 2017. Retrieved from https://en.wikipedia.org/wiki/religious_conversion

"John Frederick Elector of Saxony" *En.wikipedia.org.* Web. 24 Jan 2017. Retrieved from https://en.wikipedia.org/wiki/john_frederick_elector_of_saxony

"Exile" *En.wikipedia.org.* Web. 24 Jan 2017. Retrieved from https://en.wikipedia.org/wiki/exile

"Prague" *En.wikipedia.org.* Web. 24 Jan 2017. Retrieved from https://en.wikipedia.org/wiki/prague

"Ivan the Terrible" *En.wikipedia.org.* Web. 24 Jan 2017. Retrieved from https://en.wikipedia.org/wiki/ivan_the_terrible

"Genoa" *En.wikipedia.org.* Web. 24 Jan 2017. Retrieved from https://en.wikipedia.org/wiki/genoa

"Franciscan" *En.wikipedia.org.* Web. 24 Jan 2017. Retrieved from https://en.wikipedia.org/wiki/franciscan

"Yom Kippur" *En.wikipedia.org.* Web. 24 Jan 2017. Retrieved from https://en.wikipedia.org/wiki/yom_kippur

"Pope Paul IV" *En.wikipedia.org.* Web. 24 Jan 2017. Retrieved from https://en.wikipedia.org/wiki/pope_paul_iv

"Polotsk" *En.wikipedia.org.* Web. 24 Jan 2017. Retrieved from https://en.wikipedia.org/wiki/polotsk

"Lithuania" *En.wikipedia.org.* Web. 24 Jan 2017. Retrieved from https://en.wikipedia.org/wiki/lithuania

"Russian Orthodox Church" *En.wikipedia.org.* Web. 24 Jan 2017. Retrieved from https://en.wikipedia.org/wiki/russian_orthodox_church

"Morocco" *En.wikipedia.org.* Web. 24 Jan 2017. Retrieved fromhttps://en.wikipedia.org/wiki/morocco

"Kristallnacht" *En.wikipedia.org.* Web. 24 Jan 2017. Retrieved from https://en.wikipedia.org/wiki/kristallnacht

"Sergey Brin" *En.wikipedia.org.* Web. 24 Jan 2017. Retrieved from https://en.wikipedia.org/wiki/sergey_brin

Chapter 17

Excerpts from:

Saul McLeod, "Sigmund Freud's Theories | Simply Psychology" *Simplypsychology.org.* Web. 24 Jan 2017. Retrieved from http://www.simplypsychology.org/Sigmund-Freud.html

"Moralising Criticism and Critical Morality: A Polemic Against Karl Heinzen: Karl Marx" *Amazon.com.* Web. 24 Jan 2017. Retrieved from https://www.amazon.com/Moralising-Criticism-Critical-Morality.../dp/150777558X

"Top 10 Most Influential Jews in History" *As-i-was-saying.com.* Web. 24 Jan 2017. Retrieved from http://www.as-i-was-saying.com/2016/10/top-10-most-influential-jews-in-history.html

"Siegfried Marcus" *En.wikipedia.org.* Web. 24 Jan 2017. Retrieved from https://en.wikipedia.org/wiki/Siegfried_Marcus

"Marcus Goldman" *En.wikipedia.org.* Web. 24 Jan 2017. Retrieved from https://en.wikipedia.org/wiki/Marcus_Goldman

"Lehman Brothers" *En.wikipedia.org.* Web. 24 Jan 2017. Retrieved from https://en.wikipedia.org/wiki/Lehman_Brothers

"Julius Rosenwald" *En.wikipedia.org.* Web. 24 Jan 2017. Retrieved from https://en.wikipedia.org/wiki/Julius_Rosenwald

"Goldman Sachs chief: Rabbi, Jewish groups helped me succeed" *Jewish Telegraphic Agency.* Web. 24 Jan 2017. Retrieved from www.jta.org/.../goldman-sachs-chief-rabbi-jewish-organizations-helped-me-succeed

"Hitler's VW Beetle is a Jewish Invention" *RNW Media.* Web. 24 Jan 2017. Retrieved from https://www.rnw.org/archive/hitlers-vw-beetle-jewish-invention

Jew Week, "Mercedes-Benz Jew of the Week" J*ewoftheweek.net.* Web. 24 Jan 2017. Retrieved from http://www.jewoftheweek.net/tag/mercedes-benz/

"André Citroën" *En.wikipedia.org.* Web. 24 Jan 2017. Retrieved from https://en.wikipedia.org/wiki/André_Citroën

"Top 10 Israeli inventions you should know about" *Jewish News.* Web. 24 Jan 2017. Retrieved from http://jewishnews.timesofisrael.com/top-10-israeli-inventions-need-aware/

"Igor Magazinnik" *En.wikipedia.org.* Web. 24 Jan 2017. Retrieved from https://en.wikipedia.org/wiki/igor_magazinnik

"Talmon Marco" *En.wikipedia.org.* Web. 24 Jan 2017. Retrieved from https://en.wikipedia.org/wiki/talmon_marco

"Trappstadt" *En.wikipedia.org.* Web. 24 Jan 2017. Retrieved from https://en.wikipedia.org/wiki/trappstadt

"Kingdom of Bavaria" *En.wikipedia.org.* Web. 24 Jan 2017 Retrieved from https://en.wikipedia.org/wiki/kingdom_of_bavaria

"Goldman Sachs" *En.wikipedia.org.* Web. 24 Jan 2017. Retrieved from https://en.wikipedia.org/wiki/goldman_sachs

"Investment Banks" *En.wikipedia.org.* Web. 24 Jan 2017. Retrieved from https://en.wikipedia.org/wiki/investment_banks

Chapter 18

Excerpts from:

"A Caribbean Crime Wave" *The Economist* . Web. 24 Jan 2017. Retrieved from www.economist.com/node/10903343

"Crime and Violence Linked to Poverty in Caribbean" *The Borgen Project.* Web. 24 Jan 2017. Retrieved from http://borgenproject.org/crime-violence-linked-poverty-caribbean/

Thompson, Nicole Akoukou "UNDP Report: Afro-Panamanians Suffer Discrimination at Every Level in Panama" *Latin Post* . Web. 24 Jan 2017. Retrieved from http://www.latinpost.com/articles/4981/20131219/undp-report-afro-panamanians-discrimination-panama.htm

Ghosh, Palash "Blackout: How Argentina 'Eliminated' Africans From Its History and Conscience" *International Business Times.* Web. 24 Jan 2017. Retrieved from http://www.ibtimes.com/blackout-how-argentina-eliminated-africans-its-history-conscience-1289381

"Committee on the Elimination of Racial Discrimination" *Ohchr. org.* Web. 24 Jan 2017. Retrieved from http://www.ohchr.org/EN/HRBodies/CERD/Pages/CERDIndex.aspx

"16 Harsh Realities of being Black and/or Mixed in Brazil" *Black Girl with Long Hair.* Web. 24 Jan 2017. Retrieved from http://blackgirllonghair.com/2015/08/16-harsh-realities-of-being-black-andor-mixed-in-brazil/

Okeowo, Alexis "Breaking News, Analysis, Politics, Blogs, News photos, Video, Tech Reviews" *TIME.com.* Web. 24 Jan 2017. Retrieved from http://content.time.com/time/world/article/0,8599,1922192,00.html Tuesday, Sept. 15, 2009

Comptonherald.com, Web. 24 Jan 2017. Retrieved from http://comptonherald.com/black-mexicans-face-considerable-hurdles/

"Oppressed Dalits of Bangladesh fight for their future" *The Independent.* Web. 24 Jan 2017. Retrieved from http://www.independent.co.uk/news/world/asia/oppressed-dalits-of-bangladesh-fight-for-their-future-1205005.html

"Facts on Education in Africa" *Achieve in Africa.* Web. 24 Jan 2017. Retrieved from https://achieveinafrica.wordpress.com/2009/04/15/facts-on-education-in-africa/

Kostadinova, Gloria "Crime and Violence Linked to Poverty in Caribbean" *The Borgen Project*. Web. 24 Jan 2017. Retrieved from http://borgenproject.org/crime-violence-linked-poverty-caribbean/

Fari Jamitah "TheBurningSpear.com – Home" *Uhurunews.com*. Web. 24 Jan 2017. Retrieved from http://uhurunews.com/story?resource_name=african-population-in-colombia-struggle-freedom-and-education

Reeves. V, Richard and Rodrigue Edward "Five Bleak Facts on Black Opportunity | Brookings Institution" *Brookings*. Web. 24 Jan 2017. Retrieved from http://www.brookings.edu/blogs/social-mobility-memos/posts/2015/01/15-mlk-black-opportunity-reevescJanuary 15, 2015

"Education Is Not Great Equalizer for Black Americans" *NBC News*. Web. 24 Jan 2017. Retrieved from http://www.nbcnews.com/feature/in-plain-sight/wealth-moves-out-grasp-blacks-so-does-opportunity-n305196

"Black British" *En.wikipedia.org*. Web. 24 Jan 2017. Retrieved from https://en.wikipedia.org/wiki/Black_British#Unemployment

"Refugees Are Living in a Former Prison in Holland Giles" *Vice.com*. Web. 24 Jan 2017. Retrieved from https://www.vice.com/read/refugees-are-living-in-a-former-prison-in-holland Giles Clarke

"Black People in Spain" *Afroeurope.blogspot.com*. Web. 24 Jan 2017. Retrieved from http://afroeurope.blogspot.com/2010/01/black-people-in-spain.html

"Dalit" *En.wikipedia.com*. Web. 24 Jan 2017. Retrieved from https://en.wikipedia.org/wiki/Dalit

"Dalit: The Black Untouchables of India" *Itsabouttimebpp.com*. Web. 24 Jan 2017. Retrieved from http://www.itsabouttimebpp.com/Announcements/Daliti_Panthers_in_India.html

"Oppressed Dalits of Bangladesh fight for their future" *The Independent*. Web.. 24 Jan 2017. Retrieved from http://www.independent.co.uk/news/world/asia/oppressed-dalits-of-bangladesh-fight-for-their-future-1205005.html

"Australia | Cultural Survival" *Culturalsurvival.org*. Web.. 24. Jan 2017. Retrieved from https://www.culturalsurvival.org/australia

Chapter 19

Excerpts from:

"Rubicon Speech, President PW Botha" *En.wikipaedia.org* Wed 24 Jan 2017. Retrieved from https://en.m.wikiquote.org